T0205521

Lecture Notes in Information Systems and Organisation

Volume 36

Lecture Notes in Information Systems and Organization—LNISO—is a series of scientific books that explore the current scenario of information systems, in particular IS and organization. The focus on the relationship between IT, IS and organization is the common thread of this collection, which aspires to provide scholars across the world with a point of reference and comparison in the study and research of information systems and organization. LNISO is the publication forum for the community of scholars investigating behavioral and design aspects of IS and organization. The series offers an integrated publication platform for high-quality conferences, symposia and workshops in this field. Materials are published upon a strictly controlled double blind peer review evaluation made by selected reviewers.

LNISO is abstracted/indexed in Scopus

More information about this series at http://www.springer.com/series/11237

Elisabetta Magnaghi · Véronique Flambard ·
Daniela Mancini · Julie Jacques · Nicolas Gouvy
Editors

Organizing Smart Buildings and Cities

Promoting Innovation and Participation

Editors
Elisabetta Magnaghi
Lille Catholic University
Lille, France

Véronique Flambard
Lille Catholic University
Lille, France

Daniela Mancini
Department of Business and Economics
Parthenope University of Naples
Naples, Italy

Julie Jacques
Lille Catholic University
Lille, France

Nicolas Gouvy
Lille Catholic University
Lille, France

ISSN 2195-4968   ISSN 2195-4976   (electronic)
Lecture Notes in Information Systems and Organisation
ISBN 978-3-030-60606-0   ISBN 978-3-030-60607-7   (eBook)
https://doi.org/10.1007/978-3-030-60607-7

This Springer imprint is published by the registered company Springer Nature Switzerland AG
The registered company address is: Gewerbestrasse 11, 6330 Cham, Switzerland

Preface

Smart Buildings can be part of smart organizations and smart cities. We can define them based on the technologies used to manage resources, performance expected or see them as ecosystem of actors and systems. Interest has grown around IT-based solutions, private-public partnerships, co-creation with stakeholders in the area of Smart Buildings and Smart Cities. Publications started to increase quickly after 2010 with attempts to define the concepts, and recurring issues such as energy efficiency, Big data, IoT, planning and organizing, data security and innovations. All disciplines contributed to advance knowledge with an overrepresentation of computer science, engineering, architecture and urban studies. Contributions made by social sciences, humanities and management sciences remain relatively more modest. This book is a response to the perceived need of analysis and answers from a multidisciplinary perspective, with several contributions from the usually less represented disciplines.

This book is of interest for a large audience, from all disciplines, interested by Smart Buildings, Universities and Cities. In this book, *Organizing Smart Buildings and Cities*, you will find insights into the origin and promises of smartness and their limits, how to best engage users and real cases and experiments.

Lille, France	Elisabetta Magnaghi
Lille, France	Véronique Flambard
Naples, Italy	Daniela Mancini
Lille, France	Julie Jacques
Lille, France	Nicolas Gouvy

Acknowledgments We would like to thank Elie Joe Wakim for his editorial assistance, and our colleagues Loïc Aubrée, Hervé Barry, Fateh Belaïd, Laura Carraresi, Sabine Kazmierczak for insightful comments. Our special thanks also go to the keynote speakers, presenters and participants to the second conference on Smart Buildings in Smart Cities, which took place in Lille, on July 12, 2019 for the inspiration they gave us and their contribution with some chapters of this book.

Contents

Contributors

Monica Bruzzone University of Parma, Parma, Italy; University of Genoa, Genoa, Italy

Nicolas Cochard Head of Research and Development, Groupe Kardham, Paris, France

Peter B. Duncan Department of Business and Management, Glasgow Caledonian University, Glasgow, UK

David A. Edgar Department of Business and Management, Glasgow Caledonian University, Glasgow, UK

Véronique Flambard Université Catholique de Lille- FGES and LEM (UMR CNRS 9221), Lille, France

Nicolas Gouvy Université Catholique de Lille, Lille Cedex, France

Antoine Huerta La Rochelle University, La Rochelle, France

J. Jacques Université Catholique de Lille, Lille, France

Josias Kpoviessi Dijon, France

Vincent Lefévère Computer Science and Mathematics Departement, Yncréa Hauts-de-France, Lille, France

Yaya Li School of Finance and Economics, Jiangsu University, Zhenjiang, China

Elisabetta Magnaghi Department of Business and Economics, Université Catholique de Lille, Lille, France

D. Mancini Faculty of Law, University of Teramo, Teramo, Italy

Marco De Marco Department of Economics, University of Uninettuno, Rome, Italy

Elizabeth Mortamais ENSA Paris Val de Seine - laboratoire EVCAU, Université de Paris, Paris, France

Marta Musso Department of Economics and Business, University of Cagliari, Cagliari, Italy

Jad Nassar Computer Science and Mathematics Departement, Yncréa Hauts-de-France, Lille, France

Ekene Okwechime Lancashire School of Business and Enterprise, University of Central Lancashire, Preston, UK

Joanne Peirani ACA Sustainable Development Project Manager, Groupe Kardham, Paris, France

Roberta Pinna Department of Economics and Business, University of Cagliari, Cagliari, Italy

Rustam Romaniuc Burgundy School of Business, Université Bourgogne Franche-Comté, Dijon, France

Matteo Trombin Department of Economics, University of Uninettuno, Rome, Italy

Eleonora Veglianti Department of Economics, University of Uninettuno, Rome, Italy

Abbreviations

ACA	Assistants to the Contracting Authorities
ACLR	Agglomerate Community of La Rochelle
ADEME	Agence de la Transition Ecologique
AI	Artificial Intelligence
ANCI	National Association of Italian Municipalities
BAMB	Building as Material Bank
BCG	Boston Consulting Group
BIM	Building Information Modeling
CADM model	Comprehensive Action Determinant Model
CDP	Carbon Disclosure Project
CPC	Communist Party of China
CRiMM	Research Center for Models and Mobility
CROUS	Regional Center for University and School Works
CRUI	Conference of the Rectors of the Italian Universities
CSR	Corporate Social Responsibility
DCT	Digital and Communication Technology
DDD	Data-Driven Decision-Making
EEA	European Environment Agency
EPR	Extended Producer Responsibility
EU	European Union
FCG	Future City Glasgow
FUA	Functional Urban Area
GDP	Gross Domestic Product
GPS	Global Positioning System
HEI	Higher Education Institutions
HER	Electronic Health Records
ICT	Information and Communication Technology
IoT	Internet of Things
IS	Information System
IT	Information Technology
ITC	Information Technology Communication
MIT	Massachusetts Institute of Technology

MTurk	Amazon Mechanical Turk experiment
OECD	Organization for Economic Cooperation and Development
PPP	Public-Private Partnerships
RBV	Resource-Based View
RT	Thermal Regulation
RUS	Italian Network of Sustainable Universities
S&T	Science and Technology
SC	Smart Cities
SG	Smart Grids
SMILE	Smart Ideas to Link Energies
SU	Smart Universities
TBM	Technical Building Management
UN SDGs	United Nations Sustainable Development Goals

Organizational and Environmental Framework of Smart Cities, Universities and Buildings

Véronique Flambard, Nicolas Gouvy, J. Jacques, Elisabetta Magnaghi, and D. Mancini

Abstract Cities are complex forms of organizations. The phenomenon of smart cities (SC), smart universities (SU) and smart buildings (SB) is expanding and information systems constitute organizational frameworks for this development. In this chapter, we will come back on the evolutionary approach of SC and develop what is at stake. Then we will explain why technology enables a more sustainable response to urbanization challenges. We will describe living laboratories and SU experiences. Finally, we will address an important building block of this ecosystem, which is SB.

Keywords Smart cities · Smart universities · Smart buildings · Information and communication technologies · Digital technologies · Sustainability

1 Introduction

In a globalized and 'flat' world, do cities still matter? Scholars, policymakers, businesses and people tend to think they do. The size, location, history, infrastructure, economy, institutions, human and social capital all participate to the success of cities and people who inhabit them [37]. The size and benefits of agglomeration reduce transports costs that are commuting time for workers, transportation costs of goods to consumers, diffusion of ideas and innovations (see the pioneer work by [26], [34]). Firms locate near one another, near suppliers and consumers. Consumers and workers

V. Flambard (✉) · N. Gouvy · J. Jacques · E. Magnaghi
Université Catholique de Lille, Lille, France
e-mail: veronique.flambard@univ-catholille.fr

N. Gouvy
e-mail: nicolas.gouvy@univ-catholille.fr

E. Magnaghi
e-mail: elisabetta.magnaghi@univ-catholille.fr

D. Mancini
Faculty of Law, University of Teramo, Teramo, Italy
e-mail: dmancini@unite.it

© Springer Nature Switzerland AG 2021
E. Magnaghi et al. (eds.), *Organizing Smart Buildings and Cities*,
Lecture Notes in Information Systems and Organisation 36,
https://doi.org/10.1007/978-3-030-60607-7_1

also locate close to production and retail firms. Ellison et al. [15] have provided clear empirical evidences of those coagglomeration patterns, which explain the existence of cities. Accessible and well-connected cities tend to grow faster than others do. Institutions also explain the growth or decline of cities [37].

These agglomerations of people and activities that constitute cities put pressure on space, resources including the natural environment and drives upward prices and wages. Construction cost to build vertically tends also to be higher [21]. Congestion, pollution, exclusion add to the fact that cities exist only because density enhances higher productivity and transfer of information which counterbalance those issues. Technological progress in Information and Communication Technologies (ICT) could reduce the needs of urbanization, but it has not yet materialized [20].

Today more than half of the population lives in urban areas and this rate is expected to grow to 66% (which will represent 6.419 billion people) by 2050 according to [45]. This urbanization comes with challenges. Cities have the difficult task to meet the needs of people for housing, transportation, infrastructures and access to education, health, social services, decent work and safe environment. Concentration of people weight on air quality, the environment and can be a threat to public health due to the high-population density and concentration of economic and social activities [7]. In addition, cities are subject to pressure to compete on a global scale for their sustainability. They strive to attract skilled and educated people, successful entrepreneurs, investments and transportation infrastructures. Cities rely on ICT to meet these challenges [5] and endeavor to encourage innovation and success [38]. They also aim to meet citizen's needs [12].

Innovations help regulating traffic, responding to changing needs or availability of resources or external factors such as the temperature, facilitating citizen's participation and access to services. The objectives are to deal with congestion of space, resource management, social inclusion, environmental protection, transparency. Cities are ecosystems with stakeholders and interaction between those stakeholders. Information system (IS) facilitates the sustainable transformation by processing information flows within and between the five helices of SC, which are civil society, businesses, academia, government and external environment. This information system relies, if we adopt a resource-based approach, on the built, human, natural, social capital, augmented by the IS and altered by the "smart" way people interact with this IS and ITC.

The answer to these issues and challenges requires multidisciplinary coordination. Naturally, academic research and exchange of good practices on smart cities are also interdisciplinary, involving architecture, urban studies, computer science, social sciences, economics and business management, or engineering studies [38].

This book hopes to contribute to the sustainability of SC with an original approach focusing on the different levels of the ecosystem: from SC to SU or living-lab and then to SB. Contributions are both exploratory (defining concepts, reflections on living-lab), organizational and behavioral ones. The volume aims to advance knowledge on this important topic of management of SC initiatives, SU and SB, bringing together contributions about the key organizational success factors of current transition to smarter societies. The objective is to provide insights to build a successful IS and organizational environmental framework for SCs, SUs and SBs. Living-laboratories experiments evaluation, context dependent and behavioral responses of users are key points developed in this volume. As the title "Organizing Smart Buildings and Cities - Promoting Innovation and Participation" suggests, special care is given to enablers of SC. With this choice, we are in line with the SC concept, which evolved from, technology-led to people-centric ([3], [35]).

In this volume, ten research papers define concepts and focus on the impact of technologies on organizations, choices and processes. The volume is divided into four sections, each one focused on a specific element of the smart ecosystem as SC, SU, SB, and ICT. The content of the book is based on a selection of the best papers (original double-blind peer reviewed contributions) presented at the conference Smart Buildings in Smart Cities, which took place in Lille, on July 12, 2019. This book is of particular interest to government, firms, researchers, citizens who want to gain insights into successful information system and organizational environmental framework for smart initiatives.

2 Smart Cities

The SC concept dates back to the sustainable urbanization movement [44], starting from digital to intelligent and then to smart [35]. The digital city was born with internet, Web 2.0 technology and software applications that provided access to digital services in the early 2000 [12]. Komninos [25] introduced the intelligent city in reference to a city supporting, through its institutions and organization, knowledge, innovation and people's creativity with the aim to increase competitiveness and sustainability. The intelligent city is considered the first-generation SC because it does not emphasize enough the role of the government and civil society. A SC is more user-friendly and services are better integrated in the ecosystem [3].

Giffinger et al. [19] argues that the six dimensions (smart governance, smart economy, smart mobility, smart environment, smart people, smart living) help to understand the concept of SC. The last generation of SC has been coined as responsive city by [47] emphasizing even more that SC must foremost serve citizens' needs. Literature on SC has dramatically increase from 2009. Zheng et al. [48] published the most recent and exhaustive literature review, as far as we know, with an overview of the main clusters of research topics related to SC. Kummitha and Crutzen [27] distinguished in an earlier state of the art two main streams, a technology and a human driven approach. The keen interest for SC should not mask caveats. Opponents question the willingness and ability to take into account the social dimension of the city, social justice, human bonding, data ethics, neoliberalism, privatization of urban space and generally speaking inclusion ([11], [23], [30], [10], [13], [14], [22], [24]). Opponents are also advocates of the importance to place people first.

In the human driven orientation, 'living lab' or 'urban lab' become important places of experimentation for co-creation [46]. Leydesdorff and Deakin [30] define the important partnership between universities, industry and government as a triple-helix, which triggers innovation by sharing resources. Lombardi et al. [31] emphasize another stakeholder that is 'civil society' in the so-called quadruple-helix model. The natural environment and issues such as global warming are also brought in the roadmap of sustainable development, with the quintuple helix model, which stresses ecology and economy as determinants for research and innovation.

Based on all challenges of SC (outlined in our Sect. 1), the authors of Chapter 1 conclude that emergence of smart cities is a response to wicked problems (defined as intractable and intertwined problems), following [6]. Based on the literature, they use the six facets of smart cities [18] to identify areas of actions. The organization mode is described as a triple helix (public private partnership and academia), or quadruple and even quintuple helix when users and respectively users and organizations participate through open innovations. The Future City Glasgow initiative (FCG) serves as a case study. From 2013, an open data platform, with more than 400 data streams, has provided real-time data accessible to all with smartphone applications. Users can obtain information and contribute. The authors conclude smart initiatives must be living laboratories supported by ICT infrastructure. Most of the literature has been devoted to large-size cities.

Chapter 6 fills a gap in the literature by focusing on medium-size cities. In this chapter, structural problems common to medium-size cities are identified and serve as benchmarks to analyze Parma in a case study. The author suggests extending the concept of the functional urban area by taking into account morphological dimensions. This would increase the quality of the urban indicators and improve digitalization policies. In addition, an extended geo-referenced interactive map would be a promising organizational tool. Such a dashboard would help record and query, both material and immaterial data about the city, and its functional area, taking advantage of open-data and morphological characteristics of the city to improve urban indicators and better inform for mobility, health supply and environment policies. Working with a holistic smart vision is a key success factor for smart medium-sized cities and should guide all initiatives. The data and technology are the main enablers of these initiatives.

3 Data and ICT: Key Pillars of Smart Initiatives

Although the positive impacts of the ICT deployment in the SC have yet to be fully felt, it is hard to imagine a so-called "smart" world without them. This is due to the combination of two main factors: mass production and the continuous technological progress in microelectronics.

As a matter of fact, computing capabilities and wireless technologies are now so easily cheap to produce that they can even be printed on a tag… making it a smart-tag. Therefore, the SC is mostly envisioned as a city in which computing is ubiquitous as everyday objects embed computational capability in a way that do not require the interaction of the end user.

If each of these smart devices is inherently hardware limited with very little capabilities, they cooperate in order to create a new kind of internet, the Internet Of Things (IoT). Members of the IoT sense and collect data related to the use of smart device or to their surrounding environment, sometimes even about their users.

In Chapter 5, authors detail a smart-city project, which illustrates the ubiquitous city in the Chinese context with *The Xiong an new area* project. In this project, ICT are heavily used to improve the development of urban life.

Using a case approach authors want to understand the SC model specific to China. In this country, indeed, smart cities' projects are directly managed by the central government as strategic projects in order to solve the "urban disease". And the *Xiong an new area* project appears as a benchmark for the Chinese approach as it combines a unique position in the political and physical geography to a full use of renewable energy and urban information infrastructures with real time environment monitoring. Moreover, this project successfully involves the technological national big companies to design better solution and deliver innovative services.

Nevertheless, as most smart city in China, citizens are passive actors of the project and the city lacks a global intelligent management system making the best of all the data.

Hence, the smart side of smart cities can also be provided using Big Data technologies. The term Big Data was first introduced in 1999 [9]. Its definition may vary from one author to another. Computer specialists will generally speak of Big Data as soon as the volume of data to be processed is no longer exploitable by conventional methods. By extension, other authors will also use Big Data to refer to treatments applied to data, such as predictive analytics.

The topic of Big Data is addressed in Chapter 2. The authors make an overview of data-driven decision-making and Big Data. First, they define the concept of Big Data: its characteristics (7 V) and its five key sources. They show its applications in several sectors. Then, they focus on the different types of open data and define what is the concept of open data. Finally, the concept of Data Driven Decision-making is defined. The importance of the volume and variety of the source of data to obtain good results is illustrated. Finally, this chapter explains how it is applied in the smart cities domain and identifies some complexities that could be raised by predictive analytics, with an illustration on crime analytics.

There are concerns as well as benefits associated with these IoT and Data governed cities. One must balance innovation with associated new privacy issues.

Chapter 4 investigates the issue of data security, right to privacy and ethical use of data for La Rochelle, Barcelona and more generally for smart Universities and Cities. The ISO norms regarding security management system start to define standards. Giving back to users the control over personal data and data governance is primordial. Human and social sciences can contribute by analyzing how data management system are set up and presented to users.

4   Smart Universities

Some eco-cities have been created relying mostly on Universities to support their research on sustainability [43]. For example, Masdar City is intrinsically related to the Masdar Institute of Science and Technology established with the MIT, in 2007, in Abu Dhabi. In fact, Higher Education Institutions (HEIs) play a dominant role by the nature of their mission of education (development of human capital, dissemination of sustainable principles). Universities have the opportunity to experiment on their campuses. They can become living laboratory. Initiatives can be implemented and evaluated by researchers and users (students and staff). Amaral et al. [4], based on a literature review, identify actions in energy (most popular area of action), water, waste, transportation and food. They also discuss the barriers and enhancers. Difficulties may arise from limited funding, insufficient human or technological resources, limited administrative support, lack of leadership or resistance from users and stakeholders. The main drivers can be support from direction or community, financial incentives. Examples of initiatives on University Campuses include passive building (ultra-low energy building) or positive building (building producing more energy than they consume). Other actions include harvesting rainwater to irrigate green spaces or waste separation for recycling. Smart mobility is the subarea, which involves most the community and has the most potential for dissemination. Application of circular economy can be based on Campuses on energy generation from waste.

Universities always had an important influence in the development of cities and growth through their activities of education, research and innovations. In the definition of SC, Universities are part of the triple helix and therefore from the beginning are main actors of the SC private-public partnership. In fact, all the activities of the Universities are organically and uniquely involved in the SC development. The ranking and reputation of Universities depend on their ability to produce research and development, to innovate, to deliver high quality education to students who will succeed in their professional career. Universities therefore have incentives to reinforce their role as engines of economic growth and competitiveness. They also strive to be recognized as inspiring and able to form leaders. Local communities aim at capturing the positive externalities created by Universities to leverage local and regional development. Addie [1] however argue that universities also have the potential to shape the metropolis and become global actors (beyond their local role). HEIs interact with transnational stakeholders and their role should not be thought only as being primarily local or regional.

In Chapter 3, using a multi-case approach, the authors review how best to engage students in smart mobility in Italian Universities. They propose to use well-integrated apps on smart phones, to facilitate sustainable mobility, with solution for the last mile to the University. Programs consist in two phases, data collection from the users and engagement phase with data-informed personalized solutions for them. Social marketing is used to accompany changing habits, values, preferences. This includes rewards to improve response and engagement rates.

In Chapter 10, the authors explain how The Catholic University of Lille has implemented a Smart Grid (SG) demonstrator. This project is undertaken as a living laboratory of social innovation. With a heterogeneous stock of University buildings, the University is renovating and equipping buildings with photovoltaic power stations for production and electric vehicle charging stations for residual consumption. A dedicated Information System was set up with computer servers duplicated on two sites with cross-backup system between the two sites to improve reliability. Optical fiber connection and radio waves secure the links. Research on interoperability of SM demonstrators and architectural choices is undertaken between European Universities.

5　Smart Buildings

Nowadays, in managing their activities, organizations cannot fail to consider two main forces: firstly, the disruptive innovation represented by ICT, and secondly, the growing attention and sensibility towards sustainability, social issues and performances.

The greater part of modern economy has been grounded on digital technologies and communication technologies such as Internet-of-Things, smart devices, artificial intelligence, cloud computing, and so on. This kind of technologies has a deep impact on individuals, organizations, and cities because they radically change the way, the time and the space in which people and machines interact, with each other, in a wide ecosystem [33]. Employees and managers can interact with other people or with machines, monitoring processes and making decisions everywhere, at any time, using several different devices because today they are immersed in a digital ecosystem ([32], [41]). Moreover, thanks to the implementation of digital technologies in managing processes, organizations can collect a huge amount of detailed data and can rely on those Big Data when they need information and knowledge.

Furthermore, today there is a growing sensibility towards sustainable use of natural resources and, therefore, a growing concern on new ways to measure and disclosure non-financial performances and sustainability results. Stakeholders and legislator also demand initiatives and projects through which companies could enhance their corporate social responsibility.

According theory and practice, nowadays ICT and sustainability in some cases are intertwined; this means that digital products and services often have sustainable implications, as well as, sustainable projects often required ICT tools and infrastructure. European Union, for example, is investing great amounts of financial resources in the digitalization of the society because ICTs will play a pivotal role in achieving environmental and social aims ([2], [16]). In fact, the digitalization of organizational processes (for example e-commerce, e-health, etc.) or the implementation of cloud computing push towards a more effective and efficient use of resources, and are also a fundamental enabler for pollution and gas emission reduction, for developing climate change strategies, for paper consumption reduction and so on. Moreover,

ICTs are a fundamental support to collect data for a better measurement, monitoring and planning of sustainability strategies. For example, IoT can help organizations to collect data on environment health, on noise pollution, to take under control the consumption of pesticide in agriculture etc.

Moreover, recently we have assisted to a convergence between sustainable and smart concepts, in other words being a smart organization, a SC often means also being sustainable, as well as being sustainable often requires being smart.

SB could be key components of both smart organizations and SCs. However, literature has not yet developed a general and shared concept of SB, from a managerial and business point of view. We can identify three groups of concepts:

- the equipment-centered definitions consider the use of technologies to manage and integrate several building services, maintenance facilities and communications ([36], [17]). These are static definitions that stress the complexity of the infrastructure of an intelligent building. Buildings are seen as a complex network of equipment (i.e. cable, sensors, etc.), able to communicate with each other.
- the performance-centered definitions consider the implications of a SB in terms of output and results ([39], [8], [29]). This definition considers a SB as an environment able to produce efficiency and effectiveness for occupants, resources inside the building, and environmental impacts in the local and global context. It is a building conceived to minimize the life cycle costs, whose results, in the evolution of time, passed from quantitative to financial to environmental and to sustainable. These are dynamic definitions that stressed the way in which the building produces those results, the process and combination of things able to affect financial, social, business, environmental, sustainable matters.
- the ecosystem definitions are complex, they see a SBs as a combination of systems able to interact inside, and outside and to produce quantitative and qualitative, financial and non-financial impacts. Those definitions highlight the importance of the relationship among different and several components of the SB, they underline the interconnections and integration among objects and actors in the building ecosystem ([40], [28], [42]).

Considering these three SB models, we can develop some considerations. The first group of definitions is essentially based on hard components of a SB, in fact, structures and systems are essentially the tangible part of a building, while services and building management regard the way in which data and information are used in order to deliver services and gained insight about services consumption. The second group of definition stressed the relationship of the building with actors and objects in different context: users' environment, organization, local and global environment. The third model, the most recent, is mainly focus on the intangible components of a SB that are related with its knowledge and immaterial resources. In fact, SBs could be seen as made by three layers able to collect and deliver data and information; to generate knowledge; and, finally, to develop and deliver innovative services, using insight and deep knowledge of data collected through an interactive platform.

In conclusion, we can assert, that smart and sustainable organizations have to consider their intelligent/smart buildings as a "hybrid" and valuable asset, composed by: a tangible structure, which is the traditional asset, made by the building and the infrastructure of relevant smart devices used to collect data; a smart intangible ecosystem composed by the model developed to combine several devices, able to collect predefine type of data; the model and resources implemented to process data, generate and deploy knowledge, and deliver some customized and innovative services.

Three of the book chapters give an overview of the SB concept, shed the light on some interesting issues analyzed from an interdisciplinary point of view.

In Chapter 7, the author adopts the Simondon's philosophic conception to technics and define an intelligent building "as a network able to produce, share and record information, acting in and with the *milieu* and the inhabitants". This concept of SB underlines the relevance of the *milieu*, as a quite different and deeper concept than that of the environment, in defining the essence of such kind of buildings. An intelligent building, in fact, is immersed in a *milieu* and has the capacity to answer to the standard and predefined needs of users, but also to interact with users and other occupants of the surrounding *milieu*.

In Chapter 8, authors study the impact of a bonus system to reward sober consumption of energy in the controlled environment of a lab experiment. The paper shows that the bonuses that SBs could implement act as focal points and change the energy consumption. The least virtuous residents managed to reach bonus anchor. The most virtuous ones reduced their energy conservation efforts; their intrinsic motivation was partially crowded out by monetary incentives. Energy manager should therefore gather data not only on energy consumption, but also on consumers profile to best design the incentives.

In Chapter 9, authors discuss advantages and obstacles of the introduction of circular economy approach into the real estate sector, pointing out some interesting feedback from real business cases. In summary, although some obstacles depend from the lack of well-established systems of rules and practices (legal, fiscal, and insurance) others, as the development of a cultural and knowledge environment based on circular economy principle among employees, customers and suppliers, can be directly overcome by the real estate firms. Furthermore, to fully catching up the competitive advantages of a circular economy approach, the authors suggest a comprehensive evaluation and planning of environmental and economic implications.

6   Organization of the Book

The book is organized on different units of analysis (column 2) of the Table 1. For each chapter, we keep track of the technology (column 3) which helps organizing SC, SU and SB, the artifact (column 4) and the application (column 5).

Table 1 Book organization

	Unit of Analysis	Technology (5G; GPS; IoT, IA, blockchain…)	Artifact (smartphones, widgets…)	Application
Chapter 1	City (Glasgow)	Wireless connection	Smartphones	Online open dashboard
Chapter 2	Society	Big Data	Databases, Smartphones	Data Driven Decision Making
Chapter 3	Universities (Genova, Caglieri, Sapienza)	Data on route habits and social marketing	Smartphones	Integrated App (with an engagement tool) with accompanying measures
Chapter 4	Universities and Cities	Data collected from connected objects	Data collected on platforms	Analyse Data Management System, data security, rights to privacy
Chapter 5	City (Xiong a new area)	5G, blockchain, Autonomous vehicle		National State of the Art Smart City
Chapter 6	City (Parma)	GIS		Extended geo-referenced interactive map Applications for health, mobility
Chapter 7	Intelligent Building	Artificial Intelligence and Big Data	Buildings and their *milieu*	Philosophic approach to intelligent building concept
Chapter 8	Building	Game Based Simulation/ Bonus	Computer/Bonus based on data collected on energy consumption	Incentive mechanisms
Chapter 9	Real estate sector			Circular economy projects in real estate sector
Chapter 10	University (Lille)	IoT, wireless sensors, Technical Building Management (BMS) system	Smart Grid	Dedicated Information System for Energy efficiency

References

1. Addie, J.-P. D. (2017). From the urban university to universities in urban society. *Regional Studies, 51*(7), 1089–1099.
2. Akande, A., Cabrall, P., & Casteleyn, S. (2019). Assessing the gap between technology and the environmental sustainability of European cities. In *Information systems frontiers.*
3. Albino, V., Berardi, U., Dangelico, R. M., (2015). Smart cities: Definitions, dimensions, performance, and initiatives. *Journal of Urban Technol, 22*(1), 3e21.
4. Amaral, A. R., Rodrigues, E., Rodrigues Gaspar, A., Gomes, Á., (2020). A review of empirical data of sustainability initiatives in university campus operations, *Journal of Cleaner Production,* 250.
5. Batty, M. (2014). *The new science of cities.* Cambridge, MA: The MIT Press.
6. Bettencourt, L. (2013). The kind of problem a city is. SFI working paper, 03 (008), 1–34.
7. Bibri, S. E. & Krogstie, J., (2017). Smart sustainable cities of the future: An extensive interdisciplinary literature review. *Sustain. Cities Soc.* 31, 183e212.
8. Boyd, D., & Jankovic, L. (1993). The limits of intelligent office refurbishment. In *Property Management,* 11(2), 102–113.
9. Bryson, S., and Johan, S. (1996). Time management, simultaneity, and time critical computation in interactive unsteady visualization environments. In *Proceedings of Visualization 96,* IEEE Press, 255–261.
10. Calzada, I., & Cobo, C. (2015). Unplugging: Deconstructing the smart city. *Journal of Urban Technology, 22*(1), 23–43.
11. Caragliu, A., Del Bo, C., & Nijkamp, P. (2011). Smart cities in Europe. *Journal of Urban Technology, 18*(2), 65–82.
12. Cocchia, A. (2014). Smart and digital city: A systematic literature review. In R. P. Dameri & C. Rosenthal-Sabroux (Eds.), *Smart city: How to create public and economic value with high technology in urban space, progress in IS* (pp. 13–43). Cham: Springer.
13. Cugurullo, F. (2013). How to build a sandcastle: An analysis of the genesis and development of Masdar City. *Journal of Urban Technology, 20*(1), 23–37.
14. Efthymiopoulos, M. (2016). Cyber-security in smart cities: The case of Dubai. *Journal of Innovation and Entrepreneurship, 5*(11), 1–16.
15. Ellison, G., Glaeser, E. L., & Kerr, W. R. (2010). What causes industry agglomeration? *Evidence from Coagglomeration Patterns, American Economic Review, 100*(3), 1195–1213. https://doi.org/10.1257/aer.100.3.1195.
16. European Commission. (2018). Artificial intelligence: A European Perspective. Available at https://publications.jrc.ec.europa.eu/repository/bitstream/JRC113826/ai-flagship-report-online.pdf.
17. Fox, S., & Do, T. (2013). Getting real about big data: Applying critical realism to analyse big data hype. *International Journal of Managing Projects in Business, 6*(4), 739–760.
18. Giffinger, R., Haindlmaier, G., & Kramar, H. (2010). The role of rankings in growing city competition. *Urban Research & Practice, 3*(3), 299–331.
19. Giffinger, R., Fertner, C., Kramar, H., et al., (2007). *Smart cities—Ranking of European medium-sized cities.* Vienna UT: Centre of Regional Science. http://www.smart-cities.eu/download/city_ranking_final.pdf.
20. Glaeser, E. L., & Gottlieb, J. D. (2009). The wealth of cities: Agglomeration economies and spatial equilibrium in the United States. *Journal of Economic Literature, 47*(4), 983–1028. https://doi.org/10.1257/jel.47.4.983.
21. Gyourko, Joseph, & Saiz, Albert. (2006). Construction costs and the supply of housing structure. *Journal of Regional Science, 46*(4), 661–680.
22. Hogan, T., Bunnell, T., & Pow, C. P. (2012). Asian urbanisms and the privatization of cities. *Cities, 29*(1), 29–63.
23. Hollands, R. G. (2008). Will the real smart city please stand up? *City: Analysis of Urban Trends, Culture, Theory, Policy, Action, 12*(3), 303–320.

24. Jazeel, T. (2015). Utopian urbanism and representational city-ness: On the Dholera before Dholera smart city. *Dialogue in Human Geography, 5*(1), 27–30.
25. Komninos, N. (2002). *Intelligent cities: Innovation, knowledge systems and digital spaces.* London: E & FN Spon.
26. Krugman, Paul. (1991). Increasing returns and economic geography. *Journal of Political Economy, 99*(3), 483–499.
27. Kummitha, R. K. R., & Crutzen, N. (2017). How do we understand smart cities? An evolutionary perspective, Cities, 67. *ISSN, 43–52,* 0264–2751. https://doi.org/10.1016/j.cities.2017.04.010.
28. Le, D. N., Tuan, L. L., & Tuan, M. N. D. (2019). Smart-building management system: An Internet-of-Things (IoT) application business model in Vietnam. *Technological Forecasting and Social Change, 141,* 22–35.
29. Lee, Y. M., An, L., Liu, F., Horesh, R., Chae, Y. T., & Zhang, R. (2014). Analytics for smarter buildings. *International Journal of Business Analytics, 1*(1), 1–15, January–March.
30. Leydesdorff, L., & Deakin, M. (2011). The triple-helix model of smart cities: A neoevolutionary perspective. *Journal of Urban Technology, 18,* 3–63.
31. Lombardi, P., Giordano, S., & Farouh, and Yousef, W. (2012). Modelling the smart city performance. *Innovation: The European Journal of Social Science Research, 25*(2), 137–149.
32. Mancini, D. (2018), Evoluzione e prospettive dei sistemi di informazione e controllo, in Management Control, 2, pp. 5–14.
33. Mancini, D. (2019), Aziende come ecosistemi intelligenti. Profili informativi, gestionali e tecnologici, Milano, Franco Angeli.
34. Marshall, Alfred. (1920). *Principles of economics.* London: MacMillan.
35. Mora, L., Deakin, M., Reid, A., (2018). Combining co-citation clustering and text-based analysis to reveal the main development paths of smart cities. *Technol. Forecast. Soc.* 142 (SI), 56–69.
36. Oades, R. (1989). Cabling in intelligent buildings. *Property Management, 7*(1), 25–29.
37. Polèse, M. (2009). *The wealth and poverty of regions: Why cities matter.* University of Chicago Press, 256 pages.
38. Ricciardi, F., Za, S., (2015). Smart city research as an interdisciplinary crossroads: A challenge for management and organization studies. In Mola, L., Pennarola, F., Za, S. (Eds.), *From information to smart society: Environment, politics and economics.* Cham: Springer International Publishing, pp. 163–171.
39. Robathan, P. (1991). BRIEFING: Intelligent buildings. *Property Management, 9*(2), 162–176.
40. Robathan, P. (1991). Open protocols—the Holy Grail or the Tower of Babel. *Property Management, 9*(4), 343–347.
41. Scornavacca E. (2019). Trarre valore dagli ecosistemi intelligenti, in Mancini D. (edited by), Aziende come ecosistemi intelligenti. Profili informativi, gestionali e tecnologici, Milano, Franco Angeli.
42. Sidney, R. (1992). Planned preventive maintenance and the maintenance contractor. *Property Management, 10*(1), 10–16.
43. Sodiq, A. et al.(2019). Towards modern sustainable cities: Review of sustainability principles and trends. *Journal of Cleaner Production, 227,* 972–1001.
44. Susanti, R., Soetomo, S., Buchori, I., Brotosunaryo, P. M. (2016). Smart growth, smart city and density: In search of the appropriate indicator for residential density in Indonesia. *Procedia-Soc. Behav. Sci.* 227, 194e201.
45. UN. (2018). World urbanization prospects: The 2018 revision. Accessed on 6 June 2019. https://population.un.org/wup//Publications/Files/WUP2018-KeyFacts.pdf.
46. Waart, P., Mulder, I., V., & Bont, C. D. (2015). A participatory approach for envisioning a smart city. *Social Science Computer Review.* http://dx.doi.org/10.1177/0894439315611099.
47. Yigitcanlar, T., Foth, M., Kamruzzaman, M. (2018). Towards post-anthropocentric cities: Reconceptualizing smart cities to evade urban ecocide. *Journal of Urban Technol, 26*(2), 147e152.
48. Zheng, C., Yuan, J., Zhang, Y., & Shao, Q. (2020). From digital to sustainable: A scientometric review of smart city literature between 1990 and 2019. *Journal of Cleaner Production, 258,* 1–22, https://doi.org/10.1016/j.jclepro.2020.120689.

Smart Cities: A Response to Wicked Problems

Ekene Okwechime, Peter B. Duncan, David A. Edgar, Elisabetta Magnaghi, and Eleonora Veglianti

Abstract In this paper we investigate the underlying theoretical and practical dimensions of the smart city concept. Exploring the smart city concept is necessary for understanding its meaning and usefulness. We begin by framing the problems faced in cities, i.e. urban issues, as wicked problems: complex and intractable. Then, a review of the meaning of a smart city is carried out in order to reach a holistic working definition of the concept. We also provide a description of how stakeholders are organized in providing smart-city-based solutions to urban problems in cities. A smart city case study situated in Glasgow, Scotland is developed. By doing so, we provide a new and practical perspective to comprehend the meaning and the use of the smart city concept in addressing urban problems by synthesizing important success factors.

Keywords Smart city · Urban problems · Wicked problems · Stakeholders

1 Introduction

The preference to live and work in cities has become increasingly dominant, which has led to the growth (and predicted future growth) of cities. City authorities have to grapple with complex urban problems. Cities now need to manage issues that

The original version of this chapter was revised: The affiliation for the authors "Peter B. Duncan and David A. Edgar" was corrected. The correction to this chapter is available at https://doi.org/10.1007/978-3-030-60607-7_12

E. Okwechime (✉)
Lancashire School of Business and Enterprise, University of Central Lancashire, Preston, UK
e-mail: eokwechime@uclan.ac.uk

P. B. Duncan · D. A. Edgar
Department of Business and Management, Glasgow Caledonian University, Glasgow, UK

E. Magnaghi
Department of Business and Economics, Université Catholique de Lille, Lille, France
e-mail: elisabetta.magnaghi@univ-catholille.fr

E. Veglianti
Department of Economics, University of Uninettuno, Rome, Italy
e-mail: eleonora.veglianti@uninettunouniversity.net

© Springer Nature Switzerland AG 2021, corrected publication 2021
E. Magnaghi et al. (eds.), *Organizing Smart Buildings and Cities*,
Lecture Notes in Information Systems and Organisation 36,
https://doi.org/10.1007/978-3-030-60607-7_2

13

arise from this population growth by creating smarter cities. The problems that have served as a precursor for the prominence of smart cities are conceptualised to be wicked problems (after Bettencourt [11]).

Therefore, to understand smart cities, it is important to begin with exploring the nature of wicked problems. The rise in population and projected growth of cities require stakeholders to find innovative ways to provide more efficient amenities through the development of smart cities ([15], [56], [68], [67]).

The rest of the article is structured as follows. Section 1.2 critically evaluates—the nature of problems that have led to the adoption of the smart city concept—wicked problems. Accordingly, to arrive at a working definition of the smart city concept (as a response to wicked problems), Sect. 1.3 critically examines the meaning of a smart city. In line with this, Sect. 1.4 critically evaluates the way organisations and stakeholders come together to work on smart city initiatives, via public-private partnerships and the Triple Helix. A smart city case study is presented in Sect. 1.5. Finally, recommendations and a conclusion are provided in Sect. 1.6.

2 Wicked Problems

The purpose of this section is to critically examine the wicked problem concept. Wicked problems are problems that are perceived to be malignant (deep rooted) or vicious (cyclical), tricky (difficult to understand) and even aggressive (leading to grave consequences) ([18], [22]). The term 'wicked' does not refer to the problems under consideration as being ethically despicable but refers rather to their intrinsic nature.

The ethical undertone of the term, however, stems from how the problem-solver deals with the problem. This raises the question on whether it is morally objectionable for planners to treat a problem as a tamed one or to ignore its viciousness, cyclicality, difficulty or its impending consequences because of the failure to solve a problem [63].

The wicked problem concept was officially described in a treatise titled 'Dilemmas in the General Theory of Planning' [63]. The concept is built on the premise that tackling problems in policy areas are likely to fail due to their intrinsic nature. This is because such problems can be wicked and untameable, unlike problems in the pure sciences that are identified and tamed [63]. Rittel and Weber ([63, pp. 161–166]) then introduced ten characteristics of a wicked problem:

1. "There is no definitive formulation of a wicked problem.
2. Wicked problems do not have any fixed or stopping rules.
3. Solutions to a wicked problem cannot be binary options such as true-or-false, but rather can be good or bad.
4. There is no immediate and no ultimate test of a solution to a wicked problem.
5. Every solution to a wicked problem is a 'one-shot operation'; because there is no opportunity to learn by trial and error, every attempt counts significantly.
6. Wicked problems do not have an enumerable (or an exhaustively describable) set of potential solutions, nor is there a well described set of permissible operations that may be incorporated into the plan.

7. Every wicked problem is essentially unique.
8. Every wicked problem can be considered to be a symptom of another problem.
9. The existence of a discrepancy representing a wicked problem can be explained in numerous ways. The choice of explanation determines the nature of the problem's resolution.
10. The social planner has no right to be wrong (i.e., planners are liable for the consequences of the actions they generate)".

In line with the characterisation of a wicked problem, various scholars, Bettencourt [11], Camillius [13], Conklin [20], Ferlie et al. [28], Jentoft and Chuenpagdee [42], have reformulated their own perceptions of a wicked problem into different subject areas. Bettencourt [11] has narrowed a wicked problem to be a problem of knowledge that focuses on algorithmically calculating problems in urban planning, while Camillius [13] related it to strategy creation in business. What these variations of a wicked problem illustrate is that the ten characteristics of a wicked problem (by Rittel and Webber) are not a set of tests, but rather offer insights that could help a problem-solver determine the nature of a given problem.

A recurring theme from these variations of wicked problems is the scope and scale of the problem. For instance, solving an equation in mathematics or analysing the constituents of an unknown compound or making a checkmate in five moves in a game of chess are not wicked problems ([13], [22]). In these examples, the mission is clear, even if the problem is not solved. On the contrary, urban problems like many social ones, lack clarity in terms of a stated problem.

Bettencourt [11] argues that solving a wicked problem could require the problem-solver to produce an inventory of possible solutions ahead of time. This implies that the problem solver would not seek out the root causes of the problem but will satisfice on solutions. Von Hippel and Krogh [38] also note that with listing an inventory of solutions, satisficing a search alternative can be deployed to justify solutions that can be deemed satisfactory. However, Bettencourt [11] and Von Hippel and Krogh [38] do not specify if an inventory of more problems arising from satisficing would also need to be produced at any point of the problem-solving process.

The 'wickedness' of a problem does not mean that the latter is difficult; it otherwise means that it cannot be completely solved ([20], [28]). The inability to address it can also be due to various underlying intertwined complex causes. In effect, if one aspect can be solved, there will be currents of other issues coming from the interconnected problems emanating from the one the planner had attempted to solve [42].

The complexity of urban problems would have an impact on how planners attempt to solve problems. This problem is symptomatic in different spheres of socio-economic, organisational and political planning. For example, when top managers in organisations deal with the issue of creating strategy, whereas ecologists try to deal with fishing and coastal governance ([20], [42]).

The ten characteristics of a wicked problem are in line with the nature of urban problems; because such problems have no defining mechanism or formula and are ill structured and complex. The issues in a city are often nebulous and cannot be entirely solved and emerge from an organised and functioning social complex system. For instance, if a city faces unprecedented challenges like high crime rates and poverty; completely solving the problem could prove intractable.

This is because planners cannot possibly know how city dwellers will want to develop their city, even down to the elementary basics of planning, such as shapes of streets, houses, use of spaces and zoning. Solving problems like this makes it 'wicked' because each problem is intertwined with another and solving one exposes the planners to others (Goodspeed 2015). Given that wicked problems defy traditional problem-solving techniques, what the above demonstrates are the challenges organisational stakeholders in the public sector currently encounter. Therefore, a wicked problem can be described as problems bridled with deep complexity with unknown consequences.

This section has critically examined the nature and characteristics of a wicked problem. It has been argued that a wicked problem cannot be reduced to an equation: a low and accurate understanding of a problem. Having done so, this then raises a fundamental question of how a wicked problem can be addressed in a city. To this end, the following section critically examines the smart city concept, a proposed solution to urban problems.

3   The Smart City Concept

The purpose of this section is to critically examine the meaning of the smart city concept and its characteristics. To understand the smart city concept, a definition is pertinent. As noted in Sect. 1.2, the smart city concept has partly been adopted as a response to wicked problems. The definition of a smart city itself poses one of the most fundamental challenges to adopting the concept (Hollands 2008, [56]).

Furthermore, the issue with a definition arises partly because there are terms analogous to the smart city concept that have the same goal ([15], [73]). Albino et al. [1], in their review of definitions and characteristics of smart cities, identified the shared constituents of the various smart city labels.

There are analogous terms such as the 'creative city' by Bayliss [10]; the 'entrepreneurial city' (Hollands 2008) and 'intelligent city' by Komninos et al. [44]. Albino et al. [1] argue that underneath the quest for urban smartness—and the various smart city labels—lies a shared aim to make cities perform better in comparison to traditional ones.

Table 1 provides various definitions of a smart city; drawn from Albino et al.'s [1] review of the definition of the concept. In general, the table reveals that the smart city concept entails the diffusion and integration of ICT, the inclusion of citizens in the decision-making and creative process of the city to provide cost efficient and effective services. The first column in Table 1 contains an outline of definitions, while the second column contains the sources of those definitions.

The term 'smart city' is treated as a conceptual dimension by which being smarter involves strategic directions; because cities are the centre of economic activity and administrative control in society [32]. Governments and public agencies are rapidly

Table 1 Definitions of Smart City

Definition	Source
Smart city as a high-tech intensive and advanced city that connects people, information and city elements using new technologies in order to create a sustainable, greener city, competitive and innovative commerce, and an increased life quality.	Bakıcı et al. [6]
Being a smart city means using all available technology and resources in an intelligent and coordinated manner to develop urban centres that are at once integrated, habitable, and sustainable.	Barrionuevo et al. [8]
A city is smart when investments in human and social capital and traditional (transport) and modern (ICT) communication infrastructure fuel sustainable economic growth and a high quality of life, with a wise management of natural resources, through participatory governance.	Caragliu et al. [15]
Smart cities will take advantage of communications and sensor capabilities sewn into the cities' infrastructures to optimize electrical, transportation, and other logistical operations supporting daily life, thereby improving the quality of life for everyone.	Chen [17]
Two main streams of research ideas: (1) smart cities should do everything related to governance and economy using new thinking paradigms and (2) smart cities are all about networks of sensors, smart devices, real-time data, and ICT integration in every aspect of human life.	Cretu [23]
Smart community—a community which makes a conscious decision to aggressively deploy technology as a catalyst to solving its social and business needs—will undoubtedly focus on building its high-speed broadband infrastructures, but the real opportunity is in rebuilding and renewing a sense of place, and in the process a sense of civic pride. Smart communities are not, at their core, exercises in the deployment and use of technology, but in the promotion of economic development, job growth, and an increased quality of life. In other words, technological propagation of smart communities isn't an end in itself, but only a means to reinventing cities for a new economy and society with clear and compelling community benefit.	Eger [26]
A city well performing in a forward-looking way in economy, people, governance, mobility, environment, and living, built on the smart combination of endowments and activities of self-decisive, independent and aware citizens. Smart city generally refers to the search and identification of intelligent solutions, which allow modern cities to enhance the quality of the services provided to citizens.	Giffinger et al. [31]

(continued)

Table 1 (continued)

Definition	Source
A smart city, according to ICLEI, is a city that is prepared to provide conditions for a healthy and happy community under the challenging conditions that global, environmental, economic and social trends may bring.	Guan [33]
A city that monitors and integrates conditions of all of its critical infrastructures, including roads, bridges, tunnels, rails, subways, airports, seaports, communications, water, power, even major buildings, can better optimize its resources, plan its preventive maintenance activities, and) monitor security aspects while maximizing services to its citizens.	Hall [35]
A city connecting the physical infrastructure, the IT infrastructure, the social infrastructure, and the business infrastructure to leverage the collective intelligence of the city.	Harrison et al. [36]
(Smart) cities as territories with high capacity for learning and innovation, which is built-in the creativity of their population, their institutions of knowledge creation, and their digital infrastructure for communication and knowledge management.	Komninos [44]
Smart cities are the result of knowledge-intensive and creative strategies aiming at enhancing the socio-economic, ecological, logistic and competitive performance of cities. Such smart cities are based on a promising mix of human capital (e.g. skilled labour force), infrastructural capital (e.g. high-tech communication facilities), social capital (e.g. intense and open network linkages) and entrepreneurial capital (e.g. creative and risk-taking business activities).	Kourtit and Nijkamp [46]
Smart cities have high productivity as they have a relatively high share of highly educated people, knowledge-intensive jobs, output-oriented planning systems, creative activities and sustainability-oriented initiatives.	Kourtit et al. [47]
Smart city [refers to] a local entity—a district, city, region or small country which takes a holistic approach to employ[ing] information technologies with real-time analysis that encourages sustainable economic development.	IDA [41]
A community of average technology size, interconnected and sustainable, comfortable, attractive and secure.	Lazaroiu and Roscia [48]
The application of information and communications technology (ICT) with their effects on human capital/education, social and relational capital, and environmental issues is often indicated by the notion of smart city	Lombardi et al. [50]

(continued)

Table 1 (continued)

Definition	Source
A smart city infuses information into its physical infrastructure to improve conveniences, facilitate mobility, add efficiencies, conserve energy, improve the quality of air and water, identify problems and fix them quickly, recover rapidly from disasters, collect data to make better decisions, deploy resources effectively, and share data to enable collaboration across entities and domains.	Nam and Pardo [57]
Creative or smart city experiments […] aimed at nurturing a creative economy through investment in quality of life which in turn attracts knowledge workers to live and work in smart cities. The nexus of competitive advantage has […] shifted to those regions that can generate, retain, and attract the best talent.	Thite [71]
Smart cities of the future will need sustainable urban development policies where all residents, including the poor, can live well and the attraction of the towns and cities is preserved. […] Smart cities are cities that have a high quality of life; those that pursue sustainable economic development through investments in human and social capital, and traditional and modern communications infrastructure (transport and information communication technology); and manage natural resources through participatory policies. Smart cities should also be sustainable, converging economic, social, and environmental goals.	Thuzar [72]
A smart city is understood as a certain intellectual ability that addresses several innovative socio-technical and socio-economic aspects of growth. These aspects lead to smart city conceptions as "green" referring to urban infrastructure for environment protection and reduction of CO^2 emission, "interconnected" related to revolution of broadband economy, "intelligent" declaring the capacity to produce added value information from the processing of city's real-time data from sensors and activators, whereas the terms "innovating", "knowledge" cities interchangeably refer to the city's ability to raise innovation based on knowledgeable and creative human capital.	Zygiaris [76]
The use of Smart Computing technologies to make the critical infrastructure components and services of a city—which include city administration, education, healthcare, public safety, real estate, transportation, and utilities—more intelligent, interconnected, and efficient.	Washburn et al. [75]
Smart cities initiatives try to improve urban performance by using data, information and information technologies (IT) to provide more efficient services to citizens, to monitor and optimize existing infrastructure, to increase collaboration among different economic actors, and to encourage innovative business models in both the private and public sectors.	Marsal-Llacuna et al. [53]

Source Albino et al. ([1], pp. 6–8)

embracing the notion of smartness for targeting sustainable development goals, economic growth and a better quality of life for their citizens [7].

Given the fastmoving nature of the concept and its underlying link to information communication technology (ICT) and big data, a working definition is pertinent. Based on the review of the literature, considering the various facets of a smart city, a working definition of a smart city is one where attempts are made:

> ... to improve urban performance by using data and [ICT] to provide more efficient services to citizens; to monitor and optimize existing infrastructure; to increase collaboration among different economic actors and to encourage innovative business models in both the private and public sectors (Marsal-Llacuna et al. [53], p. 618).

The above working definition was adopted because of its emphasis on the use of (big) data and ICT in looking for ways to provide cost effective and efficient services for citizens and the means in which to achieve this. Even though this contribution focuses on smart cities as a response to wicked problems, it is pertinent to note that the concept could be adopted as a response to the impact of climate change, which makes cities focus on resilience and sustainability ([43], [64]). What this implies is that the impact of population growth goes beyond the physical characteristics of a city because it affects ecology. However, due to the evolution of the concept, it is difficult to identify an existing smart city [67]. This, in turn, makes cities who attempt to adopt a smart city approach become 'living laboratories' that host smart city initiatives [5].

3.1   Smart Cities as Living Laboratories

Table 1 provides an inference of smart cities being an experimental and developmental project, which make cities a 'living laboratory'. The vision of the cities is executed in smart city initiatives to test and demonstrate the workings of the smart city technology [2]. For example, some cities in the UK (and around the world) are testing out the use of driverless cars [34]. Living laboratories or 'living labs' "are eco-systems in which end-users and other relevant stakeholders are involved in the development of an innovation over a longer period of time" ([66] in Baccarne et al. [5], p. 161).

Cosgrave et al. [21] argue that the living lab approach is one adopted by most cities given that the smart city concept is introduced and developed in initiatives. Living labs are central to how cities test out the smart city concept by aiming to nurture a creative economy through the investment in quality of life, which could in turn attract and retain people [1].

Living labs also give stakeholders the opportunity to assess the immediate impact of the smart city initiative. These labs are also in line with the working definition of a smart city adopted for this research, which lays emphasis on attempting to optimise already existing infrastructure to provide effective services for the citizens.

Table 2 Characteristics of Smart Cities

Smart Economy	Smart People
Entrepreneurship	Affinity towards lifelong
Flexibility	learning
Internationally Embedded	Creativity
Productivity	Levels of educational
Transformative	attainment
	Participation in public life
	Social and ethnic plurality
Smart Governance	Smart Mobility
Participatory decision-making	Availability of ICT
Provision of public and social	infrastructure
services	Innovative and safe transport
	systems
	Local and international
	accessibility
Smart Environment	Smart Living
Environmental protection	Educational facilities
Pollution levels	Health conditions
Sustainable resource	Housing quality
management	Individual safety
	Provision of cultural facilities
	Social cohesion
	Tourist attractiveness

Source Giffinger et al. [31]

The purpose of a smart city initiative is embedded in the definition it adopts [12]. Furthermore, it could be deduced from Table 2, that there are recurring themes in the definitions of a smart city, which focuses on goals such as: connectivity; governance liveability and sustainability [31]. The following sub-section critically evaluates the characteristics of a smart city.

3.2 Smart City Characteristics

Giffinger et al. [31] drew up six characteristics for a smart city. The six main characteristics of a smart city are: (1) smart economy; (2) smart people; (3) smart governance; (4) smart mobility; (5) smart environment and (6) smart living. All six characteristics are encapsulated in Table 2.

These characteristics point to the areas of urban living where the smart city concept can be used to improve existing infrastructure with the use of data and ICT to provide efficient services for its citizens. Within each smart city characteristic outlined in Table 2 are the various areas of its application to urban living and problem solving.

- **Smart Economy**

The first characteristic of a smart city (smart economy) stresses on the need for a business led approach to urban development [31]. A smart economy lays emphasis on economic competitiveness for urban development, bordering on competition for economic activity as well as for people (Hollands 2008, [50]). A smart economy is a driver for growth because business friendly cities are those with reasonable socio-economic performance [31]. However, there are potential risks of putting a high premium on economic values, as the main drivers for urban development, against factors like innovation.

Soete [69] suggests that city planners should focus on innovation rather than just the economic competitiveness of the city, to ensure sustainable growth. This implies that planners should engage in a trade-off against each factor (innovation and competition). Incidentally, the innovativeness of a city affects the overall competition of the city. The rationale behind this school of thought is that through innovation, cities can remain sustainable while also remaining competitive. In other words, planning a smart city should be based on innovation as the cornerstone of competition.

Capello et al. [14] using data from EUROSTAT—via the community innovation survey—found out that a city's innovativeness was strongly linked to it urban industrial structure. Methodologically, the analysis was evaluated with industrialisation constructs, which could have impacted the results. However, such relationships depend on the presence of knowledge intensive services that are suitable for businesses to thrive. These further buttresses the point that a city's innovativeness has a direct impact on its competitiveness through the presence of knowledge intensive services and industries.

- **Smart People**

The second characteristic of a smart city (smart people) lays an emphasis on the role the high-tech and creative industries could play in the long-term sustainable growth of a city through the people that work there. This characteristic relates to fostering knowledge networks, which makes a city a suitable breeding ground for the creative industries. The creativity of a city will be the driving force of the 21st Century economy. This is because creative occupations are on the rise, businesses now position themselves to entice the creative.

Bayliss [10] argues that through an emphasis on creativity, a city can stimulate its growth by promoting itself on an international level, thereby attracting people and investments. However, Nijkamp [58] critically summarises the role of a creative culture in a city by noting that, although creative human capital jointly determines and fosters trends observed in skilled migration, a creative and skilled workforce does not inherently guarantee a high urban performance. Therefore, cities could consider strategies to attract and retain creative people.

- **Smart Governance**

The third characteristic (smart governance) lays emphasis on 'participatory governance' in a city. Participatory governance should do with the way residents of the city are included into the day-to-day decision-making for the provision of public services. In other words, smart governance entails to what extent all social classes are included into the urban fabric of the technological and economic advancements of the city. Coe et al. [19] suggest that smart city initiatives that champion social inclusion should be encouraged as they enable social cohesion and a connected citizenry.

Nonetheless, social inclusion themed initiatives might prompt city planners to pay attention to the critical issue of fostering an equitable society. Mainka et al. [52] argue that through the integration of ICT in cities, smart governance can transform and add more value to the services provided by the city. This is because there would be a wider array of stakeholders participating in the decision-making process.

- **Smart Mobility**

The fourth characteristic (smart mobility) drawn up by Giffinger et al. [31] focuses on the deployment of network infrastructure to increase the cultural and socio-economic development of a city. Here the term 'infrastructure' denotes to business services, housing and ICTs such as satellite TVs, e-commerce, mobile and fixed phones and computer networks [50]. This characteristic has guided several developmental smart city models such as the T-City project in the city of Friedrichshafen in Germany (Hatzelhoffer 37).

In this case, connectivity is perceived as the source of growth and the level of infrastructure available to the population. From a policy point of view, policymakers tend to struggle to maximize the potentials of carrying out projects that could ensure the networking of a society. To achieve the optimum networking of a city requires a combination of technology, infrastructure development, institutional reform, education and business to lever the ICT and big data to become a networked society.

- **Smart Environment**

The fifth characteristic (smart environment) focuses on social and environmental sustainability as a significant strategic component for actualising smart city plans [31]. This is because a city should be environmentally conscious and at the same time able to make use of its natural resources to sustain itself. Smart city initiatives often adopt this dimension if there is a focus on sustainability. As such, smart cities must be physically and spatially enabled to foster environmental sustainability.

For example, the way ICT is embedded into an environmental strategy of a city, i.e. where digital sensors embedded in a city enables planners to know what ways natural resources can best be managed. Given that cities tend to compete for not just people but on harnessing resources, such as in tourism, there arises a need to optimise already existing infrastructure [53]. In other words, this characteristic entails what ways natural resources are exploited for urban sustainability.

- **Smart Living**

The sixth characteristic (smart living) focuses on combating social inequality. Coe et al. [19], drawing from the absorptive capacity theory, argue that citizens are meant to be able to benefit from growing technology available in the city. A possible interpretation could be that social and economic problems that affect a city's capacity to innovate should be considered, if not it stands, the chance to be socially polarised.

Conversely, Poelhekke [61] argues that the concentration of highly skilled people in a city is adequate for urban growth despite the polarising consequences. Thus, the impact this might have on a city may have mixed results. The impact could range from a schism between the rich and poor as well as the skilled and unskilled citizens, which might invariably hinder social mobility and increase inequality.

The divisions brought about by social inequalities in cities manifests themselves in certain parameters amongst various social and economic groups. The outcomes could raise issues around life expectancy, individual safety, poor health outcomes, life prospects, poor housing, lack of social amenities, lack of social cohesion etc. In this instance, smart city initiatives would have to look for ways to address the problems around smart living, such as the provision of educational facilities

These six characteristics encapsulate the objectives of various smart city initiatives. Overall, the purpose of a smart city initiative is to address key aspects of urban living [5]. The integration of ICT ensures that cities do become smart, but this might differ depending on the initiative [9], [53]. What this then suggests is that depending on the problem to be solved different approaches can be espoused [3].

Nevertheless, regardless of the smart city characteristic chosen, it is still pertinent to probe the assertions and associations that make a city smart. From the above characteristics, and the previous analyses on the meaning of a smart city, a smart city is what the stakeholders want it to be in relation to the aforementioned six characteristics.

The section has critically analysed the meaning of the smart city concept and its characteristics. A working definition of smart city by Marsal-Llacuna et al. [53] has been adopted for this paper. The six smart city characteristics form the different areas in which the concept can be applied to address urban problems. Marsal-Llacuna et al. [53] particularly emphasise the involvement of various actors (multiple stakeholders) in a smart city initiative. Therefore, the following section critically examines the structure in which the collaborations between different stakeholders could take place in a smart city initiative.

4 Collaborations for Smart Cities: Public Private Partnerships & the Triple Helix

The purpose of this section is to critically examine the concepts of public-private partnerships (PPP) and the Triple Helix in relation to the creation of smart city initiatives; to demonstrate the shifting innovation landscape in smart cities that is typified by the participants involved and the level of intensity of their participation. In a smart city initiative, there are multiple stakeholders involved in the process of problem solving [2], [44], [53]. To address complex problems, such as wicked problems/urban problems, problem-solving heuristics can be central in determining what solutions are deployed in a smart city initiative.

The planning structure of a smart city is carried out in public-private partnerships (PPP) [37], 40, [51], [60]. The collaborative structure in which a smart city is planned depends on the stakeholders involved in the process, such as a domain-specific of smart city initiative. For example, a smart city initiative that requires more active citizens. Despite the widespread adoption of PPP, there is no single definition for the concept and few scholars agree on what it means ([24], [39]). However, a PPP has served as a replacement to traditional contracting arrangements and to get private organisations to deliver public services [45].

These perspectives on PPP are consistent with the views by Mckee et al. [54], who argue that a PPP occurs when a governmental body contracts the delivery of a service to a private organisation. On the other hand, a PPP could be an arrangement whereby private organisations are given the right to operate a service, conventionally the responsibility of the public sector. Thus, a PPP could be referred to as inter-institutional arrangements between public and private sector organisations on certain projects for the public's benefit ([45], [60]).

Within the smart city domain, a PPP could occur when services are delivered mainly through a public system for the public by private organisations. The involvement of private organisations could be because of public organisations lacking the level of expertise to provide such a service, knowledge, capability or finances for an initiative. Therefore, such collaborations are not joint ventures in a business sense, but a partnership between two or more participating organisations in the private and public (and not-for profit) sectors. However, for the development of smart cities, the input or ideas for the provision of support services are sourced from what could generally be termed as the 'private sector' [37]. Hatzelhoffer (37) demonstrates that the process of developing a smart city involves a wider array of stakeholders, namely academia. Consequently, a PPP for smart cities can be referred to as a joint venture that brings various organizations from different sectors that share certain attributes and, most importantly, a shared objective.

The participation and involvement of different stakeholders are pivotal to the creation of a smart city, especially through the triple helix model. Deakin [25] suggests that the triple helix provides the opportunity for planners to study a community in terms of getting the wider society's support for the development of an innovative eco-system that promotes environmental and cultural development.

There are two main strands of the Triple Helix concept ([25], [49], [70]). The first is one where universities play a pivotal role, which could be on par with that of industry (Etzkowtiz 2008, [27]). The second is one where there is collaboration between the three key main stakeholders—academia, industry and government—in the innovative process for smart cities [55]. The latter is more in line with the Triple Helix system of innovation proposed by Ranga and Etzkowitz [62]; the process synthesises the key features of Triple Helix interactions into an innovation eco-system format, based upon a set of components, relationships and functions.

The relationship between these components is, then further, synthesised into five main types: technology and knowledge transfer, collaboration and conflict moderation, collaborative leadership, substitution and networking ([16], [55], Nijkamp et al. 2011, [62]). Thus, the overall function of the Triple Helix system serves for knowledge generation, innovation, diffusion and application.

Moreover, Meyer et al. [55] highlight that the literature on Triple Helix has tended to focus on universities being the central body in this relationship; however, the perceived role played by universities has begun to disintegrate given the change in the innovative landscapes, especially because of new non-technological driven innovations, such as service innovation. Similarly, new institutional arrangement and advances in computing and communication technologies have created a space for the participation of new and more stakeholders in open and user-driven innovation eco-systems; thereby, moving the locus of problem solving away from a single organisation to then include multiple—in this context more than three main—agents. However, within the smart cities' domain, there is a shift in the innovative landscape, which has been facilitated by the widespread applicability of ICT and big data.

Regardless of the form a Triple Helix takes, the roles between the actors involved in creating a smart city is becoming increasingly blurred. In other words, this can be described as a hybrid helix of organisation. The blur emerges because of the core focus and interests of the respective actors in a smart city initiative and the inclusion of more stakeholders outside the traditional three. Meyer et al. [55] argue that the sphere of interest of various actors has been halted and, in some cases, began to retreat to their core businesses; for example, universities on teaching and research. Anyhow, from the Triple Helix concept reviewed for this paper, from a smart city perspective, there were no research that included the direct involvement of its citizens in the innovation eco-system. This could be due to the form and structure smart cities assume when they are commissioned. Smart city initiatives could vary in terms of how active their stakeholders can be compared to others. Consequently, mutual platforms can also involve the establishment of committees, teams and organisations. As a result, Carayannis and Rakhmatullin [16] have argued for a quadruple, and where necessary, a Quintuple Helix.

This section has evaluated PPP as an inter-institutional structure and the Triple Helix as an innovative model for the creation of smart cities. Collaborations in the planning and execution of smart city initiatives, however, still mainly remain a relationship between private and public sectors organisations. Even within a Triple Helix framework, the collaborations that occur do not have a triple inter-face. The multiplicity of stakeholders has a disrupting effect on the creative process in addressing urban issues through the development of smart cities.

5 Case Study

The purpose of this section is to present an example of a smart city situated in Glasgow in Scotland (United Kingdom) named *Future City Glasgow* (FCG) which operates on various work streams (see Table 3). In this case study, the smart city has been used by the city council to address urban problems by demonstrating how data and smart solutions can help in addressing urban issues.

Table 3 Overview of the Future Glasgow Project

Project stream	Scope	Current state (October 2015)
Active Travel	Mobility (Cycling)	Currently only 2% of journeys made into Glasgow city centre involve cycling. Increasing the number of journeys by bike and or foot should help the city cut carbon emissions, boost its air quality and help tackle obesity.
City Technology Platform	Governance (Participation)	The City Technology Platform (CTP) integrates and analyses different data streams. The data is presented in a machine-readable format, which is open for use to whoever wants to use it. It can be accessed through its website (MyGlasgow dashboard) and smart phone apps.
Energy Efficiency	Energy Consumption	The city authorities are working with housing authorities to address energy consumption in older, more difficult to heat properties.
Mapping Demonstrator	Culture and Tourism	The city has urged citizens to upload information about their communities online. This includes details of favourite bars, restaurants, shops and heritage sights.
Operations Centre	Security and Safety	The city has deployed safety cameras that detect unusual activities. Suspicious detection should trigger an alarm that would be investigated by the appropriate response service.
Social Transport	Mobility (Social Transport)	The city has deployed route optimising software and scheduling tools in conjunction with service providers to reduce route duplication—to reduce the number of unnecessary journeys made and to ensure that buses carry the optimum number of passengers. This should reduce traffic congestion, air pollution and the number of buses on the road (also cutting costs).
Street Lighting	Energy Efficiency	The city has deployed energy efficient LED lamps, which have demonstrated how the city could reduce its carbon emissions, reduce energy consumption and ensure safety.

Source Future City Glasgow [30]

FCG is a £24 million smart city initiative, which aims at demonstrating how technology can make living in the city smarter, safer and more sustainable (www. gov.uk). Glasgow beats 29 other cities to win funding for the programme in a contest run by the Technology Strategy Board (TSB), the British government's innovation agency [74]. The £24 million grant lasted for over a period of three years (2013–2016).

In doing so, the city authorities and planners are putting residents at the fore-front of the technological integration and application ([4], [29], [71]). It is a data-driven process that is meant to assist policymakers and inform future investments to improve the efficiency of the provision of services. The initiative is encapsulated in Table 3, which covers areas such as healthcare, public safety, transportation and sustainability. This case adopts an inter-institutional arrangement that involves the public, academics and businesses, which is geared towards getting these stakeholders involved in using the data and contributing their own knowledge to the initiative.

For instance, the open data work stream deploys an intelligent data platform to store, analyse and publish real-time data on an online dashboard [30]. Data can be accessed on widgets and smartphone applications (apps). Another example was given, where one of the apps allows users/citizens to bring to the attention of city authorities uncollected trash and potholes—i.e. with use of smart phones—as well as receiving updates on the problem that was reported [30]. In line with open data principles, by opening data to the public, the city can engage with entrepreneurs and application developers who come up with useful ideas and solutions that help the city address urban issues.

More than 400 data streams have been identified in Glasgow; they include infor-mation on everything from bin collections to footfall in retail areas [30]. For the active travel, there is a cycling app that records the journey of cyclists, so that the council knows what routes are regularly used, which in turn allows stakeholders to know where and how to channel resources towards having an adequate cycling infrastructure. From its inception in 2013, the city has embarked on building three-dimensional (3D) model sensors in public housing buildings to help improve the energy efficiency of the citizens and city. The city council has demonstrated that they are able to redeploy these vehicles to other divisions when not being used.

Therefore, the smart city concept is a useful way to address complex urban problems. Stakeholders—in the public, private and academic sectors—involved in addressing urban problems can combine their expertise and deploy cutting-edge technology to better the day-to-day living in a city. Hence, the smart city initiative included:

- A smart street lighting demonstrator showing how the city can deploy smarter street lighting to improve the lighting quality, reduce energy usage and ensure efficient management. The other capabilities of this scheme could be transferred in other areas, such as: noise detection, movement detection, air pollution detection and wireless internet (Wi-Fi) service.
- The active travel demonstrator highlighting how the city could be more inclusive to accommodate cyclists and pedestrians.

- The integrated social transport demonstrator helped some of Glasgow's most disadvantaged citizens access social and educational services. A smart integration and route scheduling software, thus, increased the flexibility and responsiveness transport services.

6 Recommendations and Conclusion

The preference for people to live and work in cities has led to the growth (and predicted future growth) of urban areas. This growth poses challenges for planners and city-dwellers alike, such as in the development of infrastructure and the provision of basic services. The smart city concept is perceived to be a useful way to mitigate the challenges facing urban areas. Successful smart city initiatives can be categorised into the six characteristics discussed in sub-Sect. 1.3.2. For example, the city of Glasgow smart city initiative has successfully demonstrated how the smart city concept could be put into practice (see Sect. 1.5).

Multiple stakeholders working in a smart city project can define the structure that a smart city can take. For example, Glasgow wants its smart cities to be an eco-system of developers (a triple, quadruple or even quintuple helix) and data owners who work together to release, renew and update datasets that can be used to develop solutions for urban problems. Therefore, by adopting this model the city hopes to provide bespoke services that address particular problems, such as in security and safety. Thus, by opening up datasets to the public, the city hopes to build trust with its citizenry in order to enhance (data-driven) decision-making.

Becoming a smart city requires a city to be a living laboratory—a continuous 'test bed' for the experimentation of smart city ideas in the form of initiatives. To this end, living laboratories encompass societal and technological dimensions simultaneously through a business-citizens-government-academia partnership. In other words, smart cities are a continuous living lab process were stakeholders keep trying out different solutions to problems. There is also the potential for an increase in the participation of end-users. Thus, the nature of the living laboratories determines the type of helix a city should adopt.

Furthermore, stakeholders that adopt the living laboratory process also have the opportunity to incrementally enhance their existing infrastructure. This is because by embedding IT into existing infrastructure, cities are able to be more efficient in deploying their existing infrastructure. Therefore, by embedding new smart city technology with already existing infrastructure, stakeholders can at the same time integrate solutions to multiple areas of urban living. Moreover, the introduction of new smart city infrastructure can also be deployed to serve multiple areas of urban living. As demonstrated in the Glasgow case study, the intelligent street lighting scheme allowed stakeholders to efficiently light up the city and it also served as a way to measure noise and air pollution. Hence, in designing new smart city infrastructure, stakeholders should also consider the multi-faceted and inter-linked areas of urban living in respect to problems that need to be addressed in a city.

This chapter paper has critically analysed the smart city concept, its characteristics and the collaborative structure involved in developing smart cities. To understand smart cities, it was important to begin with exploring the nature of wicked problems. In doing so, it acknowledges that the kind of issues a city in the 21st Century poses to stakeholders are complex due to their intrinsic nature. These have been conceptualised as wicked problems given that they tend to be intractable, even on computational levels. Thus, the concept of smart cities was conceptualised to be a response to these wicked problems.

By identifying a working definition of a smart city and analysing the concept, the significance of its importance and relevance to the research problem was highlighted. In addition, how collaborations for smart cities are organised, through PPP and the Triple Helix, was critically investigated. The examination of the collaborative structures and processes emphasised the shift in the innovative landscape, which have been facilitated by the rise in the applicability of ICT and the growth of big data. A smart city case study situated in Glasgow; Scotland was described to have a real example. To this end, the paper offers empirically informed practical recommendations for actors in the smart city domain.

References

1. Albino, V., Berardi, U., & Dangelico, R. M. (2015). Smart cities: Definitions, dimensions, performance, and initiatives. *Journal of Urban Technology, 22*(1), 3–21.
2. Aleksandrs, Z., Jurgis, Z., Kristina, T., & Anatolijs, B. (2014). Concept of smart city: First experience from City of Riga. *Journal of Sustainable Architecture and Civil Engineering, 7*(2), 54–59.
3. Allwinkle, S., & Cruickshank, P. (2011). Creating smart-er cities: An overview. *Journal of Urban Technology, 18*(2), 1–16.
4. BBC News. (2013). *Glasgow wins 'smart city' government cash.* Available at: http://www.bbc.co.uk/news/technology-21180007. Last accessed: 12 February 2020.
5. Baccarne, B., Mechant, P., & Schuurman, D. (2014). Empowered Cities? An Analysis of the Structure and Generated Value of the Smart City Ghent. In R. P. Dameri & C. Rosenthal-Sabroux (Eds.), Smart City: How to Create Public and Economic Value with High Technology in Urban Space. Berlin: Springer International Publishing. 157–182.
6. Bakıcı, T., Almirall, E., & Wareham, J. (2013). A smart city initiative: the case of Barcelona. *Journal of the Knowledge Economy, 4*(2) 135–148.
7. Ballas, D. (2013). What makes a 'happy city'? *Cities, 32*(1), 39–50.
8. Barrionuevo, Berrone, P. & Ricart, J. E. (2012). "Smart Cities, Sustainable Progress," *IESE Insight, 14*, 50–57.
9. Batty, M. (2013). Big data, smart cities and city planning. *Dialogues in Human Geography, 3*(3), 274–279.
10. Bayliss, D. (2007). The rise of the creative city: Culture and creativity in Copenhagen. *European Planning Studies, 15*(7), 889–903.
11. Bettencourt, L. (2013). The kind of problem a city is. *SFI working paper.* 03 (008), 1–34.
12. Buck, N. T., & While, A. (2015). Competitive urbanism and the limits to smart city innovation: The UK Future Cities initiative. *Urban Studies,* Available at: http://usj.sagepub.com/content/early/2015/08/05/0042098015597162.full. Last accessed on 10 August 2016.
13. Camillius, J. (2008). Strategy as a wicked problem. *Harvard Business Review, 86*(5), 103–109.

14. Capello, R., Caragliu, A., & Lenzi, C. (2012). Is innovation in cities a matter of knowledge-intensive services? An empirical investigation. Innovation: *The European Journal of Social Science Research, 25*(2), 151–174.
15. Caragliu, A., Del Bo, C., & Nijkamp, P. (2011). Smart cities in Europe. *Journal of Urban Technology, 18*(2), 65–82.
16. Carayannis, E. G., & Rakhmatullin, R. (2014). The quadruple/quintuple innovation helixes and smart specialisation strategies for sustainable and inclusive growth in Europe and beyond. *Journal of the Knowledge Economy, 5*(2), 212–239.
17. Chen, T. M. (2010). "Smart Grids, Smart Cities Need Better Networks [Editor's Note]," *IEEE Network, 24*(2), 2–3.
18. Clarke, M & Stewart, J (1997). *Handling the Wicked Issues—A Challenge for Government.* University of Birmingham, School of Public Policy Discussion Paper, University of Birmingham.
19. Coe, A., Paquet, G., & Roy, J. (2001). E-governance and smart communities a social learning challenge. *Social Science Computer Review, 19*(1), 80–93.
20. Conklin, J. (2008). *Wicked problems and social complexity.* San Francisco: Cognexus Institute.
21. Cosgrave, E., Arbuthnot, K., & Tryfonas, T. (2013). Living labs, innovation districts and information marketplaces: A systems approach for smart cities. *Procedia Computer Science, 16*(1), 668–677.
22. Coyne, R. (2005). Wicked problems revisited. *Design Studies, 26*(1), 5–17.
23. Cretu, G. L. (2012). "Smart Cities Design Using Event-driven Paradigm and Semantic Web," *Informatica Economica, 16*(4), 57–67.
24. Custos, D., & Reitz, J. (2010). Public-private partnerships. *The American Journal of Comparative Law, 58*(1), 555–584.
25. Deakin, M. (2014). Smart cities: The state-of-the-art and governance challenge. *Triple Helix, 1*(1), 1–16.
26. Eger, J. M. (2009). "Smart Growth, Smart Cities, and the Crisis at the Pump A Worldwide Phenomenon," *I-Ways, 32*(1), 47–53.
27. Etzkowitz, H. (2008). *The triple helix: University-industry-government innovation in action.* Oxon: Routledge.
28. Ferlie, E., Fitzgerald, L., McGivern, G., Dopson, S., & Bennett, C. (2011). Public policy networks and 'wicked problems': A nascent solution? *Public Administration, 89*(2), 307–324.
29. Financial Times. (2014b). *Glasgow aims to be first 'smart city.* Available at: http://www.ft.com/cms/s/0/d119ac06-e57e-11e3-a7f5-00144feabdc0.html#axzz3qXfYmMEy. Last accessed on 20 February 2020.
30. Future City Glasgow. (2017). *Future City Glasgow.* Available at: https://futurecity.glasgow.gov.uk/. Last accessed 20 February 2020.
31. Giffinger, R., Haindlmaier, G., & Kramar, H. (2010). The role of rankings in growing city competition. *Urban Research & Practice, 3*(3), 299–331.
32. Gil-Garcia, J. R., Zhang, J., & Puron-Cid, G. (2016). Conceptualizing smartness in government: An integrative and multi-dimensional view. *Government Information Quarterly, 33*(3), 524–534.
33. Guan, L. (2012). "Smart Steps To A Battery City," *Government News, 32*(2), 24–27.
34. Guardian. (2015a). *Driverless cars set to roll out for trials on UK roads.* Available at: https://www.theguardian.com/technology/2015/feb/11/driverless-cars-roll-out-trials-ukroads. Last accessed on 12 January 2019.
35. Hall, R. E. (2000). "The Vision of a Smart City." *Proc. of the 2nd International Life Extension Technology Workshop*, Paris, France.
36. Harrison, C., Eckman, B., Hamilton, R., Hartswick, P., Kalagnanam, J., Paraszczak, J. & Williams, P. (2010). "Foundations for Smarter Cities," *IBM Journal of Research and Development, 54*(4), 1–16.
37. Hatzelhoffer, L. (2012). *Smart City in Practice: Converting Innovative Ideas into Reality: Evaluation of the T-city friedrichshafen.* Berlin: Jovis.

38. Von Hippel, E., & Von Krogh, G. (2016). Identifying viable need–solution pairs: Problem solving without problem formulation. *Organization Science, 27*(1), 207–221.
39. Hodge, G. A., & Greve, C. (2007). Public–private partnerships: An international performance review. *Public Administration Review, 67*(3), 545–558.
40. Hollands, R. G. (2015). Critical interventions into the corporate smart city. *Cambridge Journal of Regions, Economy and Society, 8*(1), 61–77.
41. IDA Singapore. (2012). "iN2015 Masterplan". http://www.ida.gov.sg/~/media/Files/Inf ocomm%20Landscape/iN2015/Reports/realisingthevisionin2015.pdf.
42. Jentoft, S., & Chuenpagdee, R. (2009). Fisheries and coastal governance as a wicked problem. *Marine Policy, 33*(4), 553–560.
43. Kanter, R. M., & Litow, S. S. (2009). Informed and interconnected: A manifesto for smarter cities. *Harvard Business School General Management Unit Working Paper*, 9–141. Available at: http://papers.ssrn.com/sol3/papers.cfm?abstract_id=1420236. Last accessed on 5 April 2019.
44. Komninos, N., Schaffers, H., & Pallot, M. (2011). Developing a policy roadmap for smart cities and the future internet. In *eChallenges e-2011 Conference Proceedings, IIMC International Information Management Corporation*. IMC International Information Management Corporation.
45. Koppenjan, J. F., & Enserink, B. (2009). Public–private partnerships in urban infrastructures: Reconciling private sector participation and sustainability. *Public Administration Review, 69*(2), 284–296.
46. Kourtit, K., & Nijkamp, P. (2012). "Smart Cities in the Innovation Age," *Innovation: The European Journal of Social Science Research, 25*(2), 93–95.
47. Kourtit, K., Nijkamp, P., & Arribas, D. (2012). "Smart Cities in Perspective – A Comparative European Study by Means of Self-organizing Maps," *Innovation: The European Journal of Social Science Research, 25*(2), 229–246.
48. Lazaroiu, G. C., & Roscia, M. (2012). "Definition Methodology for the Smart Cities Model," *Energy, 47*(1), 326–332.
49. Leydesdorff, L., & Deakin, M. (2011). The triple-helix model of smart cities: A neoevolutionary perspective. *Journal of Urban Technology, 18*(2), 53–63.
50. Lombardi, P., Giordano, S., Farouh, H., & Yousef, W. (2012). Modelling the smart city performance. *The European Journal of Social Science Research, 25*(2), 137–149.
51. Lombardi, P., & Vanolo, A. (2015). Smart city as a mobile technology: critical perspectives on urban development policies. In Rodríguez-Bolívar and Pedro (Eds.), Transforming city Governments for Successful Smart Cities (pp. 147–161). Berlin: Springer International Publishing.
52. Mainka, A., Hartmann, S., Meschede, C., & Stock, W. G. (2015). Open government: Transforming data into value-added city services. In M. Foth, M. Brynskov, & T. Ojala (Eds.), *Citizen's right to the digital city*. Singapore: Springer.
53. Marsal-Llacuna, M. L., Colomer-Llinàs, J., & Meléndez-Frigola, J. (2014). Lessons in urban monitoring taken from sustainable and liveable cities to better address 309 the Smart Cities initiative. *Technological Forecasting and Social Change, 90*(1), 611–622.
54. McKee, M., Edwards, N., & Atun, R. (2006). Public-private partnerships for hospitals. *Bulletin of the World Health Organization, 84*(11), 890–896.
55. Meyer, M., Grant, K., & Kuusisto, J. (2013). The second coming of the triple helix and the emergence of hybrid innovation environments. *Universities, Cities and Regions: Loci for Knowledge and Innovation Creation*, 193–209.
56. Murgante, B., & Borruso, G. (2014). Smart city or smurfs city. *Computational Science and Its Applications–ICCSA 2014* (pp. 738–749). Berlin: Springer.
57. Nam, T., & Pardo, T. A. (2011). "Conceptualizing Smart City with Dimensions of Technology, People, and Institutions," Proc. 12th Conference on Digital Government Research, College Park, MD, June 12–15.
58. Nijkamp, P. (2009). E pluribus unum. *Region Direct, 1*(2), 56–65.
59. Nijkamp P., Lombardi P., Giordano S., Caragliu A., Del Bo C., Deakin M., & Kourtit K. (2011). An Advanced Triple-Helix Network Model for Smart Cities performance. *Research Memorandum 2011-45*.

60. Okwechime, E., Duncan, P., & Edgar, D. (2018). Big data and smart cities: a public sector organizational learning perspective. *Information Systems and e-Business Management, 16*(3), 601–625.

61. Poelhekke, S. (2006). "Do Amenities and Diversity Encourage City Growth? A Link through Skilled Labor", *Economics Working Papers* ECO2006/10, San Domenico di Fiesole, Italy: European University Institute.

62. Ranga, M., & Etzkowitz, H. (2013). Triple Helix systems: an analytical framework for innovation policy and practice in the Knowledge Society. *Industry and Higher Education, 27*(4), 237–262.

63. Rittel, H., & Webber, M. M. (1973). Dilemmas in a general theory of planning. *Policy Science, 4*(2), 155–169.

64. Rosol, M. (2013). Vancouver's "ecodensity" planning initiative: A struggle over hegemony? *Urban Studies, 50*(11), 2238–2255.

65. Savino, T., Messeni Petruzzelli, A., & Albino, V. (2015). Search and recombination process to innovate: A review of the empirical evidence and a research agenda. *International Journal of Management Reviews, 19*(1), 54–75.

66. Schuurman, D., De Moor, K., De Marez, L., & Evens, T. (2011). A living lab research approach for mobile TV. *Telematics and Informatics, 28*(1), 271–282.

67. Shelton, T., Zook, M., & Wiig, A. (2015). The 'actually existing smart city'. *Cambridge Journal of Regions, Economy and Society, 8*(1), 13–25.

68. Slavova, M., & Okwechime, E. (2016). African smart cities strategies for Agenda 2063. *Africa Journal of Management, 2*(2), 210–229.

69. Soete, L. (2005). Innovation, technology and productivity: Why Europe lags behind the United States and why various European economies differ in innovation and productivity. In M. Castells & G. Cardoso, *The Network Society: From Knowledge to Policy*. Washington, DC: Centre for Transatlantic Relations, Paul H. Nitze School of Advanced International Studies, Johns Hopkins University.

70. Sunitiyoso, Y., Wicaksono, A., Utomo, D. S., Putro, U. S., & Mangkusubroto, K. (2012). Developing strategic initiatives through triple helix interactions: Systems modelling for policy development. *Procedia-Social and Behavioral Sciences, 52*(1), 140–149.

71. Thite, M. (2011). "Smart Cities: Implications of Urban Planning for Human Resource Development," *Human Resource Development International, 14*(5), 623–631.

72. Thuzar, M. (2011). "Urbanization in SouthEast Asia: Developing Smart Cities for the Future?," *Regional Outlook*, 96–100.

73. Townsend, A. M. (2013). *Smart Cities: Big data, Civic Hackers, and the Quest for a New Utopia*. New York: WW Norton & Company.

74. TSB. (2012). *Future cities special interest group—definition*. Innovate.uk. Available at: https://connect.innovateuk.org/web/future-cities-special-interest-group/definition. Last accessed on 10 February 2020.

75. Washburn, D., Sindhu, U., Balaouras, S., Dines, R. A., Hayes, N. M., & Nelson, L. E. (2010). Helping CIOs Understand "Smart City" Initiatives: Defining the Smart City, Its Drivers, and the Role of the CIO. Cambridge, MA: Forrester Research.

76. Zygiaris, S. (2013). "Smart City Reference Model: Assisting Planners to Conceptualize the Building of Smart City Innovation Ecosystems," *Journal of the Knowledge Economy, 4*(2), 217–231.

Big Data: An Introduction to Data-Driven Decision Making

Ekene Okwechime, Peter B. Duncan, David A. Edgar, Elisabetta Magnaghi, and Eleonora Veglianti

Abstract The purpose of this article is to set the groundwork of data-driven decision making. Currently, there are widespread discussions on how society is shaped and changing due to the increased use of data for decision making in the private and public sector. Central to this form of decision making is big data and open data. We present a critical review of big data: it's characteristics and sources. We also provide a critical review of open data by delineating its difference to big data, i.e. the types and sources of open data. We argue that if the conditions are right, big data can be open data—and vice versa. Most importantly, we present where and how big data can be used applied in various areas of society, e.g. in smart cities. By carrying out this review, we outline the composition of data and where and how it can be applied in society at large. Ultimately, given the accessibility of data, we critically review a fast-moving ecosystem where end-users and decision makers can be guided by data.

Keywords Big data · Open data · Data-driven decision-making

1 Introduction

The purpose of this article is to critically review the literature relating to the concept of big data; to demonstrate how it could drive data-driven decision making. Despite

The original version of this chapter was revised: The affiliation for the authors "Peter B. Duncan and David A. Edgar" was corrected. The correction to this chapter is available at https://doi.org/10. 1007/978-3-030-60607-7_12

E. Okwechime (✉)
Lancashire School of Business and Enterprise, University of Central Lancashire, Preston, UK
e-mail: eokwechime@uclan.ac.uk

P. B. Duncan · D. A. Edgar
Department of Business and Management, Glasgow Caledonian University, Glasgow, UK

E. Magnaghi
Department of Business and Economics, Université Catholique de Lille, Lille, France
e-mail: elisabetta.magnaghi@univ-catholille.fr

E. Veglianti
Department of Economics, University of Uninettuno, Rome, Italy
e-mail: eleonora.veglianti@uninettunouniversity.net

the increasing use of big data in industries in the form of business analytics and smart cites, there has been a lack of published scholarship that addresses the challenges of using such a tool, or which explores the opportunities for new theories and practices emerging from the use of big data [13]. Big data as a fast-growing and evolving concept in management research has disrupted the understanding in the field between information and problem solving. Von Hippel [33] had argued that information needed for problem solving was costly to acquire, transfer and use in different locations. On the contrary, although the infrastructure needed for big data might still be costly [31]. However, given the characteristics and sources of big data (information) it is far easier to acquire and transfer. Therefore, it is important to critically evaluate the concept of big data to assess how it could be used to address complex problems and ultimately decision making.

The paper is structured as follows. Section 1.2 contains the conceptualisation of big data. It is argued in this review that another aspect of the big data phenomena is its accessibility to the public. There have been efforts by governments and organisations to open data to whoever wants it [20]. This phenomenon is referred to as open data; which is critically examined in Sect. 1.3. The accessibility of big data, in turn, creates an eco-system where end-users interact with the data that is generated. Decision-making underpinned by the use of big data (data driven decision-making) is then critically examined in Sect. 1.4. Section 1.5 contains the summary of the article.

2 The Big Data Concept

The purpose of this section is to critically examine the concept of big data. It covers the definition, characteristics, growth, sources and the use of big data. Big data is data complex in terms of volume and relativity to its sources; making it difficult to analyse with conventional database management techniques [34]. It is data generated from a growing variety of sources (see Table 1), which range from clicks on the internet, mobile transactions, business transactions, user-generated content, social media, as well as purposefully generated content through sensors [13]. The term big data is a direct reference to the size of data: a large collective volume of heterogeneous data absorbed at an increasing pace. The data in question does vary in different characteristics and sources. Thus, big data is complex diverse data that is generated from different sources.

The characteristics are referred to as the 7Vs of big data. The 7Vs—Volume: size; Variety: types; Velocity: frequency; Variability: diversity; Veracity: accuracy; Visualization: visual imagery and Value: benefits—of big data are making their way as an organisational tool and resource [7], [15], [25]). What these characteristics suggest is that big data does not necessarily depend on size (volume) but on the overall nature and quality of the data generated. However, what makes big data unique and different from any other typology of data is due to its flow in real-time.

sGeorge et al. [13] list five key sources of big data (see Table 1). The data types, the source and content are in the first, second and third columns respectively. For instance, the data source labelled as 'public data' (in the second row) is data held by governmental organisations, which could include healthcare, transport and energy usage data. The second, 'private data', (in the third row) is held by private and non-profit organisations, that contain information about private individuals, such as consumer transactions and mobile phone usage. The third, 'data exhaust', (in the fourth row) is data passively generated by individuals that reflect the everyday lives of people, such as web usage and video surveillance footage. The fourth, 'community data', (in the fifth row) is a distillation of unstructured textual data that captures social trends and phenomena. The fifth, 'self-quantification data', (in the sixth row) is data discovered through the quantification of human behaviour in controlled settings with use of wearable sensors, such as fitness wristbands. These form the state-of-art of the sources of big data. However, there has been a dearth of research into the potential impact of these five sources of data within organisational studies. These five sources overlap with each other (especially 2, 3 and 4), and do not form a rigid classification typology.

Due to the widespread applicability of big data, there are varying perspectives of what it means to various stakeholders in different industries [5]. Therefore, the value of big data to, for example, an online retailer, could mean something different to an urban planner looking to address traffic congestion. For example, Table 2 also illustrates that within e-government and politics, big data has influenced the way political parties run campaigns—which are more data-driven—and the provision of services by an e-commerce firm. Above all, big data is a complex, diverse and widely used concept, which has become more complicated due to widespread availability of data from various sources (see Sect. 1.3 for Open Data).

Moreover, the analytic use of big data has been applied to produce predictive models in different sectors of the global economy, such as in international travel, healthcare, high-speed network connections, outsourcing, retail and supply chain management ([2], [5], [19], [26]). Table 2 illustrates and gives examples of how organisations, in various sectors, are becoming more data driven. These examples (in the first row) are drawn from six sectors: e-commerce and marketing; e-government and politics; science and technology; smart health and wellbeing; security and public safety respectively. The areas of application (in the second column) illustrated in the table are also analogous to areas in which the smart city concept can be applied too, such as in the provision of healthcare and governance. The table also consists of a description on the type of data (in the third row) and its characteristics that emerge from the various sectors. The applicability of the analytic use of big data in the smart city domain has also become more dynamic and complex due to the widespread availability of urban data [17], [30]; also, see Sect. 1.3 for Open Data). The means of analysis (in the fourth row) describes the various techniques suitable for in the various sectors. Lastly, the impact (in the fifth column) in the various sectors is highlighted.

The section has highlighted that the characteristics and sources of big data influence its applicability and effectiveness. Above all, this section has demonstrated that big data is a complex, diverse and growing concept with various perspectives in different sectors. Advances in computing and data infrastructure have made it possible for different sources of data to be made available to the public—to whoever needs data [7]. This phenomenon is referred to as open data [20]. Most importantly, from a smart city context, open data leads to the involvement of more stakeholders in the creative process. The following section critically examines the implications of opening various sources of (big) data to the public.

3 Open Data

The purpose of this section is to critically examine the concept of open data. According to the *Open Data Institute*, a think tank, "open data is data that anyone can access, use or share" [20]. Most of the data produced by organisations is now machine-readable which means that data can be made available to whoever needs it. Therefore, critically examining open data is important because most of the data public sector organisations are in possession off is increasingly becoming public and machine-readable. Figure 1 illustrates the spectrum on which data is made available to whoever wants it.

Figure 1 also provides a composition of the typology and sources of open data. At the far right-end of the data spectrum is open (license) data. For example, data on bus timetables or weather forecasts. Such information is free for all that want it. At the opposing far end of the spectrum is closed data—which requires internal authorisation to be accessed. An example of such data could be the sales report of a company. In the middle spectrum—shared—are named access, group based and public access data. In general, shared data is not kept away from the public, but the end-users must show interest in wanting to gain access to such information.

The Open Data Handbook [16, p. 1] produced by, *Open Knowledge*, think tank, summarises the concept in the following terms:

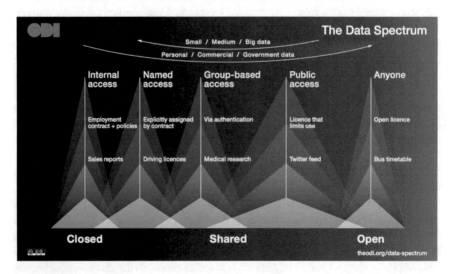

Fig. 1 The data spectrum (*Source* Open Data Institute [20])

- **Availability and Access:** the data must be available in its complete form and at no more than a reasonable reproduction cost, preferably by downloading over the internet. The data must also be available in a convenient and modifiable form.
- **Re-use and Redistribution:** the data must be provided under terms that permit re-use and redistribution including the intermixing with other datasets.
- **Universal Participation:** everyone must be able to use, re-use and redistribute—there should be no discrimination against fields of endeavour or against persons or groups. For example, 'non-commercial' restrictions that would prevent 'commercial' use, or restrictions of use for certain purposes (e.g. only in education), are not allowed.

Open data can also be big data, and vice versa. However, the difference between open data and big data is the former's insistence on availability and access; re-use and redistribution as well as universal participation [16]. For example, regarding the sources of data discussed in Sect. 1.2 (see Table 1) all sources of data, especially public data are increasingly becoming more machine-readable. Given that data is constantly collected by businesses and governments on all levels ranging from information about the urban environment, to the use of public services as well as urban and cultural activities, the open data concept seeks to make accessible 'non-personal data'—that which does not contain specific information about individuals [16]. Figure 1 illustrates to what extent the sources of data can are openly accessible for re-use and distribution that foster wider participation.

Table 1 Sources of data

Data Type	Source	Data Content
Public Data	This is data held by governmental organisations that can be accessed, in some instances, under restrictions to protect privacy.	Energy use, Healthcare and Transportation.
Private Data	This is data held by private and non-profit organisations that reflect the personal information of individuals.	Consumer transactions, mobile phone usage and radio frequency identification tags.
Data Exhaust	This is passively generated data by individuals.	Everyday activities of individuals, such as web searches.
Community Data	This is distilled unstructured textual data that can be used to infer social patterns.	Consumers' reviews and twitter feeds.
Self-quantification data	This is the quantification of personal actions and behaviours, in some cases using wearable devices.	This is quantified human behaviour, such as diets and physical exercise.

Source George et al. [13]

Open data can be based on scientific data (e.g. astronomy data), financial data (e.g. government expenditure), official statistics (e.g. socioeconomic indicators), geological (e.g. flight trackers, weather or street maps), environmental (e.g. footfall) and transport (travel routes and timetables). Thus, the availability of such data should also lead to the creation of new services that makes city living easier. For example, smart phone applications can enable citizens to plan their routes on public transportation, borrow books from the library, pay parking fees and get engaged in the broader decision-making in the city. Conversely, Reichman et al. [28] note that concerning academia, some disciplines have a tradition of sharing data, such as astronomy, while others do not, such as in genomics. Thus, scientists in specific disciplines for ethical or professional reasons [3] can withhold data. This means that organisations should question the importance of opening data; and, what premium should be placed on whatever data is opened. The opening of more data might end up empowering the empowered. Thereby widening the digital divide prevalent in cities; this leads to exclusion, low participation in governance and a lack of cohesion.

In accordance with the open data principle, by Open Knowledge [16], anyone should have the opportunity to use it. Thus, open data can foster transparency. Consequently, when organisations release data, any type of end-user, such as businesses, citizens or academics, can use open data to inform their activities [16]. There are, however, still privacy concerns about the opening data [14]; this is because with the right skills and capabilities, data subjects can be identified by matching various sources and characteristics of data.

The section has critically examined the phenomenon of open data: the availability and access; re-use and redistribution as well as universal participation of data. Opening (big) data comes with benefits and challenges. Regardless, the effective use of data by everyone still drives the move to open even more data. Open data is an important part of this thesis because most of the data public sector organisations hold is increasingly made public and machine-readable. Therefore, the following section focuses on how big and open data can be used to enhance decision-making.

4   Data Driven Decision-Making

The purpose of this section is to critically examine the concept of data driven decision-making (DDD). Considerable attention has been paid to the potential impact of big data and data-driven methods in the sciences and the social sciences ([4], [18], [19], [31]). Data driven decision-making is the practice of making decisions based on the analysis of data, rather than relying solely on intuition [4]. Thus, decision-making in organisations has increasingly undergone a change: from relying on a decision-maker's intuition to the application of data analytics ([6], [26], [29]). Okwechime et al. [19] suggest that the shift towards big data, based organisational learning indicators in firms, enables stakeholders to utilise the concept when considering different courses of action when pursuing set strategic goals.

Messelt [18] argues that DDD is the collection of suitable data analysed in a meaningful way. Data driven decision-making could also mean providing data to those who require it. In other words, it could mean using data to increase performance and improve efficiency as well as conveying data-driven decisions to key stakeholders. Moreover, DDD can also be described as the communication of data from multiple sources for decision-making to decision-makers [6]. Therefore, DDD can be conceived to be a hybrid approach to decision-making that incorporates aspects of analytics and intuition [4]. DDD has also been influenced by the relative ease in which data can be collected, stored and processed. Thus, decision-making based on the traditions of empirical science—describing a natural phenomenon or using models based on theoretical science for generalisations or even the use of computational simulation systems—has now assumed a deeper dimension due to big data. In effect, Silvestro [29] argues that big data has disrupted and changed the decision-making process in organisations, because organisations can now derive so much value from various sources of heterogeneous data.

In any of the contexts described in Table 2, the objective behind using big data for predictive modelling are "based on one or more data instances for which we want to predict the value of a target variable" [12]. The authors argue that, irrespective of the characteristics of data and sources, researchers and practitioners' alike—due to the name of the concept—keep on asking a recurring question relating to size: does bigger mean better? To empirically assess this problem, they analyse "fine-grained behavioural data" [12] from customer-generated online data (referred in Table 1 as data exhaust) and found out that such data is valuable in making predictions. They arrived at this conclusion, using a multivariate *Bernoulli Naïve Bayes* algorithm, by demonstrating that they would not have been able to arrive at their conclusion without a massive volume of data. Thus, volume forms a defining character of the concept, and could mean better analysis for decision-making [12]. Even though De Fortuny et al. [12] based their argument on size, they include that achieving a high predictive performance would also depend on the variety of the sources of data in use.

Popovič et al. [24] draw from the information technology (IT) value and resource-based view (RBV) literature to demonstrate the impact of big data on a firm's business performance. In their comparative case analysis, of three manufacturing firms, the usefulness of the analytic use of big data—"sourcing, access, integration, and delivery, analytical capabilities, and people's expertise" Popovič et al. (2016, p. 1)—alongside organisational factors, such as top-management support and financial resources, enhances a firm' decision making capabilities and (manufacturing) performance. The results from their cases under study indicate that, the analytic use of big data resulted in minimising process downtime, maximising equipment efficiency and reducing production waste.

Within the smart cities' domain, big data informs decisions in every aspect of urban development, such as in healthcare, transportation and security. Similarly, the use of big data for decision-making has been applied in different spheres of subject areas: ecology and sustainability (Guo et al. 2015); economy [10]; education [27]; healthcare [1]; innovation [21]; logistics and supply chain [32], organisational-use [31] and urban application ([9], [23]). Thus, big data has the potential not just to

Table 2 Big Data application

Sectors	E-commerce	E-government & Politics	Science & Technology (S&T)	Security & Public Safety	Smart Health & Wellbeing
Applications	Crowd-sourcing systems Recommender systems Social and virtual games Social media monitoring and analysis	Citizen engagement and participation Equal access and public services Political campaign and e-polling Ubiquitous government services	Hypothesis testing Knowledge discovery Science and Technology (S&T) innovation	Computational criminology Crime analysis Cyber security Open-source intelligence Terrorism informatics	Healthcare decision support Human and plant genomics Patient community analysis
Data	Customer generated content Customer transaction records Search and user logs	Citizen feedback and comments Government information and services. Rules and regulations	S&T instruments and system-generated data Sensor and network content	Crime maps Criminal networks Criminal records News and web contents Terrorism incident databases Viruses, cyber-attacks and botnets	Electronic health records (EHR) Genomics and sequence data Health and patient social media
	Characteristics Structured web-based, user-generated content, rich network information, unstructured informal customer opinions	Characteristics Fragmented information sources & legacy systems, rich textual content, unstructured informal citizen conversation	Characteristics High-throughput instrument-based data collection, fine grained multiple modalities & large scale records, S&T specific data formats	Characteristics Personal identity information, incomplete and deceptive content, rich group and network information, multilingual content	Characteristics Disparate but highly linked content and person-specific

(continued)

Table 2 (continued)

Sectors	E-commerce	E-government & Politics	Science & Technology (S&T)	Security & Public Safety	Smart Health & Wellbeing
Analytics	Anomaly detection Association rule mining Database segmentation and clustering Graph mining Sentiment and affect analysis Social network analysis Text and web analytics	Content and text analytics Government information semantic services and ontologies Information integration Sentiment and affect analysis Social media monitoring and analysis Social network analysis	S&T based domain-specific mathematical and analytic models	Criminal association rule mining and clustering Criminal network analysis Multilingual text analytics Sentiment and affect analysis Spatial-temporal analysis and visualization	Data mining and clustering Genomics and sequence analysis and visualization Health ontologies Health social media monitoring and analysis Health text analytics Patient network analysis
Impact	Long-tail marketing, targeted ad, personalized recommendation, increased sale and customer satisfaction	Transforming governments, empowering citizens, improving transparency, participation and equality	S&T advances, scientific impact	Improved public safety and security	Improved healthcare quality, improved long-term care, patient empowerment

Source Chen et al. [5]

change business models but also to change how decisions are made in practice. Regardless, intuition still plays an important role in decision-making, even with big data [8]. This is because when addressing complex and unstructured problems, decision-makers are influenced by their experiences and other holistic associations, such as time constraints.

To demonstrate the complexity behind DDD in relation to addressing urban problems, some cities and police forces deploy data driven technologies to combat crime, otherwise referred to as 'predictive policing' [22]. The rationale behind deploying predictive policing is to enable cities and security forces effectively predict when and where crimes are most likely to occur and by using location data to provide insight into patrol operations [11]. The police are directed to patrol areas where crimes are probable to occur. Deploying such a data driven approach, raises concerns on consent, security, safety, privacy and the ethics of efficiency, i.e. the use of proxy data—in this instance reported crime data—against the ethics of fairness, i.e. the transparency and rigour behind using such 'predictive' technology.

The section has critically examined the use of big data in decision-making in various areas of society. DDD is not an all or nothing approach [6]. In other words, it entails incorporating various sources and characteristics of data to decision-making, which is still influenced by intuition. To this end, the following section presents a summary of what was covered in this paper.

5   Summary

The present contribution has critically reviewed the evolving and fast-growing multi-disciplinary concepts of big data and open data. Thus, conceptualising big data involved describing and critically examining its characteristics (7Vs) and sources. The importance of open data to the research was illustrated. Critically evaluating the concept of open data was particularly useful in providing a holistic view on the big data concept. Thus, big data has been presented as a complex, diverse and widely used concept. Despite its complexity, it is widely used in various sectors of the economy and society. Due to its widespread applicability of the concept, there are varying perspectives of what it means to various stakeholders in different sectors. Lastly, the concept of DDD was discussed, which demonstrated that even though organisational decisions are increasingly more underpinned by big data, intuition still plays an important role in the decision-making process when dealing with complex problems.

References

1. Bates, D. W., Saria, S., Ohno-Machado, L., Shah, A., & Escobar, G. (2014). Big data in health care: Using analytics to identify and manage high-risk and high-cost patients. *Health Affairs, 33*(7), 1123–1131.

2. Bertsimas, D., O' Hair, A., Relyea, S., & Silberholz, J. (2013). An analytics approach to designing clinical trials for cancer. Working paper, MIT Available at: http://josilber.scripts.mit.edu/CancerPaper_Revision1_names.pdf.

3. Boulton, G., Rawlins, M., Vallance, P., & Walport, M. (2011). Science as a public enterprise: The case for open data. *The Lancet, 377*(9778), 1633–1635.

4. Brynjolfsson, E., Hitt, L. M., & Kim, H. H. (2011). Strength in numbers: How does data-driven decisionmaking affect firm performance?. Available at SSRN 1819486.

5. Chen, H., Chiang, R. H., & Storey, V. C. (2012). Business intelligence and analytics: From big data to big impact. *MIS Quarterly, 36*(4), 1165–1188.

6. Constantiou, I. D. (2012). Making space for intuition in decision making: The case of project prioritization. In *Proceedings of the New Frontiers in Management and Organizational Cognition Conference.* National University of Ireland Maynooth.

7. Constantiou, I. D., & Kallinikos, J. (2015). New games, new rules: Big data and the changing context of strategy. *Journal of Information Technology, 30*(1), 44–57.

8. Davenport, T. H., & Dyché, J. (2013). Big data in big companies. *International Institute for Analytics,* 3, 1–31.

9. Diamantoulakis, P. D., Kapinas, V. M., & Karagiannidis, G. K. (2015). Big data analytics for dynamic energy management in smart grids. *Big Data Research, 2*(3), 94–101.

10. Dietzel, M., Braun, N., & Schäfers, W. (2014). Sentiment-based commercial real estate forecasting with google search volume data. *Journal of Property Investment & Finance, 32*(6), 540–569.

11. Ferguson, A. G. (2012). *Predictive policing and reasonable suspicion.* Emory LJ, 62, 259.

12. De Fortuny, E., Martens, D., & Provost, F. (2013). Predictive modelling with big Data: is bigger really better? *Big Data, 1*(4), 215–226.

13. George, G., Haas, M. R., & Pentland, A. (2014). Big Data and Management. *Academy of Management Journal, 57*(2), 321–326.

14. Gkatzelis, V., Aperjis, C., & Huberman, B. A. (2015). Pricing private data. *Electronic Markets, 25*(2), 109–123.

15. Géczy, P. (2014). Big data characteristics. *The Macrotheme Review, 3*(6), 94–104.

16. Open Knowledge. (2014). *The open data handbook.* Cambridge: Open Knowledge.

17. Manyika, J., Chui, M., Brown, B., Bughin, J., Dobbs, R., Roxburgh, C., & Byers, A. H. (2011). *Big Data: The Next Frontier for Innovation, Competition, and Productivity.* McKinsey Global Institute.

18. Messelt, J. (2004). *Data-Driven decision-making: A powerful tool for school improvement.* Minneapolis: Sagebrush.

19. Okwechime, E., Duncan, P., & Edgar, D. (2018). Big data and smart cities: A public sector organizational learning perspective. *Information Systems and e-Business Management, 16*(3), 601–625.

20. Open Data Institute. (2015). *What is Open Data?* Available at: http://theodi.org/guides/what-open-data. Last accessed on 13 March, 2019.

21. Opresnik, D., & Taisch, M. (2015). The value of big data in servitization. *International Journal of Production Economics, 165,* 174–184.

22. O'Neil, C. (2016). *Weapons of math destruction: How big data increases inequality and threatens democracy* (pp. 1–220). New York: Penguin.

23. Pijanowski, B. C., Tayyebi, A., Doucette, J., Pekin, B. K., Braun, D., & Plourde, J. (2014). A big data urban growth simulation at a national scale: Configuring the GIS and neural network based Land Transformation Model to run in a High Performance Computing (HPC) environment. *Environmental Modelling and Software, 51*(1), 250–268.

24. Popovič, A., Hackney, R., Tassabehji, R., & Castelli, M. (2018). The impact of big data analytics on firms' high value business performance. *Information Systems Frontiers, 20*(2), 209–222.

25. Pospiech, M. & Felden, C. (2012). Big data–a state-of-the-art. *AMCIS 2012 Proceedings,* Paper 22.

26. Power, D. J. (2014). Using Big Data for analytics and decision support. *Journal of Decision Systems, 23*(2), 222–228.

27. Qiulin, Z. (2015). Children's reading in big data time how to think and what to do? *Publishing Research Quarterly, 31*(4), 317–320.
28. Reichman, O. J., Jones, M. B., & Schildhauer, M. P. (2011). Challenges and opportunities of open data in ecology. *Science, 331*(6018), 703–704.
29. Silvestro, R. (2016). Do you know what really drives your business's performance? *MIT Sloan Management Review, 57*(4), 28.
30. Slavova, M., & Okwechime, E. (2016). African smart cities strategies for Agenda 2063. *Africa Journal of Management, 2*(2), 210–229.
31. Tambe, P. (2014). Big data investment, skills, and firm value. *Management Science, 60*(6), 1452–1469.
32. Tan, K. H., Zhan, Y., Ji, G., Ye, F., & Chang, C. (2015). Harvesting big data to enhance supply chain innovation capabilities: An analytic infrastructure based on deduction graph. *International Journal of Production Economics, 165,* 223–233.
33. Von Hippel, E. (1994). Sticky information and the locus of problem solving: implications for innovation. *Management Science, 40*(4), 429–439.
34. Yoo, Y. (2015). It is not about size: A further thought on big data. *Journal of Information Technology, 30*(1), 63–65.

Best Practices and Strategies in Sustainability and Smart Mobility: Student Engagement in Italian Universities

Matteo Trombin, Eleonora Veglianti, Roberta Pinna, and Marta Musso

Abstract This paper is dedicated to sustainability and smart mobility in universities. In the recent period called Industry 4.0, digital technologies require the overall society to change. Studying the impact of smart society, in general, and of its components such as smart mobility has become increasingly crucial. This article fills the literature gap discussing smart mobility from a socio-economic perspective with the aim of better understanding the *state-of-art* of this phenomenon as well as to contribute to the debate about smartness in universities. Using a multi-case approach, it suggests a new way of analyzing smart mobility from a socio-economic perspective, in order to investigate the strategies and the best practices in the Italian context.

Keywords Smart mobility · Sustainability · University · Italy · Student engagement

1 Introduction

In the current period, the growth of the population, the increase in the level of urbanization, as well as globalization expose the urban realities to a continuous change. In the latest decades, concepts like smart city, smart people, smart government, smart buildings, smart mobility, smart economy acquired higher centrality in the economic, environmental and societal development process. They are becoming a focal point in the academic and professional agendas.

In other words, society is going toward the so-called smart society, which is "driven by technology, digital connectivity, knowledge, skills, common goals, and innovation

M. Trombin (✉) · E. Veglianti
Department of Economics, University of Uninettuno, Rome, Italy
e-mail: matteo_trombin@libero.it

E. Veglianti
e-mail: eleonora.veglianti@uninettunouniversity.net

R. Pinna · M. Musso
Department of Economics and Business, University of Cagliari, Cagliari, Italy

© Springer Nature Switzerland AG 2021
E. Magnaghi et al. (eds.), *Organizing Smart Buildings and Cities*,
Lecture Notes in Information Systems and Organisation 36,
https://doi.org/10.1007/978-3-030-60607-7_4

to institute political, social and economic development" [30]. In this scenario, we have a new socio-technical ecosystem with people interacting with machines [46] aiming at the improvement of the overall quality of life [26].

This raises critical issues concerning the control and management of all the encompassing "smart systems." In general, from a technological point of view, a smart system is a system imbued with advanced information and communication technologies (ICTs). These technologies can be represented by intelligent-acting products and services, artificial intelligence, and thinking machines, that allow self-configuration, self-healing, self-protection, and self-optimization. Nowadays, one of the most essential smart systems due to the overcrowding, congestion, inadequacy of the transport systems is smart mobility. A bunch of scientific contributions comes out on this peculiar topic (i.e., [47] [1], [11], [21] [23]).

In line with this critical social change and to evaluate every single sustainable initiative with a cost-benefit logic in this field of research, mobility management requires a scientific approach taking into account the flows of citizens' mobility that are part of the mobility process and that influence the final performance of this unique system.

Following this central socio-economic argument, the present paper analyses university projects in sustainable smart mobility considering the engagement of a peculiar sample of citizens, i.e. students. Students are the key actors in the smart mobility processes and evolution paths of the universities under investigation. Indeed, we use the more restrictive concept of student engagement, different from that of student involvement. Student engagement refers to the cases in which student engagement is active and influences the choices made by public administrations and institutions [37]. This is the case that seems to fit better to be applied to the current case, to take into account a broader spectrum of initiatives carried out by Italian universities.

The paper fills the literature gap discussing smart mobility from a socio-economic perspective with the aim of better understanding the *state-of-art* of this phenomenon using a multi-cases approach. Besides, it is our goal to contribute to the debate in order to foster the current thinking about smartness in general, and about smart mobility strategies, during the digital age.

The rest of the paper is structured as follows. Section 2 presents the literature review; Sect. 3 defines the research methodology, and it analyses the cases in the selected Italian universities. Finally, Sect. 4 highlights the findings, presents the limitations, and suggests further works.

2   Literature Review

Recently in the academic literature, a growing interest in the smart city concept emerged worldwide as well as in Europe. The smart city is a new city paradigm, which results from a combination of different factors such as the use of new communication technologies, mobility, environment, and energy efficiency. Its goal is to improve the overall quality of life following the needs of citizens, businesses as well as institutions ([22], [26]).

The current relevant literature does not provide a unified definition of the construct; however, there are some significant research streams in this field. The first approach is more technology-centred, based on the smartness provided by information technology for managing various city functions [36]. From this point of view, some researchers have stressed technology and infrastructure as the main components. The use of information technology (IT) has been considered as a critical factor in the smartness of a city. IT can sense, monitor, control and communicate most of the city services like transport, electricity, environment control, crime control, social, emergencies, etc. ([11], [1]). While information technology can make a city smart, the city itself is an entity with multiple stakeholders seeking diverse outcomes.

The second sample of studies (i.e., [3]) tends to find a definition balancing different economic and social factors such as human and social capital with an urban development dynamic. Then, a bunch of scholars (i.e., [9], [10], [18]) proposed various frameworks, which provide a more integrated perspective of smart cities considering different factors to highlight specific clusters or categories of the smart cities' initiatives.

From the relevant literature, the definition of a smart city presents several alternatives which, together, show the importance of promoting the scientific and political debate. Nevertheless, their potential socio-economic characteristics are key points in the public and government interest.

This article follows the socio-economic perspective analyzed in few scientific contributions ([21], [36], [37], [46], [49]), and it deals specifically with one of the six characteristics (smart governance, smart economy, smart mobility, smart people, smart living, smart environment) of the smart society, as identified by the European Smart City Project.

In other words, at the European level, among the topics regarding the smart city implementation, there is the so-called smart mobility, which is defined as the set of transport and logistics systems supported and integrated by the ICT [5]. The term embodies a series of elements: technology, mobility infrastructures (parking lots, recharging networks, signage, vehicles), mobility solutions (including new mobility models) and people [3].

In line with the above definitions and with the relevant literature, the growth of mobility in the last period requires the adoption of intelligent mobility management systems. As the World Climate Conference suggests, the population growth rate, globalization, and urbanization impact on the volume traffic that in the metropolitan area exceeds any reasonable and sustainable level. In this regard, concrete solutions are crucial, and political actions are needed towards transport transformation and innovation scenarios focused for instance, on fuel efficiency, fuel substitution, and end-of-pipe carbon capture as leverage for decarbonization.

Additional efforts should be made on the combined and synergetic effects of integrating urban energy, infrastructure, and mobility systems, including via modal-shift measures, expansion of public transport options, and sustainable land-use governance. Thus, smart mobility is a broader and more complex phenomenon that aims to offer a new mobility experience more flexible and integrated as well as more accessible and convenient to people and the overall environment.

The role of smart mobility is to manifest in our society in terms of impact and improvement. However, many issues should still be scrutinized and investigated, especially from a socio-economic point of view. For this reason, the choice of the university context is the right setting to test and analyze the innovation coming from smart mobility.

Smart mobility brings innovative solutions in different areas. Firstly, for example, smart mobility is about vehicle technology such as power trains, electric car technology, fuel technology, autonomous automation (i.e., [20]). Secondly, smart mobility is about Intelligent Transport Systems, such as cooperative adaptive cruise control, traffic management, connected automated driving. Thirdly, smart mobility concerns data which can be identified as travel information, logistics planning, advanced IT systems for matching supply and demand and big data solutions. Moreover, smart mobility means also new mobility services: seat management, car sharing, ride sharing, connecting transport modes, new cycling systems.

In other words, vehicle technology, ITS, data, new mobility services broadly define the current scope of smart mobility that finds its origins in a combination of innovation in transportation, infrastructures, and services. At the same time, new paths are booming related to smart mobility, such as e.g. autonomous things, augmented analytics.

Specifically, the Internet of Things (IoT) and the spread of 5G have significantly influenced the worldwide economy and the mobility sector [27]. Thus, the introduction of technologies leads to automation in the road, rail and air traffic with several advantages in terms of traffic (for example smartphones and GPS that show routes with less traffic in real-time), travel (access to information on timetables and locations public transport) and shared mobility (optimization of vehicle and vehicle movements).

Therefore, 5G is transforming the Internet into a network capable of progressively connecting all machines and robots allowing them to perform actions based on complicated algorithms able to process in real-time an immense amount of information and to guide the machines towards external patterns of pre-established behavior [41]. Through the cloud, AI and IoT technologies, cities can harness the power of real-time intelligence for monitoring, anticipating and managing public events, from traffic congestion and flooding to utility optimization and construction [39].

Also, thanks to machine learning and AI, it is possible to automate data analysis processes improving the accessibility to all users, thus having an essential role in citizen engagement. Moreover, the mobility sector is a crucial area of application for AI solutions with several testing examples all around the world (see e.g. [54]).

Finally, many efforts are devoted to applying the blockchain technology to mobility to improve decisive aspects and services ([46], [28], [48]). Some authors, such as Scekic et al. [46] suggest a blockchain-support smart city platform for social value co-creation and exchange.

This paper considers the approach of the value co-creation for a successful implementation of smart mobility pushing citizen's behavior towards the acceptance and adoption of new technologies.

In this stream of research, mobility, and specifically, mobility management reached increasing importance especially at the European level. For instance, since 2009 the EU has pushed the adoption of Sustainable Urban Mobility Plans (SUMPs). SUMPs are a planning tool aimed to face better the challenges posed by the transport system and the critical issues affecting urban areas with a more integrated and sustainable approach.

For example, the European Commission in 2017 defines a SUMP[1] to improve the accessibility of urban areas and to reach high quality and sustainable mobility and transport to, through and within the urban area. The latter highlights the focus on the so-called "functioning city" which emphasizes the involvement of citizens and stakeholders, on the coordination of policies and planning tools among several sectors (transport, urban planning, environment, economic activities, etc.), as well as among various institutions at different levels within and across the territory.

Here, the importance of studying the role of individual engagement is evident. This field of research focuses on the fulfillment of individual mobility needs by leveraging an active approach that involves citizens and other stakeholders from the beginning of the development and implementation of the entire process. Recently, we have a more people-centric approach, which relies more on people and mobility needs, than on traffic and infrastructure [12].

By considering the specific topic of university student's engagement toward sustainability, research was conducted in two main directions. On the one hand, some scholars focused on co-creation, co-production, and living labs initiatives tested on campuses ([13], [38], [47], [49], [53]). On the other hand, some scholars sought to highlight more general features about student's behavior, attitudes, and awareness beyond the context of the campus, from a less self-reliant perspective, and with a focus on regional stakeholders ([43], [42], [4], [8], [14], [34]).

Based on the above literature review, our research questions are as follows:

RQ1 – Which actions and initiatives are implemented at the national level to foster university student's engagement toward sustainability and, in particular, smart mobility?

RQ2 – How and to what extent do the actions and initiatives considered as a sample match a broader and institutionally aware strategy?

To answer these research questions, multi case-based research was conducted to carefully examine this phenomenon in a narrative form, which occurs within the data under analysis. The choice of Italy is the consequence of the nationality and the involvement of the authors in this country. Also, their in-depth knowledge of the relevant literature and the documentation about the subject in the original language,

---

[1] SUMPs provide local authorities with a structured approach on how to develop and implement strategies for urban mobility based on a thorough analysis of the current situation, combined with a clear vision for sustainable development of the urban and neighboring areas under consideration. Thereby, SUMPs can help cities make efficient use of existing transport infrastructure and services and ensure a cost-effective deployment of the proposed measures.

without the filter of the translation, represents a vital aspect in studying the material as well as in enhancing the tacit knowledge of the present phenomenon.

3   Research Methodology

The paper follows a case study research to allow the exploration and understanding of a complicated issue such as smart mobility using a people-centric approach. This methodology provides an in-depth investigation of the social and behavioral problems envisaged here.

The purpose is to carefully examine the data within a specific context, as Yin [55] suggests the case study research method is "an empirical inquiry that investigates a contemporary phenomenon within its real-life context; when the boundaries between phenomenon and context are not evident; and in which multiple sources of evidence are used."

This article adopts a multiple-case design ([6], [55]). In line with the relevant literature on this research methodology and with the aim of this scientific contribution, we consider a descriptive approach to examine this phenomenon in a narrative form that occurs within the data in question [31].

The choice of these methods is to design an examination of the data conducted within the context of its use that is, within the situation in which the activity takes place [55]. Following this relevant literature, the present work defines a multi-case method to describe the *state-of-art* of smart mobility in the Italian universities' context, as described in the following paragraphs.

Instead, the choice of three peculiar university cases has to do with three key factors:

a. They are the most representative and complex; we found that other similar cases aggregate around each of them, just like a galaxy (as further explained);
b. We found that, being the most complex, they are also the most structured;
c. Being the most structured, they are also very well documented (papers, projects, administrative documents, institutional agreements, international protocols, etc.).

3.1   The Context: Italian Universities—The Network of Universities for Sustainable Development (RUS)

At the European level, like for example, the Spanish case, it seems that, based on Italian context, universities usually incorporate practices and strategies on sustainability as a response to the pressure exerted by institutional forces, such as the funding systems of higher education institutions [25]. This also depends on lower student engagement, which should be reinforced.

For some years, Italian research has been trying to highlight the importance of engaging behaviors and positive attitudes towards the implementation and co-creation of best practices in sustainability within the university framework ([4], [34], [43], [42]).

However, the focus was mainly put *tout court* on both engineering and architectural aspects. Evidence of this can be drawn from the agreements signed between Universities and the Italian Ministry of Defense (especially the SPE—Structure of Energy Project). It is the case of the Memorandum of Understanding signed between the University of Genova and the Ministry of Defense, which hinges on "opportunities in acquiring collaborations in the sector of energy-saving, rationalization of consumption, and development of renewable energy sources" [35].

In 2015, the Conference of the Rectors of the Italian Universities (CRUI) spurred the RUS—Italian Network of Sustainable Universities. This network, comprising 51 Italian public universities, aims at:

– Disseminating best practices toward sustainability, by sharing skills and expertise, then causing a positive impact through sustainable actions;
– Promoting the United Nations Sustainable Development Goals (UN SDGs);
– Exploiting the experience and the outcomes of the Italian case toward international acknowledgment.

Although these best practices are suggested, they are not applied uniformly. Consequently, it happens that some universities develop a more perfunctory and cosmetic approach toward sustainability; some are profoundly involved, but only from the engineering perspective; while, others raise significant issues about the engagement of students and stakeholders. The latest approach is further taken into consideration since it shows important elements such as:

– Universities have appreciable local impacts: direct, as employment and revenue generators, and indirect, as developers of knowledge and human resources [44];
– The reaction from the local context and the students is crucial to the project's success, as the educational process cannot be separated from the social and psychological context [34].

In line with the above, we can face an increasing interest in the scientific and practical sphere on the impact of the phenomenon under investigation, especially from a socio-economic perspective. The Italian context presents various cases which highlight the different level of development and implementation strategies that need to be considered to better understand the *state of art* of smart mobility in this country. Therefore, the following paragraph describes a compendium of engagement practices to list a florilegium of initiatives supposed to have a positive impact (see e.g. [16]).

In addition, given that initiatives in sustainability are multi-pronged, the Authors chose to focus their attention on smart mobility, due to three factors:

1) Initiatives in smart mobility are implemented by all of the universities within the Network;

2) Such initiatives are accurately reported and evaluated, often in the wake of research already conducted by the relevant university itself;
3) Smart mobility, more than other sustainable initiatives, requires a cultural engagement, as well as a close link with the surrounding urban context (smart grids, smart roads, IoT, e-Government).

For these reasons, the Authors decided to target a well-established network of Italian Universities operating towards sustainable goals, in order to develop a consistent common framework by circumscribing the analysis to target universities. The same framework could be also useful in the future for scaling up the research on this specific topic, as well as for comparative purposes with coherent frameworks at international level.

3.2 Best Practices Toward Student Engagement: The Case of Smart Mobility

Among the members of the RUS, we selected three institutions meant to be representative to outline a consistent framework. The choice was made based on the features and peculiarities of these three cases, which allow identifying divergences and convergences.

The three selected universities are representative of a sample that we identified. All the approaches by other universities tend to aggregate around three main galaxies represented by the three universities (see Fig. 1). The use of the term 'galaxy' is purpose-specific, and it has to be understood here as an aggregating point for different groups of cases. These share a common background with the aggregating point and

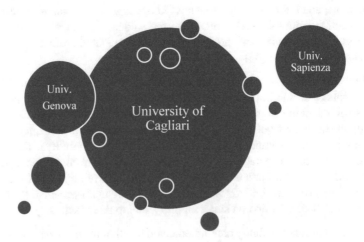

Fig. 1 Case aggregation in galaxies: An example of the galaxy 'University of Cagliari'

gravitate around it. At the same time, though, they partially differ from it in terms of formal implementation, design, efficiency, and outcomes.

Besides, the three cases deserve being scrutinized, because each of them involves a research group focused on investigating smart mobility issues. As a consequence, a broader range of publications is available than in the case of other member universities, at least in terms of the number of papers devoted to the topic, both theoretically, and in connection to tests or projects conducted on-field.

3.2.1 University of Cagliari

The University of Cagliari developed an integrated system within the city of Cagliari, in the framework of the project "Joint Innovation Center," fueled by the Research Center CRS4 and Huawei, aiming at making Cagliari a smart city, with a focus mainly on smart mobility. The city's proactivity toward becoming a smart city is testified by several academic studies aiming at highlighting significant aspects of a 'smart' transformation of the city. Many studies have been focusing on smart mobility (see e.g., [15], [40]), and user's behavior toward mobility (see e.g., [33], [45]).

As to smart mobility initiatives being implemented at the University of Cagliari, particular attention was paid to route behavior, as a voluntary program, to facilitate a sustainable lifestyle and mobility through information and communication. The projects implemented are three, called:

1. Casteddu Mobility Styles
2. Cittadella Mobility Styles
3. IPET

The theory lying beneath the projects assumes that not only hard measures are needed to modify the user's behavior (time saved, cost, etc.), but also soft measures, such as VTBC programs—Voluntary Travel Behaviour Change programs, aimed at changing habits, beliefs, values and preferences of the individual [32].

One of them is taken into account in the present framework as the most representative.

The program Casteddu Mobility Styles, conceived and implemented by the CRiMM (Research Center for Models and Mobility) of the University of Cagliari is a program of "Voluntary travel changes," aimed at the promotion of different forms of sustainable mobility. In particular, the program is aimed at increasing the percentage of journeys made on foot, with one's bicycle or bike-sharing, by all public transport, and finally by private means shared in the vast area of Cagliari. The program was articulated into two phases: the data gathering phase, based on social marketing theory, and the proactive and engaging phase, based on the personalized marketing techniques.

In particular, in February 2011, the submission of a questionnaire to the users of Metrocagliari (the underground service of the city) on their travel habits, the reasons that led them to use the underground, the pro-environmental attitudes, their current judgment on the service offered and finally some fundamental socio-economic characteristics to outline an accurate profile of the typical user. Those who use Metrocagliari were reached through postcards distributed at the metro stops and invited to complete an online questionnaire (www.metrostyles.it). As an appreciation for the interest and the time dedicated, CRiMM will offer an iPhone 4 and ten vouchers worth € 100 each. This rewarding system allowed us to reach high response rates. The data collection helped identify 5 user profiles: Car dreamers (11.91%); Sporadic pro-car (12.30%); Two clusters of loyal students (occasional frequenter, 16.99%); (regular frequenter, 20.5%), Convinced park and riders (19,75%).

Among these profiles, the group of Park and riders represent a point of reference for customized marketing, because they identified a rational use of their vehicle and can be regarded as a symbol.

3.2.2 University "Luigi Vanvitelli" of Caserta

The case of the University "Luigi Vanvitelli" of Caserta is iconic as to some features, which can be regarded as familiar to most of the Italian universities, i.e.:

- Students are not homogeneously allocated among the various buildings of the Universities, located in different areas of the city, sometimes really far from the Headquarters and the centre of the city;
- The areas that students should reach have low transport accessibility.

This is the reason why car dependence in the key Italian Universities sways between 20% and 50% [7]. The student experience at University "Luigi Vanvitelli" was profoundly frustrating due to the issue of "last mile," emerging when reaching the extra-urban buildings of the university.

To mitigate the issue and to improve the quality of student experience, an integrated platform was contrived and designed, called "Verysoon." What is interesting is that this app for smartphones is not merely functional but also an engagement tool. The app was co-designed with the students to meet their needs, and the roadmap was set up to be as efficient as possible, based on student planning, and it focuses on two practical services: carpooling and free bus shuttles.

By starting from a survey-based analysis between 2015 and 2016, the assessment phase went forth with the dissemination phase. To achieve this goal, a list of accompanying measures to the successful implementation of the app was put in place: public events, brochures, ads, social networks, videos broadcast online and on TV videos.

The project resulted in a consulting phase before being implemented. The assessment was made on data gathering based on surveys and a shared and participated methodology. The latter should be emphasized since it informs the steps followed to design the process. The different intertwined phases were:

1. listening to the needs of the stakeholders involved;
2. dissemination of the project;

3. implementation of the project;

Eventually, the project entails a follow-up monitoring phase on customer satis-faction, retention actions, and service quality assessment. This phase is performed through an online survey regarding the travel habits of the students, and the annual publication of a report, which is open to public discussion and dissemination to improve the service. No rewarding systems are envisaged here, rather an incentive system/accompanying measure system represented by the following factors: free parking for carpoolers; real-time infomobility; reliability and manageability of the consistently updated app; efficiency in booking e-tickets; clearness of signs, posters, instructions; the existence of an app failure recovery system.

3.2.3 University of Bologna

The project of smart mobility at the University of Bologna takes on a peculiar place in this regard because of the dimensions involved. The project was targeted on a complex multi-campus reality, characterized by urban integrated models, and off-centered campuses.

The institution involves 81,174 students, five regional campuses, more than 6000 employees. It is the second-largest university in Italy as to the number of registered students after "La Sapienza" of Rome [29], but it is established in a municipality counting about 390,000 inhabitants: the student ratio over resident population is then higher than the case of Rome. As a consequence, the impact upon the territory is more significant.

Besides, the project grafts onto a municipal fabric that, for a long time, has dealt with smart mobility initiatives, and has a deep-rooted cycling endorsement attitude.

While previous projects focused on agreements with the municipality on passes and improved public service quality (until 2015), the current management of the university perceived it was not enough.

The traditional strategies implemented by the mobility manager had always been three, associated with consequent actions: persuasion strategy, granting strategy, and restriction strategy.

In this framework, a focus on students was added, through a research project on behavior with the application of CADM model (Comprehensive Action Determinant Model), based on the study of Klöckner & Blöbaum [24]. In 2017, an innovative web-based questionnaire (GOTOUNIBO) was administered on the platform Qualtrics. Respondents were 5000, to assess students' mobility behavior to and from university and gauge their mobility intention. From this assessment, various projects came out:

- *Alma-bike* (connected and shared bike);
- *Web-ike* (inter-modality planning through digitization);
- *Mi muovo libero* (I move free), based on incentives allowed to the students, and previously agreed with the municipality;
- *Zeta A 2.0 & Van Sharing* (implementation of a new university interconnected eco-fleet).

Table 1 Similarities and differences between galaxies

Galaxy/Feature	Cagliari	Caserta	Bologna
Urban Integration			
Platform Development			
Co-design			
Soft Measures			
Dissemination			
Data Gathering			
Tech Enhancement			

The new model of mobility at the University of Bologna envisages three major modifications:

a) multi-disciplinarity toward engagement, by involving HR, territorial level, behavioral analysis, infrastructure system, technology culture, and innovation;
b) Service integration, which is a result of a merge between the fleet manager and mobility manager;
c) New financial tools, by kicking off the processes linked to the eco-systemic values.

As it emerges, though, a couple of elements should be stressed in order to compare the University of Bologna with the other two cases above.

First, the centrality of the bike as the main transportation means. This peculiarity depends on two specific features: bike abuts on well-established facilities and the structure of the city of Bologna.

Also, the bike is an affordable, easy-to-use, willingly and widely adopted in the context where the University operates.

Second, the specificity of incentives, which are agreed with the municipality in written form and have a twofold nature: financial benefits (integrated fare system; mitigated prices; etc.), and non-financial facilitations (easy parking; priority; etc.).

A graph showing similarities and differences between the three identified galaxies is shown below (Table 1).

4   Discussion and Further Research

The establishment of an academic Network pursuing the UN SDGs represented a breakthrough initiative in the Italian panorama.

In order to answer RQ1, within this network, we found actions and initiatives implemented at the national level to foster university student's engagement toward sustainability and, in particular, smart mobility. Among these, we selected the most significant and representative cases, intending to highlight common patterns by identifying similarities/differences.

In the examined examples, we see that the *fil rouge* is the concept of multi-modality together with environmental sustainability employing novel technologies leveraging interconnected devices to build a network [17]. Also, the systems of incentives are another primary beacon for the implementation of smart policies toward smart mobility. These main principles are embraced by most of the other Italian universities joining the Network.

However, there is too much of a disparity among the members of the network.

The University of Cagliari adopts a rewarding system of incentives and travel habit data gathering through surveys to gauge its policy toward smart mobility.

The University "Luigi Vanvitelli" stakes on the fleet sharing experienced empowered by an app, which is collectively designed to the needs of the students.

Eventually, the University of Bologna strives to apply the incentive system and technology application to its dimensions and the centrality of the bike, as acquired transportation means to be enhanced. Though, these elements are still predominantly carried out with a top-down approach and are only partially interwoven with a student engagement policy.

Starting from the analysis of these similarities/differences, we could also indulge a tentative answer to RQ2, which, however, should be further investigated.

Indeed, while the assessment phase deploys in similar ways in the three cases, we can observe a fragmentation toward the approach. Also, student engagement differs both in the operational phase and in the applied theoretical background.

What comes out converges with the pioneering study by Vagnoni and Cavicchi [52], who used the model of Glavič and Lukman [19] focusing on the Deming Cycle. Actually, the results "allow one to depict a university system addressing the challenge posed by international agendas in a fragmented way, even if many universities are showing a strong commitment to the sustainability challenge" [52]. This is valid in a general framework of sustainability as it is in the branch of smart mobility. As a consequence, the policies implemented to address the question diverge substantially.

Besides, an analysis conducted on many of the other universities of the network does not provide evidence of their full commitment, since they try to implement statutory top-down measures, which do not envisage dissemination and stakeholder engagement/involvement.

The emerging results delineate a context-targeted strategy on behalf of each of the universities. They do not seem to lock onto a coherent institutional framework deliberately. As far as we found, the overall strategy is not fully aware at a national level, although incentives, surveys, and dissemination activities seem well-established among the top players. Also, we could use a kind of distinction between innovators and followers among the members of the network to mark an essential feature of the Italian network for sustainability.

Rather, efficient institutional policies at the national/local level should be implemented to enhance a convergence between innovators and followers. This goal could be accomplished by taking into consideration the enforcement of the following measures: a performance-driven rewarding system for universities; the establishment of facilitator pools for the integration city-university; the set-up of KPIs for evaluating progress, impact, and efforts of smart mobility initiatives; the establishment of accessibility and transparency procedures aimed to foster co-creation and co-design approaches; the implementation of a quality assessment tool for mapping strengths and weaknesses of follower universities in order to evaluate appropriate policies and initiatives to let them bridge the gap.

The added value this paper would foster is just the kick-off of a systematic study of smart mobility initiatives at the academic level, seeking to investigate the role students and institutional stakeholders play in it. The research should be extended to draw a model needed to compare the Italian university innovation ecosystem with that of other countries, especially within a shared framework, which is the European Union.

Although this paper confines itself to strict limits, it should be regarded as a first attempt in the field to spur further research. The latter should involve two aspects. On the one hand, the actions concretely put into practice by universities, as well as their (more or less aware and committed) adherence to the sustainable policies; on the other hand, the unavoidable involvement of the stakeholders (in particular, students), which can only be attained by focusing on behavior, emotional aspects and, sense of belonging in a consistent framework of smart citizenship.

References

1. Akhras, G. (Autumn 2000). Smart materials and smart systems for the future. *Canadian Military Journal*, 25–32.
2. Anthopoulos, L., & Fitsilis, P. (2010). *Intelligent Environments (IE)*, 2010 Sixth International Conference on, IEEE., 301–306.
3. Arena, M., Cheli, F., Zaninelli, D., Capasso, A., Lamedica, R., & Piccolo, A. (2013). Smart mobility for sustainability. *AEIT Annual Conference, 2013*, 1–6. https://doi.org/10.1109/AEIT.2013.6666811.
4. Bachiorri, A., & Puglisi, A. (2007). Promoting education for sustainability: A challenge for the University system. In W. L. Filho, E. I. Manolas, M. N. Sotirakou, & G. A. Boutakis (Eds.), *Higher education and the challenge of sustainability: Problems, promises and good practice*. Evrographics: Orestiada.
5. Benevolo C., Dameri R. P., & D'Auria B. (2016). *Smart Mobility in Smart City*, Empowering Organizations, 13–28, Cham: Springer.
6. Campbell, D. (1975). Degrees of freedom and the case study. *Comparative Political Studies, 8*, 178–185.
7. Cartenì, A., & Henke, I. (2017). The Influence of Travel Experience within Perceived Public Transport Quality. *World Academy of Science, Engineering and Technology, International Journal of Social, Behavioral, Educational, Economic, Business and Industrial Engineering, 11*(9), 2077–2081.
8. Chaplin, G., & Wyton, P. (2014). Student engagement with sustainability: Understanding the value–action gap. *International Journal of Sustainability in Higher Education, 15*(4), 404–417. https://doi.org/10.1108/IJSHE-04-2012-0029.
9. Chourabi, H., Nam, T., Walker, S., Gil-Garcia, J. R., Mellouli, S., Nahon, K., Pardo, T. A., & Scholl, H. J. (2012) *Understanding smart cities: An integrative framework, System Science (HICSS)*, 2012 45th Hawaii International Conference on, IEEE., pp. 2289–2297.
10. Cocchia, A. (2014). *Smart and digital city: A systematic literature review. smart city: how to create public and economic value with high technology in urban space*. R. P Dameri & C. Rosenthal-Sabroux (Eds.), 13–43, Cham: Springer.
11. Debnath, A. K., Chin, H. C., Haque, M. M., & Yuen, B. (2014). A methodological framework for benchmarking smart transport cities. *Cities, 37*(C), 47–56.

12. European Commission. (2014). *Guidelines. Developing and implementing a sustainable urban mobility plan.*
13. Evans, J., Jones, R., Karvonen, A., Millard, L., & Wendler, J. (2015). Living labs and co-production: University campuses as platforms for sustainability science, *Current Opinion in Environmental Sustainability, 16*, 1–6, Amsterdam: Elsevier, https://doi.org/10.1016/j.cosust.2015.06.005.
14. Figueredo, F. R., & Tsarenko, Y. (2013). Is "being green" a determinant of participation in university sustainability initiatives? *International Journal of Sustainability in Higher Education, 14*(3), 242–253. https://doi.org/10.1108/IJSHE-02-2011-0017.
15. Garau, C., Masala, F., & Pinna, F. (2016). Cagliari and smart urban mobility: Analysis and comparison. *Cities, 56*, 35–46. https://doi.org/10.1016/j.cities.2016.02.012.
16. Garlick, S., & Pryor, G. (2002). *Compendium of Good Practice University–Regional Development Engagement Initiatives*, Supplement to the report: Universities and their Communities: Creative regional development through knowledge-based engagement.
17. Giacon, M. (2017). *La sharing mobility*, Master Thesis. Venice: Università degli Studi Cà Foscari Venezia.
18. Giffinger, R., Fertner, C., Kramar, H., Kalasek, R., Pichler- Milanović, N., & Meijers, E. (2007). *Smart Cities—Ranking of European medium-sized cities.* Cent. Reg. Sci.: Vienna University of Technology.
19. Glavic, P., & Lukman, R. (2007). Review of Sustainability Terms and Their Definitions. *Journal of Cleaner Production, 15*, 1875–1885.
20. Janasz, T. (2017). *Paradigm shift in urban mobility: Towards factor 10 of automobility.* Wiesbaden: Springer Gabler.
21. Jeekel, J. F. (2016). *Smart mobility and societal challenges: An implementation perspective.* Eindhoven: Technische Universiteit Eindhoven.
22. Kahn, M. E., & Mills, E. S. (2006). *Green cities: Urban growth and the environment.* Washington: Brookings Institution Press.
23. Karinsalo, A., & Halunen, K. (2018). *Smart Contracts for a Mobility-as-a-Service Ecosystem*, 2018 IEEE International Conference on Software Quality, Reliability and Security Companion (QRS-C), Lisbon, 135–138, https://doi.org/10.1109/QRS-C.2018.00036.
24. Klöckner, C. A., & Blöbaum, A. (2010). A comprehensive action determination model: Toward a broader understanding of ecological behaviour using the example of travel mode choice. *Journal of Environmental Psychology, 30*(4), 574–586.
25. Larràn, M., Herrera, J., & Andrades, F. J. (2015). Measuring the linkage between strategies on sustainability and institutional forces: An empirical study of Spanish universities. *Journal of Environmental Planning and Management, 59*(6), 967–992. https://doi.org/10.1080/09640568.2015.1050485.
26. Levy, C., & Wong, D. (2014). *Toward a smart society.* London: Big Innovation Centre.
27. Li, S., Da Xu, L., & Zhao, S. (2018). 5G Internet of Things: A survey. *Journal of Industrial Information Integration* (10). Amsterdam: Elsevier.
28. Lopez, D., & Farooq, B. (2018). *A blockchain framework for smart mobility.* In Proceedings of IEEE International Smart Cities Conference 2018.
29. MIUR. (2018). *National student registry of the Italian Ministry of University and Research (MIUR).* http://anagrafe.miur.it/php5/home.php?&anni=2017-18&categorie=ateneo&status=iscritti&tipo_corso=TT&&order_by=i (retrieved 28 June, 2019).
30. Manda, M., & Backhouse, J. (2016). *Towards a "smart society" through a connected and smart citizenry in South Africa: A review of the national broadband strategy and policy.* In Proceedings of the 15th IFIP WG 8.5 International Conference, 228–240, Cham: Springer International Publishing.
31. McDonough, J., & McDonough, S. (1997). *Research methods for english language teachers.* London: Arnold.
32. Meloni, I. (2017). *Misure Soft per la Mobilità Sostenibile. I programmi di cambiamento volontario del comportamento di viaggio.* Rome: Aracne editrice.

33. Meloni, I., Sanjust, B., & Spissu, E. (2017). Lessons learned from a personalized travel planning (PTP) research program to reduce car dependence. *Transportation, 44,* 853. https://doi.org/10.1007/s11116-016-9681-y.

34. Micangeli, A., Naso, V., Michelangeli, E., Matrisciano, A., Farioli, F., & Belfiore, N. P. (2014). Attitudes toward sustainability and green economy issues related to some students learning their characteristics: A preliminary study. *Sustainability, 6,* 3484–3503.

35. MoU UniGe. (2015). *Memorandum of Understanding between the University of Genova and the Italian Ministry of Defence.*

36. Nam, T., & Pardo, T. (2011). *Conceptualizing smart city with dimensions of technology, people, and institutions.* In Proceedings of the 12th Annual International Conference on Digital Government Research, 2011, 282–291, ACM.

37. O'Faircheallaigh, C. (2010). Public participation and environmental impact assessment: Purposes, implications, and lessons for public policy making. *Environmental Impact Assessment Review, 30,* 19–27.

38. Pagliaro, F., Mattoni, B., Gugliermenti, F., Bisegna, F, Azzaro, B., Tomei, F., & Catucci, S. (2016). *A roadmap toward the development of Sapienza Smart Campus.* In Proceedings of the International Conference on Environment and Electrical Engineering, 1–6, Florence: Italy.

39. Pendleton, C. (2018). *IoT for smart cities: New partnerships for azure maps and azure digital twins,* https://azure.microsoft.com/sv-se/blog/iot-for-smart-cities-new-partnerships-for-azure-maps-and-azure-digital-twins/ (retrieved 13 March 2019).

40. Pinna, F., Masala, F., & Garau, C. (2017). Urban policies and mobility trends in italian smart cities. *Sustainability, 9,* 494.

41. Principali, L. (2018). *Rivoluzione smart mobility, così la "accenderanno" 5G e IoT,* https://www.corrierecomunicazioni.it/digital-economy/rivoluzione-smart-mobility-cosi-la-accenderanno-5g-e-iot/ (retrieved 2 March, 2019).

42. Rinaldi, C., Cavicchi, A., Spigarelli, F., Lacchè, L., & Rubens, A. (2018). Universities and smart specialisation strategy: From third mission to sustainable development co-creation. *International Journal of Sustainability in Higher Education, 19*(1), 67–84. https://doi.org/10.1108/IJSHE-04-2016-0070.

43. Rinaldi, C., & Cavicchi, A. (2016). *Universities' emerging roles to co-create sustainable innovation paths: Some evidences from the Marche Region.* AESTIMUM 69, 211–224, Florence: Firenze University Press.

44. Russo, A. P., van den Berg, L., & Lavanga, M. (2007). Toward a sustainable relationship between city and university: A stakeholdership approach. *Journal of Planning Education and Research, 27*(2), 199–216. https://doi.org/10.1177/0739456X07307208.

45. Sanjust, B., Meloni, I., & Spissu, E. (2015). An impact assessment of a travel behavior change program: A case study of a light rail service in Cagliari, Italy. *Case Studies on Transport Policy, 3*(1), 12–22. https://doi.org/10.1016/j.cstp.2014.04.002.

46. Scekic, O., Nastic, S., & Dustdar, S. (2019). Blockchain-supported smart city platform for social value co-creation and exchange. *IEEE Internet Computing, 23*(1), 19–28. https://doi.org/10.1109/MIC.2018.2881518.

47. Sesana, M.M., Grecchi, M., Salvalai, G., & Rasica, C. (2016). Methodology of energy efficient building refurbishment: Application on two university campus-building case studies in Italy with engineering students. *Journal of Building Engineering, 6,* 54–64.

48. Sharma, P. K., & Park, Y. H. (2018). Blockchain-based hybrid network architecture for the smart city. *Future Generation Computer Systems, 86,* 650–655. https://doi.org/10.1016/j.future.2018.04.060.

49. Shriberg, M. & Harris, K. J. (2012). Building sustainability change management and leadership skills in students: Lessons learned from "sustainability and the campus" at the University of Michigan. *Journal of Environmental Studies and Sciences, 2*(2), 154–164, Cham: Springer, https://doi.org/10.1007/s13412-012-0073-0.

50. Sun, J., Yan, J., & Zhang, K. Z. K. (2016a). Blockchain-based sharing services: What blockchain technology can contribute to smart cities. *Financial Innovation 2016,* (2)26, Cham: Springer, https://doi.org/10.1186/s40854-016-0040-y.

51. Sun, Y., Song, H., Jara, A. J., & Bie, R. (2016b). *Internet of Things and Big Data Analytics for Smart and Connected Communities.* IEEE Access, 4, 766–773.
52. Vagnoni, E., & Cavicchi, C. (2015). An exploratory study of sustainable development at Italian universities. *International Journal of Sustainability in Higher Education, 16*(2), 217–236. https://doi.org/10.1108/IJSHE-03-2013-0028.
53. Villegas, W., Palacios-Pacheco, X., & Luján-Mora, S. (2019). Application of a smart city model to a traditional university campus with a big data architecture: A sustainable smart campus. *Sustainability, 11,* 2857.
54. Voda, A. I.; & Radu, L. D. (2018). Artificial intelligence and the future of smart cities. *BRAIN. Broad Research in Artificial Intelligence and Neuroscience, [S.l.], 9*(2), 110–127.
55. Yin, R. (1994). *Case study research: Design and methods* (2nd ed.). Beverly Hills, CA: Sage Publishing.

Digital Humanities and Smart City. University as a Service and Uni-Living Lab for the City: Thinking the Case of La Rochelle Thanks to Social Sciences and Humanities

Antoine Huerta

Abstract The methods of the social sciences (geography and present-day history) can be put to good use in a synthesis on the Smart Project in La Rochelle. The methodology applied submits to the analysis of numerous sources from the actors involved in this project, but also scientific communications dealing with the current proposal in La Rochelle (LR). It also facilitates the development of various disciplines (economics, management, computer science, ecology, sociology and other engineering, human and social sciences). The concepts of sustainability and intelligence are at the heart of this program and the issue of data allows them to be thought of jointly. This work therefore sets up an analysis aimed at clarifying the relationships to these notions and contextualizing them through various direct sources and testimonies. A comparative perspective will be put in place in relation to a similar project, in this case that of Barcelona, in order to bring out the relative deficiencies and assets of the case of La Rochelle. The case of the La Rochelle Smart City project allows a more detailed understanding of the links between urban digitization and social sciences and humanities.

Keywords La rochelle · Barcelona · Smart city · Smart campus · University as a service · Uni-living lab · Social sciences and humanities

1 Introduction: Testing *Smart Cities* for Resilience and Sustainability

The city of La Rochelle has been involved for a long time in a smart city project in which open data plays a crucial role [9]. Among the different projects developed amidst this rochelian urban reform [19], some of them have, at a subsequent time, been led in cooperation with the University of la Rochelle (ULR).

A. Huerta (✉)
La Rochelle University, La Rochelle, France

© Springer Nature Switzerland AG 2021
E. Magnaghi et al. (eds.), *Organizing Smart Buildings and Cities*,
Lecture Notes in Information Systems and Organisation 36,
https://doi.org/10.1007/978-3-030-60607-7_5

Therefore, since 2018, a smart campus project has been progressively implemented around a triple mission of:

- "Enhancing the university's environmental impact in order to create a sustainable and responsible campus;
- Evolving the campus to a smart, digital, connected and responsible one;
- Register it as part of a larger whole: a "Smart Campus in a Smart City" [12].

More precisely, from the university's point of view, the project aims at:

1. "Enhancing the efficiency of university operations and services in all its superior missions by liberating, through digitalization, new dimensions to reinvent itself and further improve student success rates;
2. Increasing competitivity and attractiveness of the institution in order to attract a much wider audience of learners and increase industrial and academic partnerships;
3. Reinforcing the quality of life of university users at work and in town" [45].

This approach is part of a context where "cities are confronted by a major challenge: to continue to develop themselves while limiting the negative effects of their growth on the agglomeration costs and the well-being of their residents" [2]. This project aims to answer these issues. We will come back to these contours and their implications, but from this point on, it should be noted that two essential axes structure the discourse: the sustainability and intelligence that a project wishes to connect. The purpose of this article is to demonstrate how this connection operates and to what extent a critical discourse on this statement can be exercised. What are the relevant and applicable notions of human and social sciences in this context?

Albert Gidari, the Consulting Director of the *Center for Internet and Society* at *Stanford Law School*, writes a bit maliciously that a smart city is too smart for your private life [16]. This subject, which transpires frequently—not to say systematically—when we evoke the question of smart cities and the Internet of Things or rather the *Internet of everything* [4].

What rapport does this point entail with a smart and sustainable city? This represents a strong approach to tackle the question of the respect of data generated by users—or rather city dwellers, *Smart Citizens*, as the term is sometimes coined. The notion of sustainability is compelling because it evokes *what represents the conditions required to sustain for a long time, what is susceptible to sustain for a long time* and henceforth *what sustains for a long time, what represents the stability and constancy in time: what lasts forever or at least for a long time* (TLFi). Sustaining and making sustainable, are two sides of the same medal.

Durability, also known as sustainability, is issued from the Latin word *durabilis* (TLFi), which means "lasting or permanent," and comes from *durare,* "to harden" which refers to, in computer sciences, the process of securing a system. This consideration is essential in a Smart City: certainty (prevention of accidents), security (prevention of malevolent acts) and the respect of privacy, form the three pillars of a Smart City. According to the *Journal of Advanced Research,* "This privacy violation is a major security risk [and] technical hardening of such systems is important, even as some early implementations do not seem to have anticipated these risks from even such vulnerabilities" [10].

Obtaining this relative security may pass, according to several commentators, through the use of open-source software, even "if where security is concerned, clearly this is not necessarily the case" [31], but the communication revolving around these questions is undoubtfully an important point. The example of the rochelian Smart City illustrates this analysis.

These are the conditions of computer-aided urban production that need to be analyzed here in order to understand to what extent the importance of data security is presented. Since there are no reasons to judge the quality of the system already implemented or in development, this work focuses on the presentation that is provided in the communication plans of the University of La Rochelle in order to restructure around these themes of sustainability and intelligence as part of a future Sustainable and Smart Urban Coast institute, an institute that is integrated in the smart campus project in the connected city of La Rochelle. This in turn does not refer to a technical analysis of the rochelian project, but rather to an attempt to historically recontextualize one of its aspects.

How should one consider the connection to data in a sustainable and smart perspective in the case of the rochelian project? What traces of this vocabulary will we find in the implementation of this project? What can we deduce from history and, more generally, social sciences? After a brief presentation of La Rochelle's living university laboratory project, certain aspects of the role that social sciences can play, in light of a better consideration of the various criticisms that may be addressed to it, will be presented.

2 La Rochelle, Words of a Living Atlantic University Laboratory

The rochelian *Smart City* project is in progress. At this stage, we can consider that it has not yet entered the phase where it would constitute, in fact, "a major innovation authorizing the fluidity of the city in the process of spatial, social and economic recomposition under the effect of globalization and the digital revolution", but remains at the stage of "narrative of "fiction" […] at the service of a technical innovation—which is eventually limited to the optimization of urban services" [15]. What are the words and actions that support it?

2.1   La Rochelle, a Context Favorable to Smart Urban Growth?

On the 7th of November 2019, the agglomerate community of La Rochelle (ACLR) organized a *Smart Cities Tour* in which the question of "transportations, data, data in transportations and the financing of projects" was addressed [36]. This approach is carved in the city's desire to develop around this question of *Smart City* [49]. Faced with "energy consumption, pollution and the social needs induced by an often-dysfunctional urban growth", this rose as the occasion for active members like the university of La Rochelle to furthermore integrate itself in this project through the already initiated work of its *Smart Campus*.

This example illustrates "the strong actual adherence of the public authorities responsible for the principles and theories of *Smart Growth*, new urbanism and, more generally, urban sustainable development" [28].

In fact, the university of La Rochelle is currently witnessing a radical restructuration of its operations and different functions revolving around a smart campus aiming at "favoring and developing sustainable mobility", "developing the environmental efficiency of the building", "limiting the environmental impacts and the campus' streams", "building a biodiver'city"; an abundance of ways to amplify "a smart digital and responsible campus" [44]. All these qualifications refer to the definition, still prevailing blurry, that we can attribute to a smart and sustainable city. In conclusion, "a smart sustainable city is an innovative city that utilizes information and communication technologies (ICT) and other means to enhance the quality of life, the efficiency of operations and urban services, and the competitiveness, while taking into account the needs of current and future generations in terms of economic, social and environmental aspects" [48]. The rochelian project corresponds to this definition of a city aiming at becoming as inclusive as possible.

In this development phase of a *Smart Campus*, the university of La Rochelle engages in a research and management project of a larger smart city. In fact, the university of La Rochelle is developing a research department revolving around the major themes related to the Sustainable and Smart Urban Coast [46]. This experience of *Smart City*, is developing around the different axes at the center of which lies the university of La Rochelle. This questions not only the way we perceive and envision the smart city but also the role attributed to the different active members of the territory based on the logic of sustainability, good management and urban intelligence. The rochelian coastal specificities make this particular case study, a type of model that allows us to better understand the relationships between the various urban and technical components. We will now explore in details the content of the project.

2.2 The Living University Laboratory of La Rochelle, a Smart Campus in a Smart City

The living laboratories or *Living Labs*, as they are often labeled, are "research and development structures created by companies, universities or territorial collectivities in various European countries that aim, in a generic way, to innovate in a particular sector of activity" [1]. In this case, this innovation takes place by taking into consideration the links between a university and a city. The laboratory project clearly articulates the energy, digital and environmental transitions [20] with each word holding its relative weight in this context.

Around this program, "favoring and developing sustainable mobility, developing the environmental efficiency of the building, limiting the environmental impacts and the campus' streams, building a biodiver'city" are the major points presented ([44, p. 3]). In fact, Jeanne Lallement[1] prompts that "the originality of a project lies in its systemic character and its large perimeter, involving several members of the university (students, personnel, teachers and researchers) and in the territory" [20].

In fact, it refers to crossing the interests of the university and its partners by constructing an exemplary campus in the city, but also to "provide an added-value and contribute reciprocally to the reputation of the territory" ([44, p. 5]). Therefore, the university becomes an experimentation field presenting itself as a center of expertise in the areas highlighted. The experimentation also aims to implement "a common system allowing a valorization of the campus' data" (*Idem* p. 6) and to benefit from the researchers' skills in the decision-making process while seeking optimal mobility, housing development and transportations or even the smart control of energy and buildings (*Ibidem*). Different points, as those that follow, are to be featured:

- Turning users and university staff into citizens users,
- Supporting students in their approaches and projects related to sustainable development,
- Mobilizing the student community of the university in light of a sustainable campus in a smart city,
- Including students in eco-responsible approaches,
- Fostering the social, unified, cultural and environmental inclusion of the user on campus,
- Raising awareness among users of their environmental impact (carbon footprint, consumption, waste),
- Favoring carpooling and responsible mobility,

All these initiatives shape the rochelian *Smart Project* into a true living laboratory (*Ibidem*) that "contains a pool of experts and a talent incubator capable of bringing precious resources to decision-makers. It is suitable to create, from this point on, the conditions of a mutual fertilization between the researchers' skills, production and

---

[1]Lecturer in management sciences at the Center for Research in Management (CEREGE) and vice-president of the Board of Directors of the University of La Rochelle.

valorization of data on one hand and the issues of public affairs and the decision-making needs on the other hand" ([43, p. 26]).

Hence, the university found itself operating as a service from a perspective of valorization of knowledges and productions [27]. In fact, we eventually know that the heart of the university service, as an apprenticeship experience, is a cocreation of emerging values, non-structured, interactive and uncertain, with a significant hedonistic reach (*Ibidem*). Therefore, "A new vocabulary is gaining respectability in academia. The terms have been appropriated from the field of marketing and, although they still stick in many an academic throat, they are spreading rapidly through the system" (Ibid.).

In light of this perspective, as of those of legal obligations to respect the standards of the *General Data Protection Regulation* of 2016, how is the communication policy of La Rochelle implemented?

We know that the discourse on innovation of large French cities constitutes an interface between a strategic approach of new public management (NPM) type inspired by the practices of companies to enhance the efficiency of public policies and a territorial marketing approach aiming at communicating the advantages of a territory and forging an identity to construct a city brand" [7]. Project management based on communication is in fact taking place, but how is data articulated in this case? And what is its vocabulary?

Even if the technical and communication aspects of this project are well presented, some equally essential aspects seem to be absent from the communications plan. A comparative solution allows the consideration of this relative gap, in regard to a similar project, albeit on a larger scale: the case of Barcelona.

3 Brief Critical and Comparative Perspective: La Rochelle, Barcelona, What Convergences?

It is in fact possible to put in comparison the rochelian project with the one set in place in Barcelona, mainly because other approaches have to be considered to contextualize the rochelian project. A method will consist to engage in a comparative study, and the case of Barcelona presents a certain interest from this point of view allowing to highlight certain differences with the rochelian method. The case of the city of Barcelona, a smart city that has greatly progressed in its project [3] and holds one of the most important trade shows in the sector—The Smart City Expo World Congress—allows to set in perspective the rochelian project.

3.1 The example of Barcelona and its data report: a model of the kind?

The project "Barcelona as a people city" aimed at promoting economic growth just as much as the well-being of its residents [6]. For this reason, five axes were privileged: "(1) Open data initiatives; (2) Initiatives of sustainable growth for cities (smart lighting, mobilizing electric vehicles and residual energy); (3) Social innovation; (4) Promotion of partnerships between research centers, universities, public and private partners; (5) Provision of "smart services" based on ICT" (Ibidem). We notice that some of these points were also applied by the rochelian project, most notably those concerning open data (1), the establishment of a sustainable city (2), and the partnerships between municipalities and research centers (4). Knowing that "Barcelona has been effectively implementing the Smart City strategy with an aim to be a Smart City model for the world" [3], nothing proves that the rochelian project was inspired from this approach. However, developing certain aspects of the Barcelonan project will allow us to put into perspective the rochelian project.

Francesca Bria, Chief Digital Technology and Innovation Officer for the City of Barcelona, is at the origin of a report on the openness and security of digitization which is a must-read report. Among the main points set forward, appears the need of "Improving access to the authority's data, respecting privacy and evaluating the ethical risks of smart cities and large databases, including legal compliance with data protection regulations, by establishing an ethical code of technological practices and defining a data strategy" ([5, p. 7]).

In her point of view, "Considering security, privacy and ethical aspects. An assessment will be made of which user data and information will be provided or stored in the digital service, taking into account the level of security, legal obligations, privacy issues and the risks associated with the service. (Consulting with experts if necessary) (*Idem*, p. 16.). Spain is therefore in the progress of acquiring a comparable legislation to the French General Data Protection Regulation (GDPR). The question of digital rights is considerably developed and presents "dispositions relative to Internet neutrality, universal access to the Internet, digital security, digital education, the right to privacy, to the use of digital devices in the workplace, the right to digital disconnection in the workplace, the right to privacy against the use of video-surveillance and sound-recording devices in the workplace, the right to privacy against the use of geo-location systems in the workplace and the right to a digital will" [34]. From this point of view, the Barcelonan case appears undeniably ahead of these questions.

Certain aspects are nevertheless promoters of good practices. Therefore, Barcelona has a very aggressive communication from this point of view since the city is also an endorser of the campaign charter "Public money? Public code!" [33], alongside a myriad of non-governmental organizations and other administrations. This Barcelonan campaign sets a valid example of what is done in terms of communication around data protection in the implementation of a *Smart City*. The rochelian *Smart Project* presents, from this point of view, a communication of lesser importance to these questions, without neglecting them in the process of an efficient implementation.

3.2   Communication Documents Versus Administrative Documents: An Aperture Between the Different Approaches to the Respect of Privacy?

We can immediately note the absence of evident references to privacy and data management issues in communications related to the rochelian *Smart Campus*. An intriguing fact, however, these themes are addressed in internal documents. We should note that these aspects are not neglected. The previously mentioned *Smart City Tour* program also provides an idea [36] which we will review later-on.

Therefore, for example "the responsible of the ULR data (*Chief Data Officer*) accompanies, consults, implements data management solutions" and, most importantly, has a mission to "Rethink governance with a stronger connection with close partner community-members, data sharing with third parties... The innovative text of the adoption of the European regulation of 27 April 2016 (relative to the protection of individuals with regard to the processing of personal data and on the free movement of such data), proposes a modern approach to data protection, relying on greater stakeholder empowerment: "*Privacy by design,* strong compliance obligation".

Because, evidently, privacy and security are part of the design that appears in the project's architecture: "these are the key elements guarantying respectful management of personal data in anticipation of the GDPR of May 2018. The infostructure and the platform natively integrate the management of profiles and access rights of all types of data. Mastering the entire chain of use of this personal data makes it possible to [highlight three points]: (i) re-using anonymously [...] the data (presenting to an application service provider only the data necessary to obtain this service, no more no less), (ii) allow the data user to have specific and differentiated access rights to these data with or without delegation of these rights to others, as well as (iii) the possibility of tracing the use of these data and ban certain uses if deemed abusive. Thus, the citizen remains in control of his data even ahead of a potential restitution" [41]. The risks related to the use of data by third-parties are also taken into account in the project's framework, notably with the "creation of a public service for data" and "privacy impact studies" (Ibidem). If the University of La Rochelle must respect the directives of the General Data Protection Regulation as it should, we see that its communication plan on these issues reveals some weaknesses.

The interventions of the *Smart City Tour* allow us to formulate an idea on the importance accorded to these aspects. We can read in the report of this event the determination to put "the open data at the service of sustainable development" ([36, p. 13]). More specifically, the data administrator for the city and the agglomeration explains that the data is meant to serve everyone: "Initially, the opening of data was intended for citizens and companies. Today, we realized that open data is also intended to be used internally to develop new services" (Ibidem).

Much remains to be said about the role of data in the La Rochelle project, and in particular the nature of the metropolitan open data portal (MODP) that the City has set up [18]. These portals "constitute at the same time the key elements of smart cities that centralize and diffuse the metropolitan data irrigating these new services, the implementation tools of territorial reform and the instruments for developing regional competitiveness" [32]. In this same case, social sciences also have a say. Therefore, the La Rochelle project seems to represent the type of portal "corresponding to the ideal-types of a Smart City" (Ibidem). Among the elements highlighted, we will note six: "(1)Transport economics, (2)the economics of information and communication technologies, (3)quality of life, (4)citizen participation in the democratic life of the city, (5)natural resources, (6)human and social capitals "(Ibid.). However, let's note that these aspects are not far from the heart of the project's communication, while legitimate fears and strong criticism exist. We believe that these critics should shed new light on this type of project, putting human social sciences back at the center of development processes.

4 Taking into Consideration Criticism, a Necessity? Reapplying Social Sciences in the Face of the Development of Smart Urbanism

As we have seen, there is no shortage of literature critically analyzing smart cities. Among the topics covered, data security issues come up regularly.

4.1 Numerous and Scientifically Motivated Criticisms

The criticisms of smart cities are varied: ethical, as in the case of the "spy sensors" in the beds of students in the Regional Center for University and School Works (CROUS) in Rennes, which had stimulated students and attracted the press. These particularly sensitive issues have been the subject of extremely shrill positions, which have been widely reported in the press. This example from Rennes is a representative of the witnessed excitement [29], and the media coverage that followed [21], forcing the authorities to take action in order to diffuse the crisis [8].

Nevertheless, apart from these sources whose documentation purpose is important, historical, philosophical and, more generally, political critics are also very abundant. The example of the radical techno-critical publications of the group "*Pièces et main d'œuvre*" from Grenoble are particularly very representative of this point. Their apocalyptical description of the "machine-world automatically controlled according to the standards of efficiency and scientific organization of life" in which humans find themselves entrapped by a world phagocytosed by connected objects, where big data is the archetype of this type of criticism ([32, pp. 61–63]). The scientific and technical aspects are not to be topped in the countless computer-related literature.[2] All these criticisms can also be found together, in a more global perspective, as is the case for example in a conference by Richard Matthew Stallman comparing the use of smart city devices to the mass surveillance implemented in the Soviet Union of socialist republics[3] [37]. We could multiply the examples, but it is difficult nowadays, from a synthetic perspective, to get rid of them. Because these aspects, at times when personal data protection could be the main issue of such deployments, are sometimes overlooked by stakeholders as well as by critics [24]. The work of Lionel Maurel on these enquiries paves the way to further advance on this task: advocate of social protection of personal data, he enlightens us from his legal point of view on these questions, taking part in the debate on the status of data. It is notably the controversy between proponents of a heritage that consists, as I cite, "of creating a private property right on personal data in a way that allows individuals to negotiate their use on a contractual basis with platforms, while being eventually paid in return" (*Ibidem*) on the one hand, and the defenders of a social vision of data, on the other hand, that "estimate in fact that personal data are less "extracted" by platforms than "produced" or "coproduced" by individuals in their interaction with the infrastructures set in place by these members" (*Ibid.*), a form of *Digital Labor*, to recur the word and idea of Antonio Casilli. These perspectives are contradictory: thinking about data in a connected city cannot be conceived without a confrontation of these points of view.

Several smart cities are therefore possible, carried out from plans prepared in advance or from a bottom-up perspective as some wish [38], or by following initiatives like the one in Barcelona praising data protection. In any case, a connected city that respects privacy is possible [23], despite the obvious risks of over-collecting data which project leaders can hardly prevent [22]. History can go back over the course of these debates and social sciences should enlighten them: the sustainability of a city will not be the same depending on whether one option or another is chosen, depending on whether the use of open-source software is privileged or not, because "social protection of personal data necessarily passes through the construction of digital commons, based on open-source software" [24].

---

[2] It would be futile to want to produce a draft bibliography on these subjects where the issues are as numerous as multifaceted, but information and communication technologies, the Internet of Things, sensor networks, geospatial technologies, intelligence artificial or even technologies for the storage and transmission of information without a control body (blockchain) are all disciplines producing knowledge linked to the smart city.

[3] For a free society, we must reduce the level of surveillance to below what the Soviet Union suffered. - a discussion between RMS, Marleen Stikker, and Francesca Bria on the need for free, fair and inclusive digital technology and infrastructures.

4.2 Disciplinary Gateways Between Formal Sciences and Social and Human Sciences Towards a Polysemic Reading of the Smart City

To demonstrate the essential contribution of social and human sciences to this problematic, we can develop a conclusion of the work attributed to answer these questions on different scales of analysis. From the implementation of public policies by the agglomeration community of La Rochelle (ACLR) and the city, the agreement of public-private partnership (PPP) between the university of La Rochelle and ENGIE in March 2018 in light of an reinforced collaboration between the two entities [42], the university restructuration projects in progress, up to the research initiatives valorizing or deepening these questions: a multitude of points whose analysis will allow a better understanding of the project at hand. Here, as elsewhere, the big firms "have identified the enormous commercial opportunities that the provision of services to cities can represent and, consequently, they devote vast resources in order to strengthen their commercial relations with urban decision-makers" [6]. The words of urbanity join, without a shadow of doubt, those of trade and industrial activity. However, at the same time, the words of human sciences seek to assert their rights on these themes.

Hence, the initiatives in the La Rochelle campus are numerous and the links are created between the components of the university to propose a more global reading, integrating essential aspects for the city's development as well as tourism [19]. The work carried out within the framework of the LUDI laboratory, coupled with the will of the human sciences to take up these questions, as during the 15th annual conference of the Institute of the Americas entitled *Americas/Europe, the digital humanities in sharing? Challenges, innovation and perspectives* organized by the University of La Rochelle and in which numerous developments have supported this Smart City initiative.[4]

This event provided a chance for the interventions of local participants, such as the president of the University of La Rochelle who presented digital humanities as an "interdisciplinary lever for systemic transformation of research and cooperation between territories" during his plenary conference, or the interventions of experts from very diverse academic backgrounds such as Agnès Montalvillo, international expert in management and public administration, who moderated the panel discussion on digital technologies, serving the territories.

Other participants came to prove this unbreakable link between *Smart City* and digital humanities. This is for example the case in the communications of Roman Arcieniega Gil,[5] on "The Smart City and the digital humanities. From digital exclusion to inclusion in a citizen perspective: The example of the favelas in Rio de Janeiro

---

[4]Organized jointly by the Center for Research in International and Atlantic History (CRHIA) of the University of La Rochelle.

[5]Doctoral student in legal sciences, University of Lille 2, CERAPS - UMR 8026.

in Brazil", but also those of Jean-Francois Claverie[6] on the "decentralized cooperation as a shared territorial development tool: the example of European programs in Latin America." These interventions witnessed so much developments that they came to enhance the comprehension of the rochelian project.

The exposition of Pascal Estraillier,[7] based on the implementation of the *CampusInnov* program and the link between universities and other participants of the socio-economic world, is from this point view very significative. It allows to understand "the deployment of activities on a campus located in a city district and has strong interactions with companies ... that are defined and with whom persists research and educational interactions" [11]. And in fact, there is a strong determination of modifying the territories in order to create "workplaces, training areas, platforms and technical services for innovative projects" [47]. Such modifications of urban spaces cannot be apprehended without the analytical contribution of geographers and urban planners, making it decisive in terms of planning, but also to understand, a posteriori, the effects of such a deployment on the city.

To highlight a final aspect of the contribution of social and human sciences, we should refer back to Yacine Ghamri-Doudane's[8] intervention on "*Smart Cities*, an application field framework for a research related to the contemporary concerns of territorial collectivities". Most notably, it teaches us that the social and human sciences allow to better comprehend the populations involved and, consequently, offer them a range of connected services appropriately to their expectations: "Somewhere, the technologies that we develop, inspired by what we learned from social and human sciences on sociology, local culture, anthropology, jurors of the evolution of laws and representations, and well, all of this influences the industries" [14]. In addition, the social and human sciences are considered as a double point of view: subsequently, preparing a research for a better integration in the economic fabric, but also, beforehand, allowing a better comprehension of the variables in its application, and therefore the possibility of making adjustments.

5 Conclusion: Decrypting the Communication on Intelligence and Sustainability, or the Role of Human and Social Sciences

The smart city, as we've seen it, "is at the heart of numerous debates and controversies, either among the participants in the city or the researchers in social sciences. The success of the expression by one of them makes it all the more suspicious in the eyes of the other." [13] From this point of view, the contribution attempts of human

---

[6]Cooperation Project Manager at the Observatory of Changes in Latin America (LOCAL).

[7]Professor at the Computer Science, Image and Interaction Laboratory (L3i) at the University of La Rochelle and Vice-President of Innovation and Socio-economic Development at the University of La Rochelle.

[8]Professor and director at the Computer Science, Image and Interaction Laboratory (L3i).

and social sciences by the University of La Rochelle, even if not sufficient, seem nevertheless to be on the right track.

The analysis generated by Christelle Menanteau on the Smart Campus is certainly an example [25]. In this text, abundant with information on the smart campus of La Rochelle, the question of "data and individual protection" is covered in a succinct manner (*Idem* p. 31). Rightly considered as one of the challenges of digital technology, data does not figure prominently in the first plan of analysis. In addition, the question of security, stakeholder in the sustainability of systems, is only presented from the definition of "the ISO 27,000 range of standards [which] helps organizations keep their information secure. ISO/IEC 27001, which sets out the requirements for information security management systems (ISMS), is the most famous standard in its range" (*Idem*, p. 35). The work of Christelle Menanteau, whose reading is essential to understand the desire to structure this intelligent campus with a view of "combining ecological transition and digital transition" (Idem, p. 1), is not intended to develop this aspect which is familiar with the project.

Therefore, we find it to be an aspect less highlighted in communication programs than data security topics. A conclusive example should allow us to get a clear idea over the matter: "The city of La Rochelle led several actions around 2017 on personal data" [26]. In fact, "While personal data is today captured and monetized without real consent by the platforms, the control and capacity of action of users are at the heart of "self-data" (or "my data"), with the ambition to put the user back at the heart of the system. Provide real means of control over personal data" is here considered to be of crucial importance. (Ibidem).

This was also what emerged from the round table held during the Smart City Tour [36]. Its title "Governance, uses, security: what challenges for local public data?" displays the interest given to the data security question "(protection of personal data, hosting in a "data warehouse", choice of system passwords, etc.) and their governance (responsibility of public authorities, role of private companies, etc.)" (*Ibidem*). The scattered sources allow us to put back the rochelian project in a broader context. We see, therefore, that setting up a smart city is done in a slightly different way from what is sometimes put forward.

Anaïs Theviot has demonstrated the importance to "historicize and sociologize digital studies" [39], by taking "as a starting point, the pitfalls of most digital work: the lack of sociological and historical perspectives" (*Ibidem*). It is what we seek to propose and we believe that the rochelian case study has allowed to confirm its demonstration: if it accords an evident importance to the question of data security, it remains nevertheless imprecise in the communication that have been made: without highlighting this question, nor evoking the choices made in advance, the users remains in the dark. If human and social sciences can contribute to reinstate these questions in the center of the academic debate, they must analyze what is said and what is not said in order to build and understand the sustainable and smart city.

References

1. Ark, C., & Smyrl, M. (2017). Innovation ouverte et living labs: Production et traduction d'un modèle européen. *Revue française d'administration publique, 161*(1), 89–102.
2. Attour, A., & Rallet, A. (2014). Le rôle des territoires dans le développement des systèmes trans-sectoriels d'innovation locaux: Le cas des Smart Cities. *Innovations, 43*(1), 253–279.
3. Bakıcı, T., Almirall, E., & Wareham, J. (2013). A smart city initiative: The case of Barcelona. *Journal of the Knowledge Economy, 4,* 135–148.
4. Bradley, J., Reberger Amitabh, C., Gupta, D. (2013). L'internet of everything, *Cisco* [online], Retrieved from: https://www.cisco.com/web/FR/tomorrow-starts-here/pdf/IoE_VAS_Public_Sector_Top_10_Insights_121313FINAL_FR.pdf.
5. Bria, F. (dir.). (2017). *Barcelona city council digital plan: A government measure or open digitisation: Free software and agile development of public administration services*, Ajuntament de Barcelona [online], Retrieved from: https://ajuntament.barcelona.cat/digital/sites/default/files/LE_MesuradeGovern_EN_9en.pdf.
6. Capdevila, I., & Zarlenga, M. I. (2015). Smart city or smart citizens? The Barcelona case. *Journal of Strategy and Management, 8*(3), 266–282.
7. Côme, T., Magne, S. & Steyer, A. (2018). Être ou ne pas être une *smart city*: une étude empirique des innovations valorisées sur le site web des villes, *Gestion et management public, 7*(2), pp. 73–101.
8. CROUS. (2017). *Communiqué de presse du CROUS qui revient sur cette expérience pour désamorcer ces critiques.* Retrieved from: https://www.crous-rennes.fr/wp-content/uploads/sites/18/2017/09/expSorimentation-Maine.pdf.
9. EESC. (2012). TEN section report on the "smart cities" project, *European economic and social committee* [online], Retrieved from: https://www.eesc.europa.eu/resources/docs/qe-07-16-089-en-n–2.pdf.
10. Elmaghraby, A., & Losavio, M. (2014). Cyber security challenges in smart cities: Safety, security and privacy. *Journal of Advanced Research, 5*(4), 491–497.
11. Estraillier, P. (2017). CampusInnov: Une initiative du territoire pour l'innovation, 15ᵉ colloque international de l'Institut des Amériques (IdA). *Amériques/Europe, les Humanités numériques en partage? Enjeux, innovations et perspectives*, La Rochelle, 18, 19, 20 octobre, Retrieved from: http://portail-video.univ-lr.fr/CampusInnov-une-initiative-du.
12. Etudiant.gouv. (2018). C'est quoi, un Smart Campus?, *Etudiant.gouv* [online], Retrieved from: https://www.etudiant.gouv.fr/pid33626-cid128863/c-est-quoi-un-smart-campus.html.
13. Eveno, E. (2018). La Ville intelligente: Objet au cœur de nombreuses controverses. *Quaderni, 96*(2), 29–41.
14. Ghamri-Doudane, Y. (2017). Smart Cities, un domaine d'application cadre pour une recherche en lien avec les préoccupations contemporaines des collectivités territoriales?, 15ᵉ colloque international de l'Institut des Amériques (IdA). *Amériques/Europe, les Humanités numériques en partage? Enjeux, innovations et perspectives*, La Rochelle, 18, 19, 20 octobre, Retrieved from: http://portail-video.univ-lr.fr/Smart-Cities-un-domaine-d.
15. Ghorra-Gobin, C. (2018). Smart city: "Fiction" et innovation stratégique. *Quaderni, 96,* 5–15.
16. Gidari, A. (2017). "Smart cities" are too smart for your privacy, *Center for Internet and Society at Stanford Law School* [online], Retrieved from: http://cyberlaw.stanford.edu/blog/2017/02/smart-cities-are-too-smart-your-privacy.
17. La Rochelle. (2016). La Rochelle, ville intelligente, *European economic and social committee.* Retrieved from: https://www.eesc.europa.eu/resources/docs/la-rochelle-ville-intelligente.pdf.
18. La Rochelle. (2019). La Rochelle pionnière sur l'Open Data, *La Rochelle.* Retrieved from: https://www.larochelle.fr/action-municipale/ville-connectee/la-rochelle-pionniere-sur-lopen-data.
19. Lagier, J., & Montargot, N. (2019). Quelle est la vision des acteurs publics, institutionnels et privés sur l'intégration du tourisme dans la *Smart City? Management & Avenir, no, 107,* 13–35.
20. Lallement, J. (2017). Le Smart Campus de l'université de La Rochelle, un Living Lab pour la cité. *Administration & Éducation, 156,* 41–47.

21. Les Inrocks. (2017). Retour sur l'étrange affaire des "capteurs espions" dans les lits des étudiants du Crous de Rennes, *Les Inrocks*. Retrieved from: https://www.lesinrocks.com/2017/09/11/actualite/actualite/retour-sur-letrange-affaire-des-capteurs-espions-dans-les-lits-des-etudiants-du-crous-de-rennes/.
22. Li, Y., Dai, W., Ming, Z., & Qiu, M. (2016). Privacy protection for preventing data over-collection in smart city. *IEEE Transactions on Computers, 65*(5), 1339–1350.
23. Martinez-Balleste, A., Perez-Martinez, P. A. & Solanas, A. (2013). The pursuit of citizens' privacy: A privacy-aware smart city is possible, *IEEE Communications Magazine, 51*(6), 2013, pp. 136–141.
24. Maurel, L & Aufrère, L. (2018). *Pour une protection sociale des données personnelles, S. I. Lex*. Retrieved from: https://scinfolex.com/2018/02/05/pour-une-protection-sociale-des-donnees-personnelles/.
25. Menanteau, C. (2018), *Smart Campus: L'université du futur peut-elle permettre de conjuguer transition écologique et transition numérique?* Thèse professionnelle du Mastère spécialisé exécutive, sous la dir. De Vincent Courboulay et Valérie Lenglart, p. 81.
26. Mission Société Numérique. (2019), Lyon, Nantes et La Rochelle jettent les bases du Self Data territorial, *Labo Société Numérique*. Retrieved from: https://labo.societenumerique.gouv.fr/2019/07/18/lyon-nantes-et-la-rochelle-jettent-les-bases-du-self-data-territorial/.
27. Ng, I., & Forbes, J. (2009). Education as service: The understanding of university experience through the service logic. *Journal of Marketing for Higher Education, 19*(1), 38–64.
28. Ouellet, M. (2006). Le *Smart Growth* et le nouvel urbanisme: Synthèse de la littérature récente et regard sur la situation canadienne. *Cahiers de géographie du Québec, 50*(140), pp. 175–193.
29. *Ouest France*. (2017). Étudiants à Rennes. Dormez, vous êtes surveillés…, *Ouest France*. Retrieved from: https://www.ouest-france.fr/bretagne/rennes-35000/etudiants-rennes-dormez-vous-etes-surveilles-5227294.
30. Paquienséguy, F., & Dymytrova, V. (2018). *Open data* et métropoles, les enjeux d'une transformation à l'œuvre: Analyse sémio-pragmatique d'un corpus de portails métropolitains. *Questions de communication, 34*(2), 209–228.
31. Payne, C. (2002). On the security of open source software. *Information Systems Journal, 12*(1), 61–78.
32. Pièces et main d'œuvre. (2017). *Manifeste des chimpanzés du futur: C11ontre les inhumains* (p. 345). Seyssinet-Pariset: Service compris.
33. Public Code. (2017). Argent public ? Code public!—Une campagne pour la publication sous Licence Libre des logiciels financés par le contribuable, *Public Code*. Retrieved from: https://publiccode.eu/fr/.
34. Recio, M. (2019). L'Espagne va plus loin que le *Règlement général sur la protection des données* en adaptant sa législation en matière de protection des données, *IRIS Merlin* [online], Retrieved from: https://merlin.obs.coe.int/iris/2019/3/article11.fr.html.
35. *Smart City Mag*. (2019). *Smart Cities Tour*—La Rochelle, *Smart City Mag*. Retrieved from: http://www.smartcitymag.fr/smartcitytour/6/la-rochelle.
36. *Smart City Mag*. (2019). Le *smart city tour*. Compte rendu : La Rochelle, territoire zéro carbone, *Smart city mag*. Retrieved from: http://www.smartcitymag.fr/src/sctour_reports/00/00/00/03/compte_rendu_sc_tour_la_rochelle_300146_a.pdf.
37. Stallman, R. M. (2018). How we can have less surveillance than the USSR?, Colloque *We make the city*, Amsterdam, Netherlands, table ronde sur *"smart city, spy city? Avenues for making a city 'smart' while respecting privacy and anonymity"*. Retrieved from: https://www.fsf.org/events/rms-20180621-amsterdam.
38. Tebbens, W. (2017). Now is LoRa: Building the smart city bottom up, *Free knowledge institute*. Retrieved from: http://freeknowledge.eu/blogs/now-lora-building-smart-city-bottom-up.
39. Theviot, A. (2015). Historiciser et sociologiser les études sur le numérique. Porter le regard sur les processus historiques et les acteurs pour étudier les dispositifs web, *Interfaces numériques, 4*(3), p. 473–490.
40. TLFi. Durable, *Trésor de la langue française informatisé*. Retrieved from: https://www.cnrtl.fr/definition/durable.

41. ULR 2. (2018). Vers un littoral urbain zéro carbone français. Appel à manifestation d'intérêt. Programme d'Investissements d'Avenir—Action Territoires d'innovation de grande ambition—Communauté d'Agglomération de La Rochelle, *Université de La Rochelle*, p. 65.
42. ULR 3. (2018). L'Université de La Rochelle et ENGIE vont collaborer sur le 1er Smart Campus de France, *Université de La Rochelle*. Retrieved from: https://www.univ-larochelle.fr/luniversite/espace-presse/communiques-de-presse/luniversite-de-la-rochelle-et-engie-vont-collaborer-sur-le-1er-smart-campus-de-france-2/.
43. ULR 4. (2017). Projet d'établissement 2018–2021, *université de La Rochelle*. Retrieved from: https://www.univ-larochelle.fr/wp-content/uploads/pdf/Projet-de%CC%81tablissement-2018-2021.pdf.
44. ULR 5. (2018). Smart campus. Construisons ensemble un campus intelligent, *Université de la Rochelle*, https://www.univ-larochelle.fr/wp-content/uploads/pdf/VF_smart_campus_juille t2018.pdf.
45. ULR 6. (2018). Un smart campus à l'université de la rochelle. Pour une préfiguration et un living lab. de l'université du futur, *Université de La Rochelle* [archive], p. 10.
46. ULR 1. (2019). 2e édition des Rencontres du Littoral Urbain Durable Intelligent, *université de La Rochelle*, https://www.univ-larochelle.fr/actualites/2e-edition-rencontres-du-littoral-urb ain-durable-intelligent/.
47. ULR 7. (2019). CampusInnov, *Université de La Rochelle*. Retrieved from: https://www.univ-larochelle.fr/luniversite/grands-projets/campusinnov/.
48. Vesco, A., & Ferrero, F. (2015). *Handbook of research on social, economic, and environmental sustainability in the development of smart cities* (p. 519). IGI Global: Information Science Reference.
49. Ville de La Rochelle. (2017). Stratégie numérique. Ville de La Rochelle, *Ville de La Rochelle*, https://www.larochelle.fr/uploads/media/Strategie_numerique_-_Pour_diff usion_web_01.pdf.

Smart City in China: The State of Art of Xiong an New Area

Eleonora Veglianti, Elisabetta Magnaghi, Marco De Marco, and Yaya Li

Abstract In the last period, we have been facing the impact of smart society and of its components such as smart cities which have become a strategic element to improve the quality of lives as well as to achieve specific needs. The aim of this work is to better understand smart cities in a unique and complex context such as China analysing the most recent example known as the *Xiong an new area*. Using a case approach, it presents a new way of studying smart city concepts to investigate on the development perspective and on the strategies as well as on the best practices used in this peculiar scenario.

Keywords Smart city · Urban strategy · China · Societal change · Xiong an new area

1 Introduction

The population migration from rural to urban areas opens an interesting discussion among scholars as well as among politicians in different countries with a focus on smart cities. The rise of urbanization and of its impact on several elements such as pollution, employment, energy demand and waste production ([18, 27, 58]) highlights the need to study the opportunities and the challenges of these new trends in several

E. Veglianti (✉) · M. De Marco
Department of Economics, University of Uninettuno, Rome, Italy
e-mail: eleonora.veglianti@uninettunouniversity.net

M. De Marco
e-mail: marco.demarco@uninettunouniversity.net

E. Magnaghi
Department of Economics, Université Catholique Di Lille, Lille, France
e-mail: elisabetta.magnaghi@univ-catholille.fr

Y. Li
School of Finance and Economics, Jiangsu University, Zhenjiang, China
e-mail: yizhi19881107@126.com

© Springer Nature Switzerland AG 2021
E. Magnaghi et al. (eds.), *Organizing Smart Buildings and Cities*,
Lecture Notes in Information Systems and Organisation 36,
https://doi.org/10.1007/978-3-030-60607-7_6

contexts. In this scenario, smart cities result from an emerging strategy with the goal of bettering the quality of life of citizens using the most innovative technologies to reach the specific needs of each city ([1, 9, 10, 14, 19, 28, 31, 43, 50, 57, 69]).

In other words, smart cities become a global phenomenon showing similar features and common principles worldwide, but they have, at the same time, unique elements due to their local aspect such as the geographical and territorial background, the cultural situation and the human capital characteristics [25].

In China recently, the government decided to set up the *Xiong an new area* which is another smart city case of highly national relevance after Shenzhen Special Economic Zone and Shanghai Pudong New Area. The *Xiong an new area* is an important strategic choice for the coordinated development of the northern part of China having an interesting effect on Beijing, Tianjin and Hebei [15, 16].

The aim of this work is to better understand smart cities in China by analyzing the case of *Xiong an new area*. This choice is motivated by the unique context of China, in terms of political and territorial organization, of its culture as well as of its life attitudes. Moreover, since 2009, smart cities witnessed a boom in China due to urban development [52] with more than 300 cities showing smart-city pilot projects [30]. Consequently, our research questions are the following: how smart is *Xiong an new area*? Which are the specific case features that have more impact on the development and on the implementation of the *Xiong an new area*?

The paper is structured as follows: Sect. 2 explores the literature review; Sect. 3 defines the methodology; Sect. 4 discusses the results and Sect. 5 concludes by analyzing the limits of the paper and suggesting further works.

2   Literature Review

In the relevant international literature, we can identify three main branches of definitions regarding smart cities:

- digital city, wired city, virtual city, ubiquitous city used to highlight the importance of high technologies, especially information and communication technology (ICT), to improve the development of urban life ([24], [23], [64], [43], [3, 65], [67]);
- intelligent city, knowledge city, learning city focused on the role of smart people as actors of the city's governance and development ([32, 51, 61]);
- green city and sustainable city to define the link between the urban life and the environment ([5], [39]).

However, the term smart city collects all the above-mentioned definitions to emphasize the relevant aspects that each branch wants to support. For example, Nam and Pardo [59] identify three domains in a smart city: technological, institutional and human. While Dameri [25] suggests a theoretical framework based on four dimensions to study smart cities:

1. the land/location: the territory on which the city is built, the geographical area with its boundaries;
2. the infrastructures: the material or technological facilities such as buildings, transport systems and the ICT;
3. the government: the public powers to govern the city;
4. the people: the citizens living in the city.

In line with the literature, some dimensions highlighted smart cities as a global phenomenon, while others show local domains. In other words, on one side, urbanization is a common trend in the world and in various countries [55, 62], especially where cities tend to grow faster, a smart city becomes a strategy to manage the issues due to rapid urbanization [17]. In addition, global problems such as pollution, land consumption, energy demand, climate change, mobility and traffic increase the attention on smart cities [47], [49], [75].

On the other side, regarding the local aspects of a smart city, there are single specificities and unique features that impact the smart city's development and implementation due for example to: the geographical localization ([36], 38, [10], [2], [72]); the national laws and governance approach ([59, 63], [63], [21], [56]) as well as the culture of citizens, along with their educational and professional skills ([6], [24], [35], [68]). Furthermore, the quality of life is viewed differently around the world and this influences the political agendas and decisions of the various governments ([60], [64]).

There are also a growing number of Chinese domestic contributions in this area of research which open to several interpretations on the smart city concept [48], [54]. For example, a smart city is a composite system with a various subsystem [88]. It is a digital, wireless, eco or low-carbon city ([70], [75], [29]). Some scholars suggest smart city as a "cyber-physical-social" system [77]. Feng and Jiang [34] taking the case of Nanjing highlight that the government has to plan building programs for the creation of a smart city, acquiring high-quality talents from the university sphere.

Another interesting contribution [89] found that policies and regulations as well as the internet penetration rate are the most important elements in the smart city development. Finally, Yu and Xu [85] suggest that the success of a smart city in China is given by the political-institutional support from the ruling party. Therefore, each smart city case requires a deeper analysis to better understand the peculiarities of the single project.

3 Smart City in China

China is a unique country due to the size of its population (around 1.404 billion people), the huge gap between rural and urban areas as well as the centralized administrative power. In fact, the government exercises jurisdiction in: twenty-two provinces, five autonomous regions, four direct-controlled municipalities (Beijing, Tianjin, Shanghai, and Chongqing) and the special regions of Hong Kong and Macau.

Therefore, the smart cities' development is dominated by the national government [33].

The Chinese cities differ from the common sense of city as they comprise, typically, a main central urban area (usually with the same name as the prefectural level city) and a surrounding rural area with many smaller cities, towns and villages spanning over kilometers [61]. Smart cities in China can use greenfield land in the suburb areas to build new smart districts ([28], [37]).

Nowadays, the most important smart cities are Wuxi, Shanghai, Beijing and Shenzhen [89, 88] and each of them presents some peculiarities, for example:

- Wuxi focuses on Internet of things (IoT) applications on transportation, agriculture, industry, and education.
- Shanghai promotes the smart city for urban development looking at the public wireless LAN coverage.
- Beijing shows various plans and has made major actions in the infrastructure construction of medical information.
- Shenzhen has always been quite a pioneer, especially in the field of logistics (i.e. developing cloud logistics).

As these cases show, in China, smart cities are often implemented in greenfield districts in the suburbs of large metropolis, to decrease the quality of life differences among cities and rural areas [53]. Moreover, they present new architectural solutions and materials [28], especially in Beijing or in Shanghai. In addition, traditional technologies like WiFi are not enough to connect all the citizens in a country such as China opening new infrastructure testing such as optical networking components [74]. In addition, the importance of infrastructures implementation is recognized at the national level [77]; thus, since 2000, the government has invested huge amounts in ICT ([46], [53]).

In addition to the infrastructure, people are actors of the smart cities with different roles and positions in the development and implementation phases, specifically they can be considered as users or players [20]. On one side, they co-produce concurring to the smartness of a city ([41], [46]). On the other side, as in the case of China, most of the citizens have a passive role in the decisional process and governance of the city ([53], [42]).

In other words, the central Chinese government with the related institutions (i.e. Ministry of Housing and Urban-Rural Development, Ministry of Industry and Information Technology), committees (Internet of Things Expert Committee) and technical agencies (i.e. Smart City Innovation Solutions Research Center) manage the smart city projects from the beginning to the end. However, some innovative cases exist as Smart Pudong area, in Shanghai, which presents a more people-oriented approach [89].

China faces the administrative powers at the central level [12], the government promotes the construction of smart cities ([13], [87]) even because resources are getting scarce, environmental pollution increases as well as traffic issues ([74], [4], (81]). Therefore, smart cities are playing a key role and, after thirty years of reform, China's urbanization has made crucial achievements with millions of rural people going to the city every year ([11], [71]). Given this huge *"urban disease"* the government has to act considering the role of smart cities in the society [79].

In line with this, the Chinese policy development is improved and it can be traced back to the 12th Five-Year Plan for National Economic and Social Development (2011–2015) and the 13th Five-Year Plan for National Economic and Social Development (2016–2020) where smart cities result as a primary goal of the national development policy ([40], [79], [87]). Furthermore, several actions guided by the government emerged, the main ones are listed below:

- in 2012, the National Congress of the Communist Party of China (CPC) proposed industrialization, informatization and urbanization and promoted digital cities;
- in 2013, the Ministry of Housing and Urban-Rural Development released the first batch of national smart city pilot list with a total of 90, of which: 37 prefecture-level cities, 50 districts and 3 towns;
- the CPC Central Committee and the State Council released the National New Urbanization Plan (2014–2020) to promote the construction of smart cities into national strategic planning;
- finally, in 2016, the CPC Central Committee and the State Council defined an Urban Planning to improve people's quality of life and network security [73]. Moreover, the Ministry of Industry and Information Technology created the "China Smart City Industry Alliance": a nationwide and non-profit organization of voluntary firms engaged in smart city development [73].

Therefore, in China, smart cities are directly funded and managed at the national level by the central government which selects those cities intended to be smart [48].

4   Research Methodology

The present paper follows a case study approach to allow the exploration and understanding of a complex issue such as smart city in China. This methodology provides an in-depth analysis of the social and behavioural problems in question. The analysis is based on a broad level activity, both looking at the theoretical and empirical spheres [7].

The aim is to closely study the data within a specific context, as ([80], p. 23) highlighted, the case study research method is "an empirical inquiry that investigates a contemporary phenomenon within its real-life context; when the boundaries between phenomenon and context are not clearly evident; and in which multiple sources of evidence are used". Moreover, the authors can read the scientific literature and the different types of data collected in Chinese as well as they can share their personal experiences about smart city in this country. Therefore, in addition to the relevant literature, to better understand the case under investigation several sources of data were collected such as institutional and professional documents, web sites information, speeches and conferences notes.

Table 1 Data sources

Knowledge source	Materials
Scientific papers	A database was built collecting more than 200 papers about smart city and similar topics written in English. At this database were added several scientific papers written in Chinese since 2012
Institutional/corporate reports	Several authoritative reports were examined, issued by national or supranational institutions such as OECD. In addition, various corporate reports were analyzed, for example issued by Boston Consulting Group (BCG)
Workshops/conferences/website	The authors collected notes and records from the participation to many international conference/workshops. Moreover, many websites were visited

The data collection was repeated several times to reach a clearer framework that leads from a broader to a more detailed level of analysis. The materials used are summarized in Table 1.

This article adopts a case design ([8], [82, 83, 84]). In line with the relevant literature on this research methodology and with the purpose of this paper, we consider a descriptive approach to analyze this phenomenon in a narrative form which occurs within the data in question [56]. The choice of this method is to design an examination of the data conducted within the context of its use that is, within the situation in which the activity takes place [80].

- The theoretical framework

Following the relevant literature [25, 26]), the present work adopted the related theoretical framework for smart cities mentioned above which is based on four dimensions: land/location, infrastructures, government and people (Fig. 1). Hence, using a case approach, the paper wants to understand the smart city model in the Chinese context as described in the next paragraphs.

5   The Case of *Xiong an New Area*: Emerging Results

- The Location

Xiong an new area, relying on its superior location advantages - a new growth pole in Beijing-Tianjin-Hebei region- having a crucial role in the economic vitality of the whole North of China [45]. Specifically, *Xiong an new area* is located in the hinterland of Beijing, Tianjin and Baoding. It is 105 km away from Beijing and Tianjin, 155 km away from Shijiazhuang, 30 km away from Baoding and 55 km away from Beijing New Airport. The planning scope of the new district includes Xiong County, Rongcheng County, Anxin County administrative jurisdiction (including Baiyangdian waters), Renqiu City Fanzhou Town, Gougezhuang Town, Qijiafang

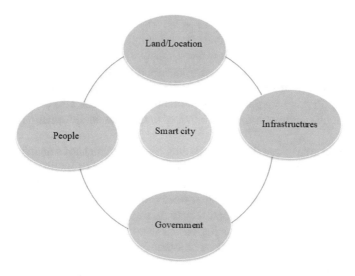

Fig. 1 The theoretical framework

Township and Gaoyang County Longhua Township, planning area of 1770 square kilometers [78].

In addition to its strategic geographical location, there is also a spatial distribution of industries in this densely populated and economically intensive area which required the coordination of the high-end industrial agglomeration with the urban service functions. In this context, the concept of urban layout should be changed from the service industry to the service people, and *Xiong an new area* shows an innovative display (*Xiong an* government website).

In other words, the geographical location of this city regards its position in the political and physical geography, highlighting this dimension is crucial because it also takes place in the decision to start the development of the *Xiong an new area*.

- The Infrastructures: material and technological facilities

A smart city is an advanced stage of urban development which requires to consider the infrastructural dimension including both the tangible and intangible facilities. On the one hand, the main material strategies are focused on: buildings efficiency, sustainable transport and lower energy consumption. On the other hand, the main technological elements regard the ICT, specifically the implementation of Internet connection broadband, IoT, open data, system security etc [76, 86].

From the perspective of the material urban infrastructure, the *Xiong an new area* has a Civic Service Center, it uses more than 30 new building technologies, and the concept of green intelligence runs through the whole process of the construction of the public service center [44]. There is also a real-time monitoring of the environment with a full use of renewable energy, to achieve heat exchange with the deep soil to meet heating and cooling.

In terms of transportation, the "bus + bicycle + walking" formula is considered to increase the proportion of green traffic and public transport. Moreover, with data flow, the intelligent transportation system framework presents a real-time perception, specifically there is an instantaneous response and intelligent decision-making based on the technology of object-linked sensing, mobile interconnection and artificial intelligence. In this scenario, the infrastructure construction also presents vehicles and roads realized through the integration of transportation, information and energy network.

The application of smart driving vehicles, the development of demand-responsive customized public transport systems and the widespread of intelligent generation routes and dynamic response requirement are done thanks to the creation of a global dynamic traffic control system. In other words, the creation of data-driven intelligent cooperative management and control system, together with the exploration of the network control of intelligent driving vehicles and the adoption of intelligent distribution of traffic rights ensure a better system operation safety as well as a higher level of system operation efficiency.

Furthermore, *Xiong an new area* presents a high standard of intelligent social security prevention and control system to enhance the ability to respond to public emergencies. The construction of a full-time, global and multi-dimensional data fusion urban safety monitoring system and of an intelligent decision-making and response ability of man-machine integration are both important contents in the creation of a smart environment.

Compared with the security application in other smart cities, the smart city construction in *Xiong an new area* is more integrated with the security industry. On the one side, a large number of infrastructures demands in *Xiong an new area* bring broad development opportunities for the security industry. On the other side, the application of intelligent security technology in this case also promotes the construction progress and provides safe and efficient technical facilities support. At the present, security products, such as video monitoring, access control intercom and anti-theft alarm, are playing an incomparable role in the construction of this new area.

Firstly, in *Xiong an new area*, China is improving the construction of urban information infrastructure in accordance with the requirements of smart cities. Secondly, China considers the local water resources' conditions, the flood control and drainage, the environmental protection and other requirements, to build the *Xiong an new area* into a national sponge city demonstration area. Thirdly, this country establishes a fast, convenient, green, clean and shared urban transport system and it tries to take the lead in piloting unmanned vehicles.

Fourthly, China presents a clean energy supply system with photovoltaic power generation as the main body. Specifically, this happened through the roof distributed photovoltaic, the ground parking distributed photovoltaic, the construction of energy storage system, combined with geothermal resources and gas energy supply system in this new area. Finally, it strictly implements the green building standards, all the buildings must be green buildings, forming a beautiful environment, supporting services and high quality ecological residential areas (*Xiong an* government website).

In addition to the material side of the infrastructure dimension, smart cities require the development of technological facilities. In line with this, modern technologies such as cloud computing, big data and the Internet are narrow in the application fields of *Xiong an new area*. Moreover, in this case, intelligent facilities such as smart medical care, smart government affairs, and smart environmental protection are still in the development stage, and there is no unified integrated smart city management platform among various systems. The lack of high-level talents has not yet formed an intelligent management system for this smart city, so the level of urban informatization and infrastructure construction needs to be improved.

- The Government

On April 2017, the CPC Central Committee and the State Council issued a notice and decided to set up the *Xiong an new area* which represents another case of national importance after Shenzhen Special Economic Zone and Shanghai Pudong New Area. The *Xiong an new area* is an important strategic choice for deepening the coordinated development of Beijing, Tianjin and Hebei. Therefore, this location was identified to create regional growth in the Beijing's urban subcenter.

With the goal of having new patterns of synergy development with complementary advantages and harmonious sharing, the planning and construction of *Xiong an new area* is significant and far-reaching for China that faces an economy characterized by high-speed growth and high-quality development [58].

To solve the *"urban disease"*, China is exploring a new approach for optimizing the development of densely populated areas, fostering a new engine for building a modern economic system. Among the historical smart city cases in China, there are Shenzhen Special Economic Zone and Pudong New Area that form two world-class urban agglomerations: The Pearl River Delta and the Yangtze River Delta. Both these examples play a pilot role in the economic improvement.

Today, *Xiong an new area* is for China a very important case with the aim of: releasing the market vitality, optimizing the industrial structure of Hebei, developing new industries, making up for the shortcomings of regional development, cultivating new growth poles and gathering more human resources. In line with this, *Xiong an new area* creates an innovative example implementing new concepts and becoming a national model of high-quality development.

In other words, innovation marks a key word in the construction of *Xiong an new area* which has become the benchmark set of China's urban development. Innovation is not only reflected in the path of urban development, but also in the governance of the city.

The Chinese government considers this phenomenon looking at the significance of optimizing urban spatial structure and urban industrial structure, but also at the strategic features of carrying out the concept of green development, the innovative economic growth, the convenient and efficient public services as well as the better urban management.

In this scenario, the development of *Xiong an new area* is an important answer toward the trend of building a high-level modern city with green, low-carbon, intelligent information, suitable for industry and people in China. Nowadays, it is considered a new engine of the modern economic system.

- The people

In *Xiong an new area*, the core in its construction is to provide more efficient and convenient public services for the people. There, the integration of information resources and the construction of public service system need to be strengthened since it is still in the basic stage.

The effective utilization rate of existing information resources is not enough. There are some problems such as information barriers, low resource sharing, information monopoly and so on. It is also a challenge to solve the practical problems related to the employment and household registration of the masses as well as to grasp the degree of control and service.

Also, in this case, China faces a lack of interaction between the government and the people. Citizens are passive actor in the construction and implementation of this smart city, consequently, having an impact on its development.

In addition to the above-mentioned dimensions, the analysis of the *Xiong an new area* highlights another important layer for the implementation and development of this new smart city in China. This layer is the cooperation with important companies in the Chinese industrial settings. These big players cooperate to create solutions and innovative answers in several sectors which foster the improvement and the smartness of *Xiong an new area* (Fig. 2).

- Cooperation with Chinese companies

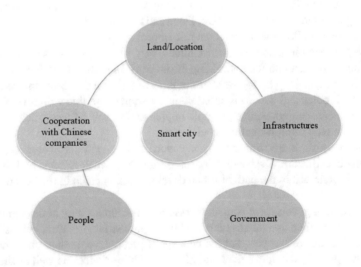

Fig. 2 The implementation and development of *Xiong an new area*

Firms, especially the technological big companies, play a pivotal role in the development of *Xiong an new area*. They cooperate to design better solutions and to deliver innovative services.

For example, on September 2017, the Hebei *Xiong an new area* Administrative Committee affirmed that 48 companies were approved to be stationed in the first batch. Among these important firms, there are: Alibaba, Tencent, Baidu, Jingdong Finance, 360 Qihu, Shenzhen Guangqi, China Development Investment, China Telecom and China Insurance. This clearly shows the influence of giant industrial players in the development of *Xiong an new area*. These important entrepreneurial entities promote different projects in several areas such as the technical support, the logistics and the traffic. In *Xiong an new area*, the principal examples are the following:

– Smart technical support—5G

China Mobile, China Unicom and China Telecom, leaders of the telecommunications industry, focus on the information network construction and on big data. Therefore, these three entities of the 5G construction industry give high importance to the construction of 5G network in the *Xiong an new area*, building high-end technical support and cloud computing. The construction of the Internet of Things (IOT) is also related to *Xiong an new area*.

– Smart logistics

On October 2017, *Xiong an new area* signed a strategic cooperation with Alibaba Group and Ant Financial Group. On one side, Ant Financial cooperates in terms of urban infrastructure, environment, industry, urban operation and management. On the other side, the two companies build the Ant Financial Service Innovation Center and the blockchain infrastructure platform.

– Smart traffic

On December 2017, Baidu and *Xiong an new area* Management Committee formally signed a strategic cooperation agreement. The two sides announced that they will make full use of their superior resource technologies to jointly build *Xiong an new area*. They will use automatic driving and dialogue. The focus on artificial intelligence promotes the pilot demonstration of intelligent industries and services including intelligent transportation.

In this field, for instance, China Mobile completed the first 5G automatic remote driving test in *Xiong an new area*. The new area becomes a test ground for autonomous driving technology. Furthermore, on December 2018, Baidu Apollo self-driving team took the lead in *Xiong an new area* opening platform in multi-vehicle, multi-scene and multi-dimensional applications such as passenger cars, commercial buses, logistics vehicles and road sweepers.

– Smart finance

Xiong an new area is an innovative demonstration place also in terms of smart finance. As an important carrier of modern finance, banks will play an important role in the construction and development of this new district.

For instance, entering the automatic deposit and withdrawal business hall of the Agricultural Bank of China Rongcheng Branch, with no need to enter a password, just check the phone number implies that the whole process is less than half a minute long to take the cash.

As suggested by Wu Xuemei, deputy governor of the Agricultural Bank of China Rongcheng Branch, the brush face withdrawal technology uses the latest infrared in vivo detection technology to completely resist photos, face-changing videos, remake, masks and other risks.

The face recognition and withdrawal technology have never been wrong during the trial period, which has facilitated the spread in *Xiong an new area*.

6 Discussion and Conclusions

Xiong an new area is in line with the urban construction in China and in accordance with the requirements of green, intelligent and innovative, low-carbon production and lifestyle.

This case presents the urban construction and operation mode that face the advanced environmental protection with energy-saving materials as well as with technical and technological standards. In other terms, it presents a synchronous planning and construction of smart city focusing on an advanced layout of intelligent infrastructure as well as promoting intelligent application services controllable in real-time framework. In addition, it establishes a large data assets management system, it builds digital facilities with in-depth learning ability, etc.

From our analysis, the *Xiong an new area* follows the smart city theoretical framework identified in the relevant literature ([25] Dameri et al. 2018), especially it is characterized by a large territory in the northern part of China which offers an important opportunity to build greenfield smart areas and to solve the urbanization issues. This confirms that the localization of smart cities is a dimension of interest also for the creation of *Xiong an new area* which requires a strategic geographic position. In China, as mentioned above, smart cities are expected to produce deeply changes especially in the suburbs, addressing collective well-being and working as an engine of the national economic and social development.

In addition to the strategic location, the infrastructure in *Xiong an new area* presents a double development taking into account the materials as well as the technological facilities. Specifically, the focus is, on the one side, on buildings and transportation and, on the other side, on ICT improvement. It emerges, therefore, that *Xiong an new area* follows the smart cities model giving a concrete evidence of the role of the infrastructure dimension in their development and implementation.

Furthermore, the *Xiong an new area* case analysis shows the central role of the government in this unique context confirming the Chinese top-down approach.

Hence, the government defines a national smart strategy that manage from the beginning to the end. In other words, the central state finances the smart city development in large and it determines the smart city implementation considering the overall national goals and needs.

Regarding the involvement of citizens, *Xiong an new area* improved compared to other cases in China by aiming at a more active role of people in the creation process to enable the public well-being in a more efficient way. Finally, a new dimension emerged, as described above, the cooperation with giant companies in the development of different elements of the smart city suggesting the peculiarity and the importance of Xiong an new area which can be the base for future projects and smart cities experiences.

This result has important implications for further scholarly research alike and for practitioners. Further studies could deep the analysis of smart cities applying a multi case approach as well as designing an analysis enlarged to other countries. Moreover, additional investigations can consider the re-configuration of smart cities business models studying the building blocks (i.e. [66]) in different cases or contexts. Despite the relevance of the topic, the article fails in developing a theoretical understanding of the phenomenon and in generating implications for politicians. However, it can present important hints for practitioners and companies that want to invest in China.

Acknowledgements This study was supported by the National Nature Science Foundation of China Project (No. 71704069)

References

1. Alawadhi, S., Aldama-Nalda, A., Chourabi, H., Gil-García, J., Leung, S., Mellouli, S., ... Walker, S. (2012). Building understanding of smart city initiatives. *Electronic government*, 40–53.
2. Angelidou, M. (2014). Smart city policies: A spatial approach. *Cities, 41,* S3–S11.
3. Anthopoulos, L., Fitsilis, P. (2010, July). From digital to ubiquitous cities: Defining a common architecture for urban development. *In Intelligent Environments (IE), 2010 Sixth International Conference* on (pp. 301–306). IEEE.
4. Baoxing, Q. (2013). Smartly promoting new-style urbanization in China. *Urban development studies.*
5. Batagan, L. (2011). Smart cities and sustainability models. *Revista de Informatica Economica, 15*(3), 80–87.
6. Berry, C. R., & Glaeser, E. L. (2005). The divergence of human capital levels across cities. *Papers in Regional Science, 84*(3), 407–444.
7. Bryman, A., & Bell, E. (2011). *Business research methods.* Oxford University Press.
8. Campbell, D. (1975). Degrees of freedom and the case study. *Comparative Political Studies,* 178–185.
9. Caragliu, A., Del Bo, C., & Nijkamp, P. (2013). 10 smart cities in Europe. *Smart cities: Governing, modelling and analysing the transition,* 173.
10. Caragliu, A., De Bo C., & Nijcamp, P. (2009). Smart city in Europe. *3rd Central European Conference in Regional Science.*
11. Champion, T. (2017). Understanding China's urbanization: The great demographic, spatial, economic, and social transformation. *The Town Planning Review, 88*(3), 379.

12. Chan, K. W. (2007). *Misconceptions and complexities in the study of China's cities: Definitions, statistics, and implications.* Eurasian Geography and Economics: University of Washington.
13. Chang, E. Y., & Zheng, F. (2017). 常恩予,甄峰. 智慧社区的实践反思及社会建构策略——以江苏省国家智慧城市试点为例[J]. 现代城市研究, (05), 2–8. (Practice Reflections and Social Construction Strategies of Smart Community: A Case Study of National Pilot Smart City in Jiangsu Province. *Modern Urban Research*).
14. Chen M., Wang Q. C., Zhang X., & Zhang, X. W. (2011). 陈铭,王乾晨,张晓海,张晓伟. "智慧城市" 评价指标体系研究——以"智慧南京"建设为例[J]. 城市发展研究, *18*(05), 84–89. (Study on the System of Evaluation for Wisdom City Construction ——*Nanjing as the Case. Urban Studies*).
15. China Smart City Planning and Construction Promotion Union. (2019). http://www.cnscn.com.cn/com/smartcity/. Accessed 10 March 2019.
16. Chinese society of Urban Studies (2019). http://www.chinasus.org/chinasus/. Accessed 20 March 2019.
17. Chourabi, H., Nam, T., Walker, S., Gil-Garcia, J. R., Mellouli, S., Nahon, K., ... & Scholl, H. J. (2012, January). Understanding smart cities: An integrative framework. *In System Science (HICSS), 2012 45th Hawaii International Conference* on (pp. 2289–2297). IEEE.
18. Cohen, B. (2015). Urbanization, City Growth, and the New United Nations Development Agenda. 3 (2). Cornerstone, *The Official Journal of the World Coal Industry.* pp. 4–7.
19. Commission, E. U. (2014). *The EU explained: Digital agenda for Europe.* Luxembourg: Publications Office of the European Union.
20. Dameri, R. P. (2013). Searching for smart city definition: A comprehensive proposal. *International Journal of Computers & Technology, 11*(5), 2544–2551. (Council for Innovative Research).
21. Dameri, R. P., & Benevolo, C. (2016). Governing smart cities: An empirical analysis. *Social Science Computer Review, 34*(6), 693–707.
22. Dameri, R. P., & Cocchia, A. (2013, December). Smart city and digital city: Twenty years of terminology evolution. *In X Conference of the Italian Chapter of AIS, ITAIS* (pp. 1–8).
23. Dameri, R. P., & Cocchia, A. (2014). La valutazione socio-economica della città digitale [Transl. The socio-economic evaluation of the digital city]. In CTI Liguria (Eds.), *La città digitale. Sistema nervoso della smart city* [Transl. The digital city. Nervous system of the smart city]. Franco Angeli: Milano.
24. Dameri, R. P., & Ricciardi, F. (2017). Leveraging smart city projects for benefitting citizens: The role of ICTs. In *Smart city networks* (pp. 111–128). Springer, Cham.
25. Dameri, R. P., & Rosenthal-Sabroux, C. (2014). *Smart city: How to create public and economic value with high technology in urban space.* Springer.
26. Dameri, R. P., Benevolo C., Veglianti E., & Li Y. (2019) Understanding smart cities as a glocal strategy: A comparison between Italy and China. *Technological Forecasting and Social Change, Elsevier*, 26–41.
27. Demographia World Urban Areas. (2014). http://www.demographia.com/dbworldua.pdf. Accessed April 2019.
28. Di Paola, A. (2012). Smart City: Utopia o realtà?. XV conferenza nazionale Società Italiana degli Urbanisti (SIU), Pescara, 10–11 Maggio, 2012. Planum—*The Journal of Urbanism, 25*(2).
29. Ding H. F., & Wang Y. H. (2016). 丁焕峰,王璎卉. 中国城市经济智慧指数的评价与分析.统计与决策, 13, 16–20. (Evaluation and analysis of urban economic intelligence index in China. *Statistics & Decision*).
30. EU-China Smart and Green City Cooperation. (2014, March). Comparative study of smart cities in Europe and China, White Paper (Draft), *EU-China Policy Dialogues Support Facilities II.*
31. EU Parliament. (2014). *Mapping smart cities in the EU.*
32. Ergazakis, M., Metaxiotis, M., & Psarras, J. (2004). Towards knowledge cities: Conceptual analysis and success stories. *Journal of Knowledge Management, 8*(5), 5–15.

33. Fang, Y., Wang, G.Z. (2017). 房勇,王广振. 智慧城市建设:中外模式比较与文化产业创生逻辑. 河南师范大学学报(哲学社会科学版). 44(06), 54–59. (Smart City Construction: Comparison of Chinese and Foreign Patterns and Creation Logic of Cultural Industry. *Journal of Henan normal university*).

34. Feng, M., & Jiang, L. (2011). 冯茂岩, 蒋兰芝. 浅谈 "智慧城市" 与 "智慧产业" 发展——以南京为例改革与战略, 9, 127–128,155. (On the Intelligent City and Intelligent Industry Development—Taking Nanjing City as an Example. *Reformation & Strategy*).

35. Fu, S. (2007). Smart café cities: Testing human capital externalities in the Boston metropolitan area. *Journal of Urban Economics, 61*(1), 86–111.

36. Gabrys, J. (2014). Programming environments: environmentality and citizen sensing in the smart city. *Environment and Planning: Society and Space, 32*(1), 30–48.

37. Gartner. (2010). Market insight: 'Smart cities' in emerging markets, *Gartner Report*.

38. Giffinger, R., Fertner, C., Kramar, H., Meijers, E. (2007). City-ranking of European medium-sized cities. *Centre of Regional Science*. Vienna UT, 1–12.

39. Gordon, D. (1990). Green cities: ecologically sound approaches to urban space (No. 138). *Black Rose Books Ltd.*

40. Gu, S., & Wang, M. (2012). 辜胜阻, 王敏. 智慧城市建设的理论思考与战略选择. 中国人·资源与环境, 5, 74–80. (Theoretical Considerations and Strategic Choice on the Development of Smart City. China Population, *Resources and Environment*).

41. Hamari, J., Sjoklint, M, & Ukkonen, A. (2013), The sharing economy: Why people participate in collaborative consumption, *Helsinki Institute for Information Technology*.

42. Hao, L., Lei, X., & Yan, Z. (2012). The application and implementation research of Smart City in China, International *Conference on System Science and Engineering, June 30—July 2, 2012*, Dalian, China.

43. Hollands, R. G. (2008). Will the real smart city please stand up? *City: Analysis of Urban Trend, Culture, Theory, Policy, Action, 12*(3), 303–320.

44. Hu, W., & Shi, B. H. (2019). A Study of the Realistic Foundation and Path Selection of the Joint Development of Tianjin Xiong'an New Area. *Journal of Tianjin Normal University* (Social Science), 2019 (04), 15–22. 胡伟,石碧华.天津—雄安新区联动发展的现实基础与路径选择.天津师范大学学报(社会科学版), 2019 (04), 15–22.

45. Huang, Q. H. (2018). Industrial Positioning of Xiong'an New District in the Coordinated Development of Beijing, Tianjin and Hebei. *Review of Economic Research*, 2018 (1), 3–6. 黄群慧.京津冀协同发展中的雄安新区产业定位[J].经济研究参考, 2018 (01), 3–6.

46. Ishida, T. (2000). Understanding digital cities. In T. Ishida & K. Isbister (Eds.), *Digital cities*. LNCS, 1765, 7–17. Berlin: Springer.

47. Jin, J., Gubbi, J., Marusic, S., & Palaniswami, M. (2014). An information framework for creating a smart city through internet of things. *IEEE Internet of Things Journal, 1*(2), 112–121.

48. Johnson, D. (2014), Smart city development in China. *China Business Review*.

49. Kitchin, R. (2014). The real-time city? *Big data and smart urbanism. GeoJournal, 79*(1), 1–14.

50. Komninos, N., Pallot, M., & Schaffers, H. (2013). Special issue on smart cities and the future internet in Europe. *Journal of the Knowledge Economy, 4*(2), 119–134.

51. Komninos, N. (2008). *Intelligent cities and globalization of innovation networks*. London: Routledge.

52. Li, S., Da Xu, L., & Zhao, S. (2015). The internet of things: A survey. *Information Systems Frontiers, 17*(2), 243–259.

53. Liu, P., & Peng, Z. (2014, October). China's smart city pilots: A progress report. *IEEE Computer Society*, 72–81.

54. Lu, S. (2011, May 13–15). The smart city's systematic application and implementation in China. *International conference on Management and Electronic Information (BMEI)*. Guangzhou, China, 116–120.

55. Martínez-Ballesté, A., Pérez-Martínez, P. A., & Solanas, A. (2013). The pursuit of citizens' privacy: A privacy-aware smart city is possible. *IEEE Communications Magazine, 51*(6), 136–141.

56. McDonough, J., & McDonough, S. (1997). *Research methods for English language teachers.* London: Arnold.
57. Meijer, A., & Bolívar, M. P. R. (2016). Governing the smart city: A review of the literature on smart urban governance. *International Review of Administrative Sciences, 82*(2), 392–408.
58. Meng, W. D., Wu, Z. Q., & Si, L. B. (2017). Discussion on the construction strategy of green smart new city in xiongan new area. *Administration Reform*, 2017 (7), 23–27. 孟卫东, 吴振其, 司林波. 雄安新区绿色智慧新城建设方略探讨. 行政管理改革, 2017 (7), 23–27.
59. Nam, T., & Pardo, T. A. (2011). Smart city as urban innovation: Focusing on management, policy, and context. In Proceedings of the 5th international conference on theory and practice of electronic governance, pp. 185–194. *ACM.*
60. Neirotti, P., De Marco, A., Cagliano, A. C., Mangano, G., & Scorrano, F. (2014). Current trends in Smart City initiatives: Some stylised facts. *Cities, 38,* 25–36.
61. OECD. (2013). *Vers une croissance plus inclusive de la métropole Aix-Marseille: Une perspective internationale.* Paris: OECD.
62. OECD Observed (1999). *Learning cities: the new recipe in regional development.*
63. Paskaleva, K. A. (2009). Enabling the smart city: The progress of city e-governance in Europe. *International Journal of Innovation and Regional Development, 1*(4), 405–422.
64. Portney, K. E. (2003). *Taking sustainable cities seriously: Economic development, the environment, and quality of life in American cities* (Vol. 67). MIT Press.
65. Qi, L., & Shaofu, L. (2001). *Research on digital city framework architecture.* IEEE International Conferences on Info-Tech and Info-Net, vol. 1, (pp. 30–36). Proceedings ICII.
66. Schiavone, F., Paolone, F., & Mancini, D. (2019). Business model innovation for urban smartization. *Technological Forecasting and Social Change, Elsevier*, 142(C), 210–219.
67. Schuler, D. (2002). Digital cities and digital citizens. In M. Tanabe, P. van den Besselaar, T. Ishida (Eds.), *Digital cities II: computational and sociological approaches.* LNCS, vol. 2362, (pp. 71–85). Berlin: Springer.
68. Shapiro, J. M. (2006). Smart cities: Quality of life, productivity, and the growth effects of human capital. *The review of economics and statistics, 88*(2), 324–335.
69. Shapiro, J. M. (2003). *Smart cities: Explaining the relationship between city growth and human capital.*
70. Si, K. L. (2014). 司开林. 智慧城市:价值、内涵与模式. 江苏城市规划, (03), 7–13. (Smart City: Value, Connotation and Mode. *Jiangsu Urban Planning*).
71. Tan, Y., Xu, H., & Zhang, X. (2016). Sustainable urbanization in China: A comprehensive literature review. *Cities, 55,* 82–93.
72. Vanolo, A. (2014). Smartmentality: The smart city as disciplinary strategy. *Urban Studies, 51*(5), 883–898.
73. Wan, B., Li, J., Zhou, W., Jiang, D., & Zhang, G. (2015).万碧玉, 李君兰, 周微茹, 等. 智慧城市试点创建实践分析.现代城市研究, 1, 2–6. (Analysis on practice of smart city pilot. *Modern Urban Research*).
74. Wang, G. B., Zhang, L., & Liu, H. L. (2013).王广斌,张雷,刘洪磊. 国内外智慧城市理论研究与实践思考. 科技进步与对策, *30*(19), 153–160. (Research and Practice on the Theory of Smart City at Home and Abroad. *Science & Technology Progress and Policy*).
75. Washburn, D., Sindhu, U., Balaouras, S., Dines, R. A., Hayes, N., & Nelson, L. E. (2009). Helping CIOs understand "smart city" initiatives. *Growth, 17*(2), 1–17.
76. Wu, B. B., & Lin, C. L. (2016). 吴标兵,林承亮. 智慧城市的开放式治理创新模式:欧盟和韩国的实践及启示, (05), 55–66. (Innovative Open Governance of Smart Cities: Practices and Policy Implications of EU and Korea. *China Soft Science*).
77. Xia, H. X., & Wang, Z. T. (2017). 夏昊翔,王众托. 从系统视角对智慧城市的若干思考. 中国软科学, (07), 66–80. (Systemic Thinking on Smart Cities. *China Soft Science*).
78. Xiogan Governement. (2019). http://www.xiongan.gov.cn/. Accessed 10 March 2019.
79. Xu, Q., Wu, Z., & Chen, L. (2012). 许庆瑞, 吴志岩, 陈力田. 智慧城市的愿景与架构. 管理工程学报, *26*(04), 1–7. (The Vision, Architecture and Research Models of Smart City. *Journal of Industrial Engineering and Engineering Management*).

80. Yin, R. K. (1984). *Case study research: Design and methods*. Beverly Hills, A: Sage Publications.
81. Yin, C., Xiong, Z., Chen, H., Wang, J., Cooper, D., & David, B. (2015). A literature survey on smart cities. *Science China Information Sciences, 58*(10), 1–18.
82. Yin, R. K. (1994a). *Case study research design and methods: Applied social research and methods series* (2nd ed.). Thousand Oaks, CA: Sage Publications Inc.
83. Yin, R. K. (1994b). *Case study research: Design and methods* (2nd ed.). Beverly Hills, CA: Sage Publications Inc.
84. Yin, R. K. (2013). *Case study research: Design and methods*. Sage publications.
85. Yu, W., & Xu, C. (2016). 于文轩,许成委. 中国智慧城市建设的技术理性与政治理性——基于147个城市的实证分析. 公共管理学报,13(04):127–138 + 159–160. (Technological and Political Rationalities of Smart City Initiatives in China ——An Empirical Analysis Based on 147 Cities. *Journal of Public Management*).
86. Zhang, A. (2015). 张爱平. "互联网+" 引领智慧城市 2.0[J]. 中国党政干部论坛. (6), 20–23. (Internet + lead the smart city. *Chinese Cadres Tribune*).
87. Zhang, X., & Xia, Y. (2017). 张尧, 夏颖. 智慧城市建设的经验比较及实现路径分析. 商业经济研究. (13), 186–187. (Experience in the construction of SMART cities in China. *Journal of Commercial Economics*).
88. Zhang, Z. G., & Zhang, X. J. (2014). 张振刚,张小娟. 智慧城市系统构成及其应用研究. 中国科技论坛, (07), 88–93. (Research on the System Components of Smart City and its Application. *Forum on Science and Technology in China*).
89. Zhang, Z. Q., Zou, K., Xiang, S., & Mao, T. T. (2017). 张中青扬,邹凯,向尚,毛太田. 智慧城市建设能力评估模型与实证研究. 科技管理研究, *37*(02), 73–76 + 96. (Model Construction and Empirical Study on Smart City Construction Ability Assessment. *Science and Technology Management Research*).

Medium-Sized Smart Cities: A Smart Vision for Urban Centralities and Buildings. From the European Case History, to a Proposal for the City of Parma, Italy

Monica Bruzzone

Abstract Smart city arouses the image of metropolis or even megacities, and many Smart city models aim at enhancing the performances of big cities. Yet in Europe, it is necessary to deal with a fact: most people dwelling cities, live in Medium-sized cities. These cities therefore create an important critical mass, both because they are very numerous, and because they suffered the greatest criticalities in terms of environmental pollution, life quality, mobility and also building sustainability. Beginning from the scientific literature and the rankings of Medium-sized cities, as well as the concept of Functional Urban Area, this research deepens medium city as a territorial issue, with an urban attractive core, and a wider complex landscape. The boundaries definition of a medium city, and the analysis of its geomorphological, infrastructural and functional criticalities, may be the key for a new interpretation of Smart strategies for their sustainable development. The research output is the proposal of an innovative tool, addressed to leaders and planners of the Smart Medium-sized city. This tool may allow a critical reading of the city, by georeferencing material and immaterial data about the city and its functional area, crossing open data and morphological characters in an interactive dashboard. After the case history of European Medium-sized cities, the research focuses on the role of Parma, Italian Medium-sized city, with a proposal about a future smart development, for consolidating results obtained during 2020, with the cultural leadership of the Italian Cultural Capital award.

Keywords Smart city · Smart building · Medium-sized city · Territory · Resilience

M. Bruzzone (✉)
University of Parma, Parma, Italy
e-mail: monica.bruzzone@unipr.it; monica.bruzzone@economia.unige.it

University of Genoa, Genoa, Italy

© Springer Nature Switzerland AG 2021
E. Magnaghi et al. (eds.), *Organizing Smart Buildings and Cities*,
Lecture Notes in Information Systems and Organisation 36,
https://doi.org/10.1007/978-3-030-60607-7_7

1   Smart Policies for Medium-Sized Cities: A Still Open Research Field

The words Smart city concern the city growth in relation with the disruptive development of new technologies and digitization; it embraces a wide range of meanings and approaches. The Smart city process may be developed at several dimensions: from the large scale of new megacities in emerging countries, to the small size of the provincial cities, up to the new phenomenon of Smart villages ([10], [22], [21], [23]), dealing with the Smart strategies for little towns and the rural areas.

The social necessity to design an intelligent city, appropriate for the ever-changing needs of contemporary culture is a problem crossing the history of civilization. Giving intelligence to the space we live, in order to adapt its vocations to the community needing [11], has always been a target, in any masterplan addressed to the city and the landscape transformation. As well, what qualifies the Smart city development process, from a traditional approach?

First of all, there is a change in the timeframe. Smart city is an innovative process, based on the growth of competitiveness and economic development, and it requires quick actions. It includes the concept of immediacy, both in the execution and in the impact evaluation: this attitude may often create negative results, when a smart strategy is not aligned with the rhythms of nature that requires a long time to respond to the anthropic transformation [18].

Then, there is a change in the methodological approaches. A Smart city aims at improving the quality of life, increasing attractiveness; but it also aims at preserving and enhancing the environment with adaptive strategies nowadays called *Resilience*. However, the Smart strategy policies often seem to give partial answers to general problems especially in Medium-sized cities. The punctual solutions they create seem to contrast with the landscape complexity, that goes beyond its administrative limits, and requires a systemic strategy, to be checked in medium and long terms. Designing a city strategy, in particular for Medium-sized cities, therefore needs a dynamic vision of the territory as well. Both in its spatial terms, considering the city as a core element of a wider landscape, and in temporal terms, considering the nowadays cities as the result of a morphological, historical and cultural development, with cyclic repetition of physical and geological events.

The aim of this research is to provide a definition of Medium-sized Smart city, with particular reference to the European condition, as well as to propose an approach model based on the interactive territorial analysis, useful for governance and planning processes. The research is divided into 4 points, described in Sects. 2–5, as follows. Section 2 provides a definition of Medium-sized Smart cities, in accordance with the European vision, and focusing on the creation of specific rankings and on the Functional Urban Area concept. Section 3 identifies Parma as a Medium-sized Italian city: a good case study for an urban analysis model, aiming at integrating environmental, cultural and functional issues with a digital dataset based on the big data georeferencing, in order to create an operational tool for policy makers and planners. The Section also summarizes the results of a case history of 10 medium Smart cities in Europe, for better understanding the Parma conditions, in order to create a new approach model to the urban phenomenon, preliminary for any governance and planning Smart strategy. Section 4 deals with the premises for a geo-referenced interactive map, as a multilevel analysis on the urban phenomenon. This dashboard will help recording and querying the three types of memory acting on the city and involving citizens: the form memory and the function memory based on the "brick and stones" city, and the recent digital memory, based on the relationship between the real city and the big data or digital traces left by sensors and people living and moving in the city. This new map may geo-reference spatial data, and also hook intangible data to real places. The interpretation model could also be useful to define an ideal area of intervention on the city, where the effects of Smart strategies can be maximized, and also to monitor the impacts of Smart policies extended to the landscape over time. Section 5, summarizes the first conclusions and explains guidelines for activating the following research.

2 The Medium-Sized Smart City: A Context Analysis

The scientific community begins a discussion about Medium-sized cities' smartness with a certain delay. The first topic concerns the performance indicators, for checking and evaluating impacts of Smart projects in Medium-sized cities, on medium and long terms. In a first phase, indicators were inherited by the big cities, with negative results for smaller cities, constantly obscured by the larger impact of the larger Smart cities. Projects with big effects on Medium-sized centers did not emerge in the international rankings: this lower visibility also determines a low competitiveness and attractiveness for stakeholders and entrepreneurs. A very bad goal for the Smart strategies' implementation process [19].

2.1 Smart City: Project and Governance. a European Approach

For a scientific definition of the medium city smartness, a premise is needed: through the meanings of the word Smart city, held by the scientific community over the last 10 years, we may identify a kind of European approach [8]. The increasing interest in smart policies for Medium-sized cities could be better understood if contextualized in the European physic and cultural landscape.

A shared definition of Smart city concerns the development of urban life quality, using new technologies and digitization [5]. From this perspective, many models have been developed around the world: each of them responds in a different way to a specific geography, culture, economic development, social needs, governance strategy [3]. In North America, where Smart policies are strictly connected with urban development models, we may appreciate the foundation of new cities and neighbor-hoods, often funded by hyper-technological global corporations, as experiments for innovative ideas. In other parts of the world, particularly in emerging countries, Smart cities are also utopian experiments of fully technologically controlled organisms. They aim at responding to individual daily needs, using artificial intelligence and big data, for integrating a wide control process, managing the citizen's life as well ([16], [17]).

In the most cautious and dense countries of European identity, cities and communities have strong historical roots. They have generally little dimensions, and their historic centers and first expansion areas, almost saturated, are the main elements of an extensive and complex territorial system. It is no longer conceivable to have political unpreparedness that proposes innovative projects without a dynamic interpretation of the historical environment, and also without a methodological approach based on the definition of a wider area and of a long-term period strategy. Also, in Europe we appreciate the need to replace a former urban expansion model, based on land consumption, with virtuous processes of regeneration and building replacement, and also with new projects of Smart building infiltration strategies, in the density of the historical texture. Another objective is to encourage a development of environmental quality: for instance, the enhancing of green lungs for the city, as new smart and sensitive models of public space.

This kind of European approach has roots in the guidelines proposed by the European Union to direct governance actions. The approach has been implemented by national and local laws, and more recently it also entered into the daily practice of the local communities. It is also necessary to take into account the 2030 Global Agenda for Sustainable Development: here the United Nations promotes the best Smart strategies and practices, for developing topics as the environmental sustainability, economy, innovative industry, energy efficiency, sustainable mobility, reduction of social inequalities [20]. As we may see, the development of Smart city processes in Europe, has got very different approaches and purposes than in other parts of the planet. The first result of this character is a deep interaction between the notions of smartness and sustainability, two sides of the same development process, improving urban life quality with Smart processes and enhancing the domestic comfort and effectiveness with the Smart building projects and the Smart grid planning.

2.2 The Medium-Sized Cities in Europe: Guidelines for a Smart Approach

The Smart approach to urban design is an almost recent issue, which has been growing in the scientific literature since the mid-1990s, and the 2000s [8]. Scientific debate documents how Smart city processes were focused, at the very beginning, on big cities and metropolis. Here an exponential dimensional growth quickly amplifies ancient problems, such as pollution, mobility, accessibility to services; and creates new challenges. The first researches on urban development strategies, the first Smart city projects and the first impact evaluation, are about the big cities, where the most innovative governance models and best practices were tested. In Europe, Smart cities such as London, Amsterdam, Helsinki, Stockholm have firstly been distinguished and then consolidated. In this first phase, and in the subsequent development of good practices and models, a focus on the development approach for Medium-sized cities was missing. Medium cities inherited the Smart approach models from big cities, based on the big size of the metropolitan problems, as well as the evaluation parameters and indicators created for cities with very different dimensions and challenges.

Yet, in Europe most of the urban population lives in Medium-sized cities, where environmental, social and cultural criticalities are revealed in a most disruptive way. Scientific literature began to deal with Medium-sized cities in the 2000s, addressing specific problems within emblematic or paradigmatic case studies.

The main challenges of these cities are: the increase of environmental pollution [15], the land consumption, and the critical mobility between the center, suburbs and rural areas. The leading cause could be a wide fragmentation of governance and service facilities, which prevents the adoption of large-scale governance measures.

2.3 What Is a Medium Sized City?

For a deep discussion it is necessary to adopt a definition about the smart development of Medium-sized cities. Firstly, by fixing dimension and boundaries, then analyzing the common challenges and potential solutions, and lastly examining the specificity and uniqueness of each city, in order to create a balance between the replicability of some models, and the uniqueness of a social and morphological landscape system, that often represents the main richness of a medium city.

From this perspective some notions register an increasing importance. The first one, identifies analogies and the common challenges between medium cities: it is the notion of *Smart Medium-sized city*, well expressed by some scientific researches since the 2000's ([1], [2], [12]). The second one aims at considering Medium-sized cities as the core of a wider identity system, and it demonstrates the inefficiency of Smart action plans based on the administrative boundaries of the single municipality. It is the notion of *Functional Urban Area* (FUA), used by OECD (since 2011–2013), to identify how the city center is often a big attractor, capable of a large influence area.

Then, what does "Medium-sized city" mean? The commonly used tools for measuring a city (small, medium, large, extra-large [13]) are, in the scientific literature, the bigness (how many sq.km?), and the inhabitants (how many residents? We will see how the concept of "who lives the city?", may be variously interpreted). From these parameters, a density index emerges (how many inhabitants/sq. Km?):

Table 1 Medium-sized city:
A comparison between
definitions

Medium-sized City. Dimension		
Institution	Inhabitants min.	Inhabitants max
Giffinger (2007—UE)	100,000	500,000
OECD-FUA (2012—UE)	100,000	250,000
ANCI-CNSPU (2015 IT)	50,000	250,000

an issue for better understanding the compactness of the city built, neighborhood-by-neighborhood. A diagram of the Medium-sized cities definition will better explain the distance between the researcher's positions (Table 1).

In Italy, the National Center for Urban Studies,[1] gives a definition of Medium-sized city based on the number of inhabitants, also acquired by the ANCI: National Association of Italian Municipalities. According with this definition, Medium cities have a population of between 50,000 and 250,000 people, they provide coordination policies between urban and internal areas, and they have a high development potential [6]. ANCI, created a list of 105 Medium-sized cities,[2] and stressed on the analogies between critical issues, problems and potential. Other scientific researchers consider Medium-sized, the cities with a population of between 100,000 and 500,000 inhabitants. A broader classification especially if compared to the small size of Italian cities, where the 14 metropolitan Italian cities host about 34% of Italian population, and the majority of the remaining 66%, lives in cities between 50,000 and 500,000 inhabitants. This information well represents the impact of medium cities: a critical mass where it is decisive to intervene with innovative policies. In Fig. 1 we may see the graphic of the high soil dispersion index in some Italian cities, according with the XIV Report by Ispra, 2018, and compared with the dataset of the air pollution (Pm10 level) in the main city of the Emilia region.

2.4 About a Ranking of the European Medium-Sized Cities' Smartness

The first issue concerns the relationship between the characteristics of a Medium-sized city and its development potential: a matter for evaluating the scientific parameters for smart performances. A first contribution comes from the mentioned research published in 2007, from a team composed of the Polytechnic Universities of Vienna, Delft, and Ljubliana, under the coordination of Professor Rudolph Giffinger. This research verifies European Medium-sized cities as a critical mass with a high development potential and also with big criticalities. In percentage terms, the largest number

---

[1] Urban@it. The Italian Study Center for the Urban Policies, an association established in 2014 with the cooperation of the Italian Universities.

[2] Medium cities have in Italy a dispersion index higher than the European in 59% of analyzed cities (Source: Ispra Dataset 2018).

	Parma	Taranto	Brescia	Trieste	Padova	Prato	Modena
Sup. Comunale Kmq	261	299	90	84	93	97	183,2
% suolo consumato su tot. Comune, nel 2017	23,60%	23,10%	45,40%	34,80%	50,10%	33,70%	25,80%

The Urban dispersion index, according with the XIV Report ISPRA "Qualità dell'ambiente urbano" (2018)

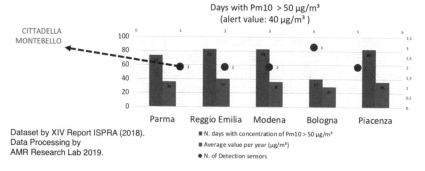

Days with Pm10 > 50 μg/m³
(alert value: 40 μg/m³)

CITTADELLA
MONTEBELLO

Dataset by XIV Report ISPRA (2018).
Data Processing by
AMR Research Lab 2019.

■ N. days with concentration of Pm10 > 50 μg/m³
■ Average value per year (μg/m³)
● N. of Detection sensors

Parma   Reggio Emilia   Modena   Bologna   Piacenza

Fig. 1 The soil dispersion index and the air quality in some Italian Medium-sized cities (dataset Ispra 2018 report—data process: AMR Research lab)

of European cities are Medium-sized. They host the majority of the population living in cities, and they show similarities in critical issues and potentials, which are very different from the ones witnessed in big cities.

The Giffinger ranking places cities with a population of between 100,000 and 500,000 inhabitants under a magnifying glass: urban centers with high growth potential, needing attentions for a sustainable development. In 2007, the European cities with these characteristics were about 600, with a total of 120 million inhabitants. About 40% of European population living in urban areas, dwells cities of medium size. The website created to disseminate the results: www.smart.cities.eu, is a support for checking the transformations of these cities over a period of a few years, from 2007 to 2014. The proposed ranking coordinates the Medium-sized cities starting from 6 major topics or specialization strategies: Economy, People, Governance, Mobility, Environment, Living.[3] The second research goal concerns the timeframe, and aims at monitoring these cities over time, in order to obtain data about their development ability in medium and long terms.

---

[3]The choice by Giffinger includes cities with a population of between 100,000 and 500,000, with an overall catchment area of less than 1.5 million people and the presence of a University. This scientific selection criteria allows researchers to reduce the number of cities from 600 (Medium cities in UE) to 256. The lower number of 94 includes cities with a homogeneous database to deal with: Urban Database and Eurostat Audit.

2.5 The Concept of Functional Urban Area by OECD: Potential and Limits of the Definition

The second issue concerns the definition of *Functional Urban Area (FUA)*,[4] proposed by the OECD in 2011–2013. This concept is very important to outline a systemic vision of the Medium-sized cities, and meaningful for the governance models [9]. The FUA area is defined by the attractiveness of the city center on the peripheries, and it may define the bigness of the city for urban governance. Scientific literature considers today the administrative limits of any urban agglomeration, less and less representative of the city and the citizen's needs. OECD investigates the functional relationships between the more attractive center, and the peripheries and small centers around. The dossier outlines two reference perimeters: the attractive heart of the system, called *Core area*, surrounded by a wide area of functional influence, called *Commuting zone*, which establishes a boundary for the daily migration. These two perimeters make up the *FUA*.[5]

The OECD dossier distinguishes the FUA in cities of different sizes, and defines medium cities with a FUA population of between 100,000 and 250,000 inhabitants. Here, the wide or small attractiveness of the center on the boundaries, can mark a difference between population living in the Core area, and people moving every day, at certain times, from their municipality, towards the most attractive city. The scientific criterion applied by OECD is based on the workers' flows, and it includes all those municipalities, near the Core area, where at least 15% of the population is working in the chief town. The report and the open data made available by OECD, are very important for studying the Medium-sized cities. For instance, we may verify that the mobility flows between the center and the periphery, may create some critical issues concerning infrastructure conditions, services availability and pollution levels.

The model proposed by OECD has some structural limits that make it only partially applicable. First of all, in order to have homogeneous data, it standardizes the process, using only data available for all the examined cities. As well, the minimum unit for the analysis is the municipality. An aspect affecting the real definition of Core area for Medium-sized cities, where population density is often higher in the historic center than in the first expansion zones, characterized by a high dispersion index and sometimes by small settlements and rural areas too.

The second problem reflects the differences between residents and inhabitants of the Core area. The FUA Commuting zone, just analyzes commuter's flows, but there are many other flows moving daily from the periphery to the center. For instance, commuters moving for educational services (high schools and universities), health services (hospitals and diagnostic centers), culture and sports (sport facilities, theaters, cinemas, museums, libraries). We also have flows of visitors and tourists, which can affect the urban population, especially concurrently with some

---

[4]Definition of Functional Urban Areas (FUA) by OECD. Internet open database: www.oecd.org/cfe/regional-policy/functionalurbanareasbycountry.htm, last accessed 20 February 2020.

[5]OECD provides a database of georeferenced vector maps, connected with an open data protocol, which allows the upload of the Core area and the Commuting zone.

topic events: temporary exhibitions, fairs and trade shows, or special awards like in Parma, Italian Cultural Capital. For these reasons, inhabitants referred by the FUA dossier, may represents a conservative estimate, compared to the real people who daily live the city.

3 The Italian Medium-Sized City of Parma: A Smart Development After the Cultural Capital 2020–2021?

The research takes into account Parma as a good Italian case study. Parma is nowadays interesting, because of its cultural and urban regeneration process, enhanced by the role of Italian Capital for Culture in the year 2020, extended to 2021 after the Covid-19 pandemic. The application research aims at developing the basis for an urban strategy project for this city after the year 2020, analyzing its characteristics and renewed identity and outlining an urban interpretation tool studied for Parma, but replicable in other Medium-sized urban conditions.

3.1 Research Methodology and Case-History

The methodological approach was conducted as follows. First it deepened the city of Parma as a morphological and functional organism. Then it focused on the people's need: both resident population and inhabitants of the FUA area. The first results highlighted some structural problems, with strong analogies to the main topics that emerged in other medium-sized cities from the scientific literature. This report reveals three major problems: the unsustainability of private mobility (both connected to traffic and infrastructure congestion, and to the vehicle pressure on the urban center); the low air quality level and the pollution (Pm10 levels connected with many related heath diseases); the serious issue of land consumption. The main cause for the inefficiency of some Smart strategies concerns the difficulty of planning at a landscape scale beyond the municipality borders, involving both the Core Area and the Commuting zone in the strategic choices.

Beginning from a scientific literature review and the analysis of the rankings proposed by the website www.smart.cities.eu, the research selected 10 medium-sized cities, characterized by analogies with Parma, for performing a scientific analysis and comparison of Smart visions, models and good practices. Of course, the morphological and cultural conditions of the 10 cities, all in northern Europe, are very different from the Parma situation. The aim of the selection is to highlight the Smart models applied and, above all, to deepen the strategic governance process for choosing the most suitable Smart specialization strategy for each city.

Finally, the compared results of the 10 cities analyzed became a grid for an optimal interpretation of Parma Medium-sized city, with its values and criticalities. The aim is not to replicate virtuous Smart projects in a very different context, but to create a model of urban reading, capable of enabling the rulers and choosing the best way for a good Smart governance process.

3.2 The Medium-Sized City of Parma and the Morphological-Functional Basin

One purpose of the research is to identify the best wider area for extending the Smart city strategies.

Other purposes include facing the territorial challenges with favorable impact on the city and landscape, respecting the short timeframe required by Smart strategies without contrasting with the environment's medium and long reply time. The proposed tool, takes into account the city as a system, consisting of a center and a complex area around. It aims at specifying the concept of Functional urban area proposed by OECD, widening the criteria. The purpose is to shift from the concept of Functional area to the concept of Morphological-Functional basin, matching, in a systemic perspective: attractiveness, accessibility, city vocations, potential, as well as critical issues and environmental risks. The tool can also be used for defining the performance indicators, checking the effectiveness of Smart strategies for the life quality in Medium-sized cities, and planning verification steps on the short, medium and long term. This interpretation key may enhance the impact of urban planning strategies, supporting governance, helping the identification of a Smart specializations and driving the best practices for increasing urban Resilience.

As we may see in Fig. 2, Parma is a Medium-sized city: it has an urban area of 208.8 sq. km and about 195,000 residents. The former Province (dotted line) is 3449 sq. km and the overall resident population stands at 447800 units [7]. Data available from the OECD definition of FUA, verify that, in addition to the 195 thousand residents in the Core area of Parma municipality (dark gray), there is a Commuting zone (light gray) to better analyze from a morphological and cultural point of view. The Functional urban area of Parma defines an attractive zone, more realistic than the extension of the old province. It is limited to the south by the morphological boundaries of the Apennines, breaking on the Cisa Pass, while to the north, the river Po [14] is a natural border. Along the via Emilia, an axis with the main infrastructures of highway and railway, the FUA could hypothetically expand its boundaries, instead it is contained from the attractiveness of the Fidenza city to the west, and from the city of Reggio Emilia to the east, confirming the role of the via Emilia as a polycentric corridor, where the quick pace of many cities, limits the expansion possibility for each of them. According with OECD, the Parma Core area coincides with the Municipality extension and the Commuting zone includes 18 municipalities with a very low population density (as reported in Fig. 2): 17 are part of the former Province of Parma, and one, Brescello, belongs to Reggio Emilia, marking a gap within the cultural and administrative continuity. People who daily

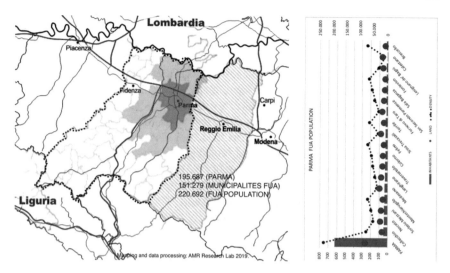

Fig. 2 The Parma FUA. On the right a representation of the Commuting zone density by municipalities (data process and mapping AMR Research Lab, 2019)

live in Parma are estimated at about 220,000 units: almost 25,000 people more than the resident population (Fig. 3).

The FUA population by OECD, concerns, as already mentioned, only the municipalities around Parma, where about 15% of the population works in the chief city, moving daily. As well, the number of people could be higher.

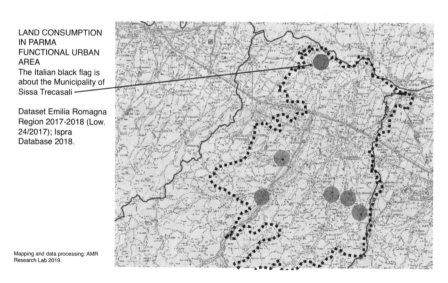

Fig. 3 A diagram of the land use in the Parma FUA (ISPRA and Region Emilia-Romagna database. Data processing and mapping by AMR Research lab, 2019)

The research proposes a redefinition of the FUA borders, based on the real perimeter of the Core Area, which can be reduced by the whole municipality to the historic center and the first suburbs. In fact, zones furthest from the historic center, are characterized by small villages and rural areas. At the same time, people living in the belt municipalities, are attracted by the Core area, for work and other purposes like education, health, culture, sports services. It is necessary to identify the Morphological-Functional basin and the real flows, for checking landscape criticalities such as, traffic, air quality and land use, detecting the overlap between Functional area and Geomorphological boundary, aiming at managing some criticalities at a higher level than the municipality governance. As we may see in Fig. 2, the land use, could appear for instance as a less complex problem if managed at the FUA level. While the Core area has been pursuing the zero-consumption target for some years, some municipalities of the belt have pursued a hard land use policies. This new perimeter must be used to overcome punctual intervention and plan in a systemic view, for a better risk mitigation.

3.3 Case History: Mapping Medium-Sized Smart Cities in the EU

Aiming at creating a systemic approach for Medium-sized Smart cities, the research developed a case-history. The analysis is held by the AMR Research Lab,[6] with the Project Works by the students in *Architectural design for the Smart City,*[7] Parma University. Each smart model is studied on the basis of its ability to face the main urban problems and challenges, its capability in creating quality and competitiveness, the expected results, and the impact found. All the data should have been represented as georeferenced maps, enriched with graphics and tables, to communicate directly and effectively the results. The Project Works involved 10 European Medium-sized cities, chosen as representatives of good Smart policies and practices. Each model can lead the city to a different Smart strategy, when dropped in contexts with different vocations, cultural identities, morphological structure, economic resources, and ability to attract financial and human capital. The scientific criteria for selecting the 10 Medium-sized cities are:

1. Cities with a FUA population in the same slot of Parma.
2. Cities in the first 30 positions in the ranking by Giffinger [12] which maintained good positions in the following checks (2013–2014).
3. Cities with a University strictly connected with the landscape activities.

---

[6]The Research lab AMR—Architettura Musei Reti is, since 2005, an observatory on the dynamics of territorial development. It also gives third mission activities of scientific support to private companies and public administrations. Coordinated by Aldo De Poli and Monica Bruzzone, from the University of Parma, Department of Engineering and Architecture—Architecture Unit.

[7]Course of *Architectural design for the Smart City,* year 2018–2019; teacher: Monica Bruzzone; contributors: Michela Montenero, Matteo Casanovi, Simone De Lisi, Ilaria Russo.

Table 2 The 10 cities selected for the benchmark

Table	City	KMQ Municipality	KMQ province	Muncipality Population	Province Population	FUA Population	Ranking 2007 position
Italia	Parma	260,80	3.449	197.132	447.779	330.000	N.D.
Denmark	Aarhus	91,00	6.846	336.411	865.830	490.000	2
France	Nancy	15,00	5.246	108.000	734.403	480.000	23
France	Clermont Ferrand	42,67	7.970	144.817	649.819	480000	26
Finland	Tampere	523,40	687,9	226.696	477.000	440.000	9
Austria	Graz	127,48	1213,68*	286.292	439.236*	420.000	16
France	Angers	42,70	7.106,64	151.229	810.934	410.000	11
Neder lands	Enschede	142,75	3.420,74	158.969	1.156.886	400.000	29
GermanY	Gottingen	116,89	1.753,41	119.529	328.036	370.000	24
Austria	Salzburg	65,64	1070,64*	153.377	304633*	350.000	3
Neder lands	Nijmegen	57,60	5.136,31	176.508	2.072.328	320.000	22

4. Cities (or Regions) with a Smart specialization strategy.

The selected cities main data are resumed, in Table 2.

Each group of students,[8] analyzes a city. Every city is equipped with an open dataset, a digital plan, the vector file of the Core area and the Commuting zone boundaries, and also with a first bibliography and sitography. Every group needs to integrate this data with a profound research, to obtain the tools for enhancing the analysis and answer, with a mapping representation, to the five questions grid, reported in Table 3:

The maps in Figs. 4, 5, 6 held by the groups of students, are graphic representations of the Smart strategies applied in some Medium-sized European cities. Tampere, in Finland, part of a regional Smart strategy based on the Helsinki centrality, is specialized in the Smart people aspect, involving citizens in a digitalization process mainly focused on social issues. In Aarhus, Denmark and in Gottingen, Germany we have a Smart vision based on mobility, with different solutions. Aarhus focuses on multimodality, and the creation of zero-carbon central areas, while in Gottingen prevails the theme of Digital mobility and the Smart communities with a deep people involvement. The maps allow a morphologic visualization of the smartness level in each Medium-sized city, identifying projects and connections between the Core and the Commuting areas. The geo-referencing of physical and immaterial data, is

---

[8]Students engaged in the Project works (with city): Martina Bacchi (Enschede), Andrea De Padova (Aarhus), Stefano Gobbi (Gottingen), Davide Mansanti (Graz), Sara Leber Luis (Nancy), Lucia Vidal Iglesias (Angers), Silvia Herrera Ojeda (Clermont Ferrand), Alessandro Castronovo (Nijmegen), Pietro Fontana and Marco Ricci (Tampere), Nazariy Sydiy and Alberto Brozzi (Salzburg).

Table 3 The 5 questions grid for the analysis

1Smart vision vs smart projects (what model for the city)?
City vs Area. Are the smart strategies applied to the city, to the province, or the region?
Specialization. Has the city a smart specialization strategy? (e.g. Green, digital,) and what are the main planning directions? (e.g. Mobility, Smart Grid, Smart Building, Energy efficiency, People, Social Inclusion …)
New buildings vs urban regeneration. The policies about land consumption.
Citizenship. How important is the citizenship involvement? Do we have hints of bottom up projects?
Funding. What are the funding sources (public funding, private funding, public-private agreement)?

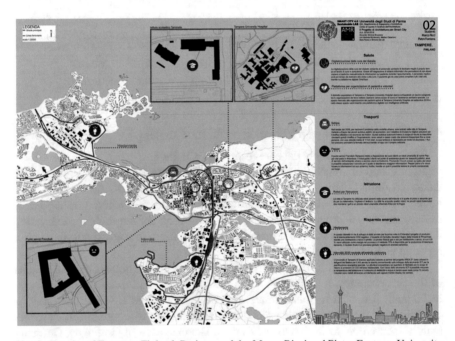

Fig. 4 The city of Tampere, Finland. Project work by Marco Ricci and Pietro Fontana, University of Parma. Smart specialization strategy: People

represented with graphics and diagrams, and aims at specifying the purposes of the Smart strategy; testing the coherence between the urban development strategy, and highlighting the impacts. The comparison is summarized in Table 4.

In the best performing cities, Smart visions coordinated by governance are applied both to the city and to a larger area. In the cities that do not take off, the spot creation of smart pilot projects with good quality is prevalent, but which hardly keep the growth constant over time. All the Smart city strategies with a better impact, have a focus on issues related to the pillars proposed by the EU (People, Environment, Mobility,

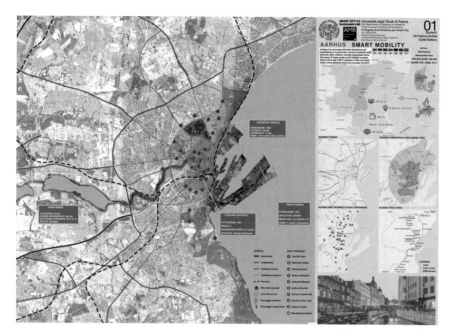

Fig. 5 The city of Aarhus, Denmark, Project work by Andrea De Padova and Stefano Gobbi, University of Parma. Smart specialization strategy: Mobility (Comparison with Gottingen)

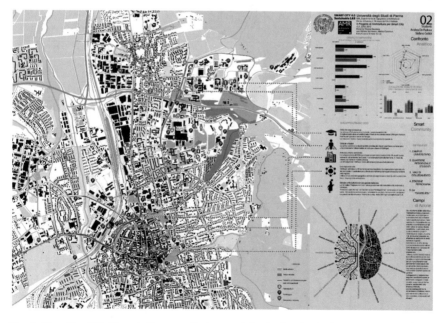

Fig. 6 The city of Gottingen, Germany, Project work by Andrea De Padova and Stefano Gobbi, University of Parma. Smart specialization strategy: Mobility and digital community (comparison with Aarhus)

Table 4 A comparison between the 10 European cities analyzed by the project works. The sign + or − specify the continuity or not of the Smart strategy. (*) Enschede is a city in decrease since 2007 to 2014, today the smart growth seems to have a stop

Smart city	Vision vs projects	City vs area	Land use vs regene ration	Active citizenship	Fundings
Parma	—	—			—
Aarhus (+)	Vision: Smart Mobility	Area: intermodal mobility projects	Regeneration	High involvement top-down (Smart people—communities)	Public funding (scientific supports by University and research centers)
Nancy	Vision: Digital city	Area: digital connections with green policies of Commuting zone	Regeneration	High Digital involvement top-down; Smart communities	—
Clermont Ferrand	Projects: Energy efficiency, green	City (with projects extended to the Area)	Regeneration	Medium involvement (information, communication)	Public funding (mainly by municipality)
Tampere (+)	Vision: Smart people Smart health & wellbeing	Region and Area (Smart neighborhood specializations)	Regeneration	High involvement top-down (Communities for healthcare)	Mixed: Public-Private funding (agreements)
Graz (−)	Projects: (Mobility, tradition—innovation)	City (mainly)	Regeneration	Light involvement of citizens	—
Angers	Projects: Innovation for Cultural and natural Heritage	Area	Regeneration	Light involvement of citizens	—
Enschede (*) (−)	Projects: Mobility Smart environment	City: Mobility and inclusion. Environment green tours	—	Light involvement (top-down, inclusion)	Private funding (after a pilot phase driven by the public)

(continued)

Table 4 (continued)

Smart city	Vision vs projects	City vs area	Land use vs regene ration	Active citizenship	Fundings
Gottingen (+)	Vision: Smart people	Area (Connections University historic centers)	Regeneration	High involvement top-down cultural goals—soft localization	Mixed: European and National public funding; private investors
Salzburg	Projects: Smart energy; Smart buildings & neighborhoods	Area (Connection with FUA districts—river green axis).	Land use & Regeneration	Light citizens involvement	Mixed: Private investors and public funding; Partnership
Nijmegen (+)	Vision. Green city (mobility, junks, green spaces, energy)	Area Commuting zone	Regeneration	High involvement top-down (University people—recycle)	Mixed: Private investors and public funding; Partnership

Digital, Energy). It may be considered as a testimony of the rewarding role of the EU funding policy, particularly in the first approach to the smart development (where public financing is a necessity for every city). As well, there is a strong prevalence in projects of regeneration policies than in the land use and soil consumption. The Medium-sized cities with the higher level of smart growth, always adopted a mixed model of public funding supported by private investors (stakeholders and companies interested in enhancing competitiveness of the city), and almost all of them improve the model by involving people in the communication of the strategy and the performances. The more virtuous cities also demonstrate a good level of integration between two smart identities: on one hand we always have mobility as a support for city accessibility and traffic reduction, and on the other hand, we may appreciate the development of a specific smart vocation in different fields. The regional projects of Smart policies are very few and limited to specific conditions, with a low density of people and towns. In the research, the virtuous case study of Finland is an excellent model of a regional Smart strategy, but also an exception.

The citizens involvement is quite an effective tool for sharing and increasing the awareness of the Smart policies. However, in the best projects, the citizens' role does not arise from *bottom*-up strategies, but is foreseen in the Smart strategy, and coordinated by urban policies.

From this case history, an abacus of policies and good practices to be replicated did not emerge, rather, it determined that most of the Medium-sized cities have the common need to implement urban accessibility with smart models and requires each of them to then develop their own Smart vision based on of their specific identity and vocations.

4   An Innovative Tool for Designers, Planners and Leaders of the Smart City

The main research objective is to create an interpretation model for Medium-sized cities. It could be an interactive grid or dashboard, simple to use, update and implement, by mapping and georeferencing material and immaterial data about the city. This map will be addressed to designers, planners, leaders and managers engaged in the Smart city development process.

After deepening a European case history, the research comes back to Parma, with the aim of creating a tool to help stakeholders in reading effectively the city, defining the best area for the Smart strategies application, detecting analogies with other contexts and territorial uniqueness to be enhanced. The comparison between the definition of a good area for developing Smart strategies in Parma, and the case history of the European Medium-sized cities, leads to some considerations.

4.1 Switching from the FUA to the Morphological-Functional Basin Concept

First of all, the research verified the effectiveness of a strategic vision that may define a Smart vocation for the city and its commuting zone, rather than the sum of individual projects, which rarely lead to continuity in urban development. If we compare the European case history with Parma, we understand how the creation of an intermodal mobility plan between the core area and the commuting zone could be important, as well as an optimal mobility solution for the connections between small villages and their rural areas: a support for any future Smart specialization strategy. Lastly, it is necessary to coordinate the governance of municipalities with a multilevel approach, aimed at encouraging strategic and transversal actions, more incisive and wide-ranging over the medium and long term. A key role is played by the attractiveness of public and private capitals.

From this research a first document emerges: a grid that can be considered a basis for the future dashboard planning. The grid, represented in Table 5, has two objectives. On the one hand, it aims at identifying the Morphological-Functional basin of Parma, that may specify the FUA boundaries with geographic and physical indicators, infrastructures and real people flows, daily attracted by the main center. On the other hand, it aims at mapping policies related to mobility, environment and digitalization, checking its effects, impacts and criticalities on the nowadays city. The grid includes material and immaterial data, to be referred to the real city, and particularly open data available from the public administration and research structures (of course deprived by personal data and augmented with the database of the city of origin).

The grid has got two main purposes: firstly, the identification of the morphological -functional basin where to extend the smart city policies in order to obtain the best results in raising life quality and competitiveness. Secondly the interaction between spatial and immaterial data that, thanks to the georeferencing protocols, can be literally linked to specific points in the city for enhancing the level of knowledge of the city itself. The grid reported in Table 5, summarize the results of this research.

4.2 Mapping the Social Media Feelings: A Quality Perception for #Parma2020?

For testing, provocatively, the effectiveness of georeferencing intangible data, a very virtual theme was chosen: mapping the empathy between people and the historic center of Parma through the social hashtag# Parma2020. It's a big data analysis, aiming at matching expectations and needs of citizens and visitors, as digital traces left on the social media, for creating a kind of digital city memory [4]. The social media language is used for testing connections between places and people's feelings towards the perceived quality of the historic center. Using the example of the social

Table 5 The research grid base of the dashboard

Functional urban area re-definition
People policies and land use

1. People flows	Work	Checking people working in the Core and living in the Commuting zone (OECDS FUA Database)
	Health services	Lists of admissions (patients and day hospital) linked with the city of origin
	High schools & Universities	Lists of inscriptions linked to the city of origin
	Cultural services	Ticketing of museums, exhibitions, libraries, theaters, cinemas, linked with the city of origin
	Sport services	Selection of the main sport facilities (sports fields, gyms, swimming pools), users with city of origin
	Temporary events	Trade fairs and salons, local fairs, data per month, from on-line ticketing, linked with the city of origin
	Visitors and tourists	Checking tools: hotel arrivals and presences (Open Data Emilia Romagna Region); origins of the cultural services users; Social media activity links between origin of the users, and GPS big data
2. Mobility policies	Railway traffic	Traffic of people of the Railway Stations (Open data Trenitalia and MIT)[a]
	Bus Traffic	Bus frequency and users (both for urban and suburban lines) (TEP dataset)
	Highway exits	Incoming and outgoing traffic at the main booths.
	Parking—parking lot	Parking lot fee, interchange Parking (Municipality dataset)
	Slow mobility and green mobility	Car-sharing and bike-sharing dataset
3. Green policies	Pm10 Value Alert	Monitoring how many alert-days per year: data per month and Phenomenon repetition (Ispra dataset)

(continued)

Table 5 (continued)

Functional urban area re-definition
People policies and land use

	Parma, Taro Enza and Po flood events	Monitoring how many alert-days per year: data per month and Phenomenon repetition Ispra AIPO Municipality, Protezione civile dataset.
	Landslide	Monitoring number, dimension and position of the landslide (data per year and per month) Ispra—Protezione Civile dataset
	Land consumption	Cubic meters of new buildings per year/per municipality (Ispra dataset)
4. Digital policies	Digital infrastructures in the cities and the rural areas	Digitalization of rural areas Telephone company dataset; free wifi, social media actions
	Digital service—online desks	Monitoring the number of people using online desks linked to the origin city (dataset Health services - Municipality of Parma)
5. Smart building	New Buildings and regeneration goals	Tax relief database for energy efficiency, and home automation service implementation (dataset Agenzia delle Entrate)

Definition from UNESCO: Cultural and Creative Industry

[a]Trenitalia (www.sciamlab.com/opendatahub/it/dataset/fs_o-s-trenitalia); MIT Ministero delle Infrastrutture e Trasporti dataset (http://dati.mit.gov.it/catalog/dataset). Last accessed 20 February 2020

media platform Instagram, people use to publish an image, as a representation of a specific feeling in the personal social profile. The photo is often connected with a message underlined by a #hashtag, expressing empathy, pleasure, happiness, rather than disapproval or hate. The test aims at giving GIS coordinates to these feelings, creating a map representing the people engagement within the city.[9] The research collected all the images posted on the social network Instagram, about the historic center of Parma, from the 1st to the 31st of January 2020. Each image has to be connected with the tag #Parma2020, localized with GPS coordinates, and scheduled to report a positive or negative opinion (Fig. 7).

The results led both to investigate the places considered "to remember" in the historic center, and to understand the overall quality perception of each of them.

---

[9]This research is held by the architects Matteo Casanovi and Simone De Lisi, from the AMR Research lab. Researcher analyzed open big data of the social media Instagram, tagged with the official hashtag **# Parma2020**, selecting the images posted by people, on the historic center of Parma. Every picture has a GIS reference, a connection to the #Parma2020. The research also excluded all the inappropriate or promotional images.

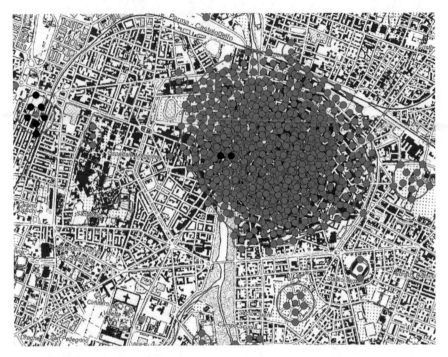

Fig. 7 A GIS elaboration of big data. Instagram images of the city with the #Parma2020 (*Source* AMR Research Lab)

The first results brought an interesting finding. There are many places, in the historic center of Parma where we have a strong digital memory, or a digital density composed by big data and virtual traces left by people, generally reporting a positive feeling. The deepest aim of this test, however, is not to give answers, but to create a provocation. What about the digital memory of a place? Is there a scientific criterion for analyzing the quality perception from immaterial dataset as well as social media? What conclusions can be drawn from mapping and geo-referencing big data and social shares? Even this research may become a useful tool, if it is considered a part of a wider interactive grid, able at mapping material and immaterial data, and giving a route for designers, planners and leaders of Smart strategy, interpreting the general models of Medium-sized cities on the basis of a specific and contemporary urban identity (Fig. 8).

Fig. 8 A detail of the big data collected on the Instagram post about #Parma2020 (*Source* AMR Research Lab)

5 Open Topic and Conclusions. Notes About a Tool for a Smart Development After #Parma2020

The research results about Smart strategies on Medium-sized cities, provide a good basis point for a future innovative model aiming at querying the city and collecting material and immaterial data based on dataset grid, linked point by point to the real city. This model, thanks to an interactive geo-reference map, may give an augmented knowledge of the city.

After a comprehensive definition of Medium-sized Smart cities, in accordance with a European vision, the research highlighted the most important problems affecting cities of medium dimensions, and verified their presence in the case study of Parma. Main problems are traffic and mobility, land consumption and pollution, especially related to the air quality control. Then the research created a benchmark of 10 Medium sized cities in Europe, characterized by analogies and differences with the case study of Parma [7]. This further research has allowed some conclusions about the development of effective Smart models for Medium-sized cities with particular reference to the European context. The study noticed that cities with higher development, adopted a Smart vision (rather than a collection of individual Smart projects), based on two elements: a systemic approach to the mobility problem, faced both with effective public transport projects and a widespread strengthening of the digital infrastructures; and a Smart specialization strategy that takes into consideration vocations and characteristics of that specific city, enhancing its potential, without forgetting its identity. The research also verified that the main obstacle to the

Smart strategy implementation for Medium-sized cities concerns the administrative fragmentation which gives a stop to all the strategic decisions capable of involving a larger area, and therefore adequate to tackle smartness not as a punctual phenomenon but with a systemic perspective.

Then the research focused again on Parma, analyzing the landscape and the open data related to the city, with the aim of proposing a grid for the creation of a dataset, composed by material and virtual data, useful for defining the best area where a Smart city process can be more effective, and for distinguishing it from many points of view. This area may define a kind of Morphological-Functional basin: it takes into consideration both the territory as a physical and morphological question, and the Parma area of influence: an attractive center for city commuters and users.

The future research aims at deepening this grid, creating a dashboard simulation, with interactive maps based on open data and administrative dataset. This dashboard, from the city of Parma, may be extended to other Medium-sized cities, with the aim of creating a replicable device for reading the urban phenomenon, helping managers and planners of the Smart city, to both face new challenges, and to choose the best Specialization strategies for a smartness process extended from the city to a wider landscape.

References

1. Balsas, C. (2000). City center revitalization in Portugal: Lessons from two medium size cities. *Cities, 17*, 19–31. https://doi.org/10.1016/S0264-2751(99)00049-9.
2. Berardi, U. (2013). Sustainability assessment of urban communities through rating systems. *Environment, Development and Sustainability: A Multidisciplinary Approach to the Theory and Practice of Sustainable Development, 15*(6), 1573–1591.
3. Bruzzone M. (2018) Costruire utopie urbane. Città perfette di nuova fondazione. In *Area, Rivista di Architettura e arti del progetto* (pp. 84–85). New Business Media, Milan, n. 157+.
4. Bruzzone M. (2014). Time, memory, architecture and public spaces for the contemporary city. Eurau 2014, *Composite cities, European symposium on research in architecture and urban design, technisches Universitat*, Istanbul.
5. Bruzzone M., & Dameri R. P. (2018). *Smart City. Pianificazione e sviluppo economico territoriale*, AMR—DIA.
6. Ciapetti L. (2015). Centro nazionale di studi per le politiche urbane Urban@it.
7. Comune di Parma stats. (on line jan 2020). www.comune.parma.it/comune/Dati-statistici.aspx.
8. Dameri, R. P., & Rosenthal-Sabroux, C. (Eds.). (2014). *Smart city: How to create public and economic value with high technology in Urban Space*. Springer International Publishing (on line January 2020). https://doi.org/10.1007/978-3-319-06160-3.
9. Dijkstra, L., Poelman, H., & Veneri, P. (2019). *The EU-OECD definition of a functional urban area*. In OECD Regional Development Working Papers (2019/11; OECD Regional Development Working Papers). OECD Publishing. https://ideas.repec.org/p/oec/govaab/2019-11-en.html (on line January 2020).
10. Doloi, H., & Donovan, S. (2019, October 31). *Affordable housing for Smart villages*. CRC Press (on line January 2020) https://www.routledge.com/Affordable-Housing-for-Smart-Villages-1st-Edition/Doloi-Donovan/p/book/9780367190781.
11. Gambi L. (1972). I valori storici dei quadri ambientali. In *Storia d'Italia Einaudi*. Vol I. I Caratteri Originali, Einaudi, Torino.

12. Giffinger, R., Fertner, C., Kramar, H., & Meijers, E. (2007). *City-ranking of European medium-sized cities*. Centre of regional science, 1–12.

13. Koolhaas, R., & Mau, B. (1995). *S, M, L, XL: *Small, medium, large, extra-large*. Monacelli Press.

14. Masotti, L. (2019). La ricerca geocartografica per la gestione di territori esposti a rischio: riflessioni e percorsi. In *Acque di terraferma, il Padovano*. Marsilio.

15. Pilidis, G., Karakitsios, S., & Kassomenos, P. (2005). BTX measurements in a medium-sized European city. *Atmospheric Environment, 39* (33).

16. Ratti C., & Claudel M. (2013). *Le smart cities di domani*. Aspenia, n. 63.

17. Rosenzweig, C., Solecki, W. D., Romero-Lankao, P., Mehrotra, S., Dhakal, S., & Ibrahim, S. A. (2018). Climate change and cities: Second assessment report of the urban climate change research network (pp. 703–704). Cambridge University Press.

18. Salgaro, S. (2018). *Il paesaggio agrario tra obsolescenza e degrado*. Patron, Bologna: Riflessioni e materiali per il recupero e la valorizzazione.

19. Stathakis, D., & Tsilimigkas, G. (2015). Measuring the compactness of European medium-sized cities by spatial metrics based on fused data sets. *International Journal of Image and Data Fusion, 6*(1), 42–64. (on line January 2020). https://doi.org/10.1080/19479832.2014.941018.

20. United Nations. (2015). *Transforming our world: The 2030 Agenda for Sustainable Development*. United Nations (on line January 2020). https://www.un.org/ga/search/view_doc.asp?symbol=A/RES/70/1&Lang=E.

21. Visvizi, A., & Lytras, M. D. (2020). Sustainable smart cities and smart villages research: Rethinking security, safety, well-being, and happiness. *Sustainability, 12*(1), 215 (on line January 2020). https://doi.org/10.3390/su12010215.

22. Visvizi, A., Lytras, M. D., & Mudri, G. (2019). *Smart villages in the EU and beyond*. Emerald Publishing Limited (on line January 2020). https://books.emeraldinsight.com/page/detail/Smart-Villages-in-the-EU-and-Beyond/?k=9781787698468.

23. Zavratnik, V., Kos, A., & Stojmenova, E. (2018). Smart villages: Comprehensive review of initiatives and practices. *Sustainability, 10*, 2559, 411–424 (on line January 2020). https://doi.org/10.3390/su10072559.

What Is an Intelligent Building?

Elizabeth Mortamais

Abstract The word *intelligent* to talk about a city, building and so on, is so overused today that one carefully avoids delimiting its contours. We admit the existence of varied and variable intelligences based on our knowledge, requirements, and necessities. Among living beings confronted with the environment, some have a more efficient form of intelligence than others. We refer to three concepts as developed by Gilbert Simondon: associated *milieu* (2005a, 2005b); concretization (1958); *mécanologiques* generations (2005a); invention (2008). After a very short analysis of the today's French Thermic Regulation we note the difficulties to exceed the question of standards, and be able to go beyond the addition of technical devices to respond to the question. To go further we need to abandon the concept of environment and rethink the whole complex systemic problem using the concepts of *milieu* and associated *milieu*. The presentation of the different generations of technical objects (Lafitte in *Réflexions sur la science des machines*. Paris, 1932) helps us to locate today's main challenge. The reasoning from the *milieu*, enables us to reach the concretization of apparatus and obtain intelligent solutions gathering several co-actors interacting in the same network: the external *milieu*, the inner one (*stricto sensus* building), the apparatus, and the inhabitants, sharing information.

Keywords Concretization · Information · Interaction · Milieu · Memory · Network · Operation

1 Hypothesis

Let us start from the following definitional hypothesis, which will consider the intelligence of a building as the faculty of what I will call "an artificial device" to solve a set of complex problems. For these elements have to be organized to communicate in a network system, with memory, a certain capacity of analysis and expertise relative

---

In the present text the French quotations are translated in english by the author herself.

E. Mortamais (✉)
ENSA Paris Val de Seine - laboratoire EVCAU, Université de Paris, Paris, France

© Springer Nature Switzerland AG 2021   125
E. Magnaghi et al. (eds.), *Organizing Smart Buildings and Cities*,
Lecture Notes in Information Systems and Organisation 36,
https://doi.org/10.1007/978-3-030-60607-7_8

to the complexity of the problems to treat. This set will be able to propose solutions, in interaction with the occupants integrating an internal *milieu*, and the external one formed by the natural, anthropogenic, and entropic conditions.

2　What Is the Problematic Context?

To meet, in particular, the requirements of the current RT 2018 (RT for Thermal Regulation), the insulation of buildings must be carried out according to the inevitable norms, that of the so-called passive house.

RT 2020 website clarifies:

> … by additionally including elements of energy production such as ventilation with heat recovery on stale air, enhanced thermal insulation, passive solar energy capture passively, windows of high quality, limitation of energy consumption of household appliances, rainwater recovery. (2016)

And so, the passive house will even become "house with positive energy" from 2020. [5] …

Current normative solutions respond to declared emergencies. Yet they are not without problems. In fact, we qualify them as willingly prosthetics. The building remains designed as a structure and an inert volume, around which are installed prosthetic futures. This is a common attitude of adding elements, each, in its own specialization area, responding to the request, even if their additions don't really redetermine the whole system.

In the name of performance, we see intervening, for each technical field, a set of professions and engineering offices. This tends to transform the building into a sum of technical devices, each of them assigned to handle and fix specific problems.

What Gilbert Simondon [9] would call abstract technical object, or even, sometimes, hypertelic.

The criterion of performance, the desire to characterize the technical activity by the yield cannot lead to a resolution of the problem; the yield, in relation to the technical activity, is very abstract and does not allow to enter this activity to see its essence; several very different technical schemes can lead to identical yields; a number does not express a scheme; the study of yields and the means of improving them leaves the obscurity of the technical zone as completely as the hylemorphic schema; it can only contribute to confusing the theoretical problems, even if it plays a practical role in the current structures.(p. 254)

The technique, in its most prosthetic forms, is precisely summoned in the name of this performance (can we see a translation of the practical technical dichotomy versus theoretical technique according to the Simondonian model above?). Add to that, each device or set of devices is controlled to ensure its performative abilities. Thus, the temperature standards inside a building are defined and applied. But they do not take into account changes in outside temperature, or perceptions of users moving from an outside at minus 5 degrees to an interior at +19 degrees or from +30 outside to +19 inside. They define a state that refers only to itself. Far from the very logic of ecology that develops a systemic reasoning (including living, non-living and atmospheres).

The control can go as far as preventing the opening of the windows, in order to maintain a constant temperature, requiring an extraction of stale air (with double flow), whereas the open window obeys natural behaviors and other spontaneous goals such as talking to someone in the street, breathing outside air, listening to the song of a bird, watching and listening to children in the garden, etc.

Prostheses are therefore also restraints that define and impose specific behaviors.

3 The Notion of *Milieu Associé*

The thermal standard is considered one of the most efficient to adapt what is called "built environment" to the environmental requirements. When we say environment, we think we have said everything about what really interests us in nature.

Dominique Lecourt quotes Georges Canguilhem [7]:

> Living is radiating, it is to organize the *milieu* from a reference center which cannot itself be referred without losing its meaning. (p. 83)

4 Let's Start by Talking About *Milieu* Rather Than Environment

The environment is, in our opinion, a dogmatic translation (and a reduction) of Nature, according to certain types of knowledge. The environment, in a way, is a performative decoding of Nature for the use of the human species. But in this decoding, there is obviously loss of information and a gap between the subject we are and what surrounds us.

Hence, we prefer the concept of *milieu*, which makes the general "bath" prevail and does not detach the elements from the context.

For Uexküll [14], the characteristic of the living is to "make oneself" one's *milieu*; the *milieu* is relative to the living who dominates and accommodates it.

Canguilhem [7], in turn, clarifies his conception of the relation of the Being with the *milieu:*

So, he says:

> From the biological point of view, it must be understood that between the organism and the environment, there is the same relationship as between the parts and the whole within the organism itself. The individuality of living-beings does not stop at its ectodermal borders, nor does it begin at the cell. The biological relation between a being and its *milieu* is a functional, and consequently mobile relation, the terms of which successively exchange their role. The cell is a medium for subcellular elements, it lives itself in an internal "milieu" with dimensions sometimes of the organ and sometimes of the organism, which the organism itself lives in a *milieu*. (as cited in [7], p. 184)

There is here a form of adjusted conciliation and cooperation between "objects" (including living beings on all scales) and the «milieu». The simple distinction between natural and artificial does not provide any understanding of what is happening. It is ineffective to describe and construct such situations.

In the words of Gilbert Simondon [10]:

> Recourse to the notion of the associated *milieu* to think the technical object makes it possible to confer on the latter a kind of autonomy and remarkable power, since it is said that it conditions itself precisely by its relation to its associated *milieu*, which is conditioned by it at the same time as it conditions it. (p. 25)

And also [9]:

> The associated *milieu* mediates the relationship between the technical elements manufactured and the natural elements in which the technical being functions. (p. 57)

Even better, for the philosopher [9] the categories are hybridizing:

> On the contrary, by technical concretization, the object, originally artificial, becomes more and more similar to the natural object. (p. 47)

The artifice spends its time borrowing from Nature as its associated *milieu* (also medium). Without Nature, there is no concrete technical object. The technical scheme originates in its relation to the *milieu*. It may be argued that the *milieu*, (and so medium), is the language by which Nature is expressed in the schema of the technical object. Here, we accept the word schema as defined by Jean Piaget [8]:

> … not constituting an object of thought but reducing itself to the internal structure of actions, while the concept is manipulated by representation and language. (p. 22)

The question of intelligence is not beyond reach.

5   The Concretization of the Technical Object According to Simondon

Let's go through the concept of concretization of the technical object according to Gilbert Simondon [10]: the technical object appears in a phylogenetic line where each step corresponds to the resolution of an identified problem. The lineage makes it possible to think of the technical object in an evolution from the abstract to the concrete. Jean-Yves Chateau [2] recalls that according to Gilbert Simondon:

> A particular thing is a technical object only by its relation to a lineage, i.e. a series (lineage) of objects that are more and more concrete, in so far as they solve, in a more and more integrated way, their problems of working: in a lineage, the primitive technical object is more abstract, it is close to the logical diagram of assembly of elementary structures realizing each one a proper function (…); (when) the technical object becomes concrete, it progresses simultaneously with the progress of the convergence of functions in a central unit, the overdetermination of the functions of the organs, which makes the entity more and more coherent with itself. (p. 80)

This, in our opinion, constitutes an important key to understanding the criticisms we formulated above, and the obstacles we encounter in apprehending the problems posed by normative practices.

To illustrate very briefly the phenomenon of concretization, let's look at the phone we have today. It contains complex functions around integrated devices: technically a 4G device connection is fourth generation of standards for mobile telephony corresponding to a high data transmission rate, as well as a reception and transmission device. It is therefore this specific transmission device that is the heart of a device that has become hyper-communicative. For the user, in practical terms, the current mobile phone is translated into a small flat box mainly comprising, on one of its faces, a touch screen that can activate a keyboard letters and numbers, but also images, sounds. It is both a simple phone, but also a receiver and emitter of emails, word processor, small calculator, calendar, data manager (health for instance), receivers and transmitters of multiple data for very extensive activities from simple GPS consultation to buying goods, transferring money, etc. The communication has spread to very wide activities from a device whose shape has been singularly simplified, compacted into a flat object, rectangular in shape, essentially equipped with a multi-functional touch screen. We can describe this object as a "concrete" one in the lineage that connects it to (and distinguishes it from) the ancient wall phone (so-called abstract), or even to the telegraph, in so far as many functions of communication and processing of the information aggregated to the first function of audio communication, and converged into a single object. It incorporates a very large number of functions formerly handled by separate devices, to be melted into a powerful object of simple appearance, multiple affordances and user-friendly features, ensuring "overdetermination of organ functions, which makes the whole more and more coherent with itself" to use the words of J. Y. Chateau [2].

6 Mechanological Generations: To Understand the Current Situation of the Building in a Lineage and Its Different Phases of Development and Improvement

In his lessons [10], Gilbert Simondon, referring to Jacques Lafitte and his book [4], establishes 3 successive generations of machines.

6.1 Those of 1st Generation

Passive machines according to Lafitte, they are referred to as machines in steady state of equilibrium according to Gilbert Simondon. As such they are:

> ... pre-scientific inventions (...) the internal logic of the objects they have produced is the in-deformability, by primacy of stable equilibrium. (p. 232)

These machines depend on the medium in terms of stability. There is search for longevity.

Let us try to identify some devices present in the construction, or the architecture, such that they could translate a belonging to each of these generations, as Simondon ([10], pp. 160–161) tried himself, on occasion.

We can identify that of simple mechanical communication—search for stability—notion of adaptation in construction field:

- Trench + footing: exhaustive summary of the relation of the soil and the building.
- Framework + roof: exhaustive summary of the relation of the sky and the building.
- Please note that the current issue of research and invention is no longer structural stability, well-acquired knowledge.

Traditionally buildings fall into this category of this first generation of machines: the first aim that motivates building is to provide a stable protection for people to be out of rain, cold, and wind, in a secured and strong place. The elemental wish is a maximum of inertia and stability for each housing. We can declare that the origin of any building is as simple as what is named here "machine of the first generation". Roman architecture expresses this aim very well with massive walls and vaults as Viollet le Duc [17] explained.

6.2 Second Generation Machines

Lafitte considered them as "Active machines". For Gilbert Simondon they are machines as assembly of tools with energy transformation, ideal of reversibility of the transformations (or control by negative feedback), maximum yield and indifferent state of equilibrium.

The active machine is, however, insensitive to the *milieu*, except for the removal of energy. It is characterized by a search for power. It is about keeping the machine in these intrinsic qualities, for a goal to accomplish. In these machines, there is a non-distinction between energy channel and information channel.

For this second generation we could identify:

binary mechanical system—reversibility of transformations - search for auto-correlation—existence of negative feedbacks to maintain homeostasis according to Norbert Wiener's ([15], pp. 189–217) terms.

Gilbert Simondon [10] gives some examples:

> … in some constructions, account is taken of unavoidable displacements (metal bridges resting on pebbles to allow the expansion, Eiffel tower resting on jacks allowing to maintain the verticality in spite of settlements of the ground. (p. 180)

If, overall, buildings stay in first generation category, were inserted little by little, more sophisticated technical apparatus, the building conception would move to second generation.

At the beginning, during the very first generation itself, we could consider chimney and hearth as self-correlated proto-system (control of the air intake). Later on, technical devices were developed for second generation machines, like the central heating with the boiler, the radiators and the thermostat: what constitutes really a system with thermal regulation and corresponds at the birth of a more complex set.

Natural ventilation devices, with manual closing and opening, are also proto-systems. Water networks, followed later on by electric ones, introduced other steps. The networks of ventilation and electric refrigeration constitute real machines for the thermal regulation.

In its way of designing, Modern architecture included other machines like elevators, a machine that establishes a relationship between two levels in a building. Modern architecture tried to promote the *Machine à habiter*, according to Le Corbusier [6] wordings (that suggested a way of living beyond technical devices, of course, but implied them).

It's reasonable to note that the current issue of research and invention is no longer a search for the now acquired functional efficiency of embedded devices. It is also clear that the energy autonomy directive requires going beyond this stage.

6.3   Third Generation: Corresponding to Reflex Machines According to Lafitte's Terms

Given the current technological evolution, I consider that there are, at least, two third generation stages.

The first stage is the one that Norbert Wiener [15] defines as having a positive feedback regulator (pp. 189–217), including the notions of servo and homeostasis. This means that it allows the amplification of a phenomenon, where the negative feedback machines are only intended to bring the machine back to its initial stage, by correcting defects or creating/making changes in the state generated by the very operation of the machine (simple self-correction).

At the early phases of aforementioned stage of third generation machines, we could distinguish a category of technical objects with positive feedback but not interdependent, therefore, their positive feedback is limited.

So-called smart elevators (optimized management of the displacements) could be included in this category: there is positive feedback thus amplification but there is still servo loop (in the cybernetic sense).

And automatic closing of openings, according to criteria of normative comfort and energy saving for instance, or the coupling of the productions of hot water (electric and solar …) could also be included in this category.

There is here a notion of amplification.

The current issue of research and invention is no longer a search for complex functional efficiency already acquired.

We can affirm this stage of fitted building does not belong to the smart building category, because it is still a set of assistant technical devices enrolled into the building, to answers separated standards.

The second stage: according to Gilbert Simondon [10], these more advanced machines are characterized by the sensitivity and importance of amplified signal transmission. There is a search for metastability responding to variations and hazards of the *milieu*. Here the machine is able to produce a close relationship between adaptation and self-correction.

The second-stage machines of this 3rd generation would be, if we use the terms of Gilbert Simondon, technical packages of reduced size or tending to be reduced for better reliability, better information output. This requires the search for signal fidelity. Here communication is not only exchange and transmission, it is original, it founds and constitutes—it translates the principal act of organization. This technical being is entirely understood as and in information, as origin and finality, element and totality.

In this configuration, it involves designing and setting up a network of communicating machines (transmit, receive, process, store, etc.) between themselves and with the *milieu*-medium ...

It is therefore the advent of a coextensive network in the world.

On this topic, the philosopher [10] mentions:

> ... in its last stage, the technicality of the networks concretely finds the *milieu* by becoming coextensive with the world, while the human operator is only in contact with the terminals, which are also initials. The medium is technicized. (p. 86)

and also:

> ... By taking the dimension of networks, the technical reality returns at the end of evolution towards the "milieu" that it modifies and structures (or rather textures). (p. 101).

Autocorrelation is then intrinsic, since the language of transmission, of positive regulation, and even of co-evolution, is entirely that of information - not information that would dominate matter (hylemorphic and/or dialectical conceptions) but an integrative information that can be (and manifested in) matter, movement, or temporality.

If we go back to the beginning of our remarks, we could say that the most emblematic current issue, as it is advocated, is that of energy stability. Nevertheless, if we translate it into Simondonian terms, what would be relevant would be to speak of energy metastability for this second step of the third generation to respond to variations and uncertainties, through a close relationship between adaptation and self-correction, a productive relationship with the *milieu*.

In this case (second step of 3rd generation) the operation ratio is carried out with the complex and technicized medium—one could advance the notion of global cross-linking. This would mean that parts of the same building communicate to produce, distribute, regulate energy for instance. But it also means better distribution and mini-mization through communicating with the inside and the outside (i.e. Producing and circulating information that can involve energy management). We must also consider the communication between the different uses of specialized spaces according to user needs, as well as the communication between specialized spaces and indeterminate spaces. Relaying on the demands of the occupants in real time, providing varied conditions for non-standardized situations, considering more widely than any inhabited place is immersed in a *milieu,* associated with it, but that it is itself an associated *milieu* for users. In this frame "intelligent" means able to provide answers, not only to standards, but able to interact with *milieu* and occupants. This supposes intricate and immediate situations and answers. Let us insist that this remark is valid not only for the building but for any place occupied, inhabited, borrowed, crossed, whether it is precise and surrounded or wide and open.

In this sense, we could go further by following the words of the architect Toyo Ito [3], who said:

> If as McLuhan said, clothing and architecture are both extensions of our skin functioning as mechanisms for controlling energy and protecting us from the world outside, then their function as membranes would certainly be very important.
>
> (…)This epidermis (…) must operate as a highly efficient sensor capable of detecting the flow of electrons.
>
> (…) Rather than being rigid and dens like a wall, architecture as epidermis must be pliant and supple like our skin and be able to exchange information with the world outside. It would be more appropriate to call architecture clad in such a membrane a media suit. (pp. 123–124)

The energetic and ambient issue is typically behind the invention of this generation of beings-objects; they are not treated with static matter, because they cannot be constituted with machines of pure control: we must consider them as emission and reception flux, realizing kinds of emulsions, and metastable states. We must now think of them as being complex backgrounds, wholly understood as and in information as origin and finality, element and totality. Here, the form is only the result of a relational process and complex tensioning as Gilbert Simondon [13] claimed.

The ways of thinking about design are shifting from the classical and modern projective method to a processual elaboration, where time as flow is imposed on space as a stable support.

Of course, the invention of these *machines-beings-milieu* is not isolated from the previous stakes (static structure, operation of embedded "machines"). But this tends to re-define their relationships, from the moment we admit the interlocking and the interaction of different beings and their associated *milieux.*

And Gilbert Simondon [12] explains the characteristics of invention:

> The invention provides a wave of condensation, concretizations that simplify the object by loading each structure of a plurality of functions; not only are the old functions preserved and better fulfilled, but the concretization brings in addition new properties, complementary functions that were not sought after, and that could be called superabundant functions, constituting the class of a real advent of possibilities in addition to the expected properties of the object. (p. 171)

We will come back to this point later.

It should be noted that Gilbert Simondon [10] himself does not envisage watertight categories, particularly as he regards buildings:

It is difficult to declare without reservation that buildings are passive machines, they are not all the same degree of individualized technical objects. (…) the passive machine is above all an irreversible machine made up of elements that maintain and adhere to each other, the real estate character of the building lies especially in the irreversibility of its genesis, if the buildings became movable and dismountable, they would have the main characters of active machines, which are open, admit repairs, changes in rooms (…) architecture integrates and propagates a cultural barrier (distinction of land and furniture) that a technological deepening can lead to revocation. (p. 182)

7 To Deepen More Precisely What Building Intelligence Is, Let's Go Through the Notion of Operation

Mechanologie is not a pure science, it is for Gilbert Simondon (1958): "… a science of correlations and transformations …" (p. 48).

He uses the concept of *operation*. According to Gilbert Simondon [11], thinking the word relation is relative to the essential notion of tension, to that of communication—especially between medium and object—in particular in the situation of invention (p. 29).

In the passive object, first generation, the operation relation is simple and finished (closed)

In the active object, the operation relation is binary (open or closed)

In the "intelligent" object, the operation relation is the very definition of the object (permanent computation).

Could it not be said that this is a report of operations requiring otherness, interaction and relationship?

This operation relation is a framework, or structure, or beacon, if you will, the path towards a clearer definition of the notion of intelligence associated with the building.

To understand this point, you have to stop for a moment on the elements of this operation relation:

We can establish four types of actors:

1. users
2. The outside *milieu*
3. The indoor *milieu*
4. to which is added a set of technical devices: informational and effectors (Fig. 1).

In the diagram above, elements of the general situation are shown:

An external *milieu* of definition and complex composition, with fluctuating contours because the conditions that make it exist are multiple, not fixed. Thus, climatic conditions, living elements such as plants and animals, fluid elements such as air and water are not stable or static; entropic data in perpetual evolution continuously modify the state of the outer *milieu*.

An internal *milieu*, whose stability we will seek, is the very purpose of the building: to create a controlled interior *milieu*. One could consider it "stable" in

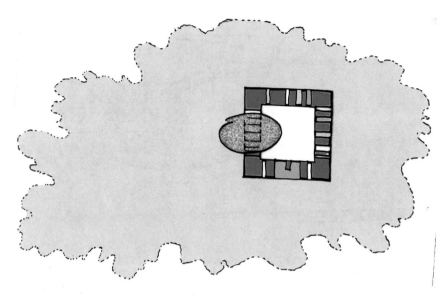

Fig. 1 Outer milieu: light grey—internal milieu: white—user: granite—buildings and technical apparatus: dark grey (*Source* Author's diagram)

a first-generation version of mechanics. However, it will be called "metastable" in a contemporary search for "intelligent building".

A set of more or less sophisticated technical devices, making up what we will call the building, which encompasses and "protects" or rather makes this internal *milieu* exist. A roof, a window, a chimney, a central heating, the electric light, are part of these devices that appeared over the generations of building (lineage).

The user, with his or her demands, vital requirements, or more elaborately taking into account the social, economic and today contexts, is the "key" actor of this system.

What is the operation relation that connects them?

In a simple context the scheme is clear:

The external *milieu* acts directly on the building: gravity, wind, rain, sun, lift of the ground, the function of the building is to resist without feedback.

The external *milieu* also acts on the user (perception, sensations of comfort, embarrassment, etc.) which will in turn affect some of the elements of the technical device of the building: open a window, turn on the light, turn on the heat, and thus retain certain desired qualities of the inner *milieu*. This is a negative feedback system to maintain internal stability (Fig. 2).

The diagram above shows a more ambitious operation relation:

The *milieu* is connected to devices that respond to the programmed demand of the users or to their request in real time (even remotely) by processing the information and sending it to effectors who make corrections or new operations and return the information. In this scheme, there is also stored processed data and past actions that are also returned to indoor *milieu* detection devices.

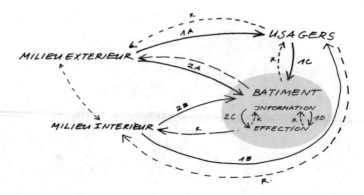

Fig. 2 Author's diagram

The relation of operation interior *milieu* and apparatus of the building makes it possible to constitute a memory, an intelligence by learning, from already produced situations which will have been correctly analyzed and translated into algorithms. The notion of feedback plays a strategic role.

This complex system with positive feedback is then considered between all partners at different scales of time and space. Thus, the external *milieu* and the building (understood as a set of artificial technical devices in interface with the interior and the external *milieu*) can collaborate to co-produce (for instance ambiances, energy, information) to the user's address or directly towards the inner *milieu*.

The internal *milieu*, the external one and the user interact, via the elaborate devices that form a "building".

The connectionist model and the contributions of AI and *Enaction* Varela et al. [16] could be very useful to deal with these complex interactions. This would need to be developed in another paper.

In order for the building to be truly intelligent, all the devices that surround the interior *milieu* and serve as interface with the external one, must be able to solve all the problems: i.e. both the primary questions (functions of the older devices in the building) but "at the same time" is able to respond to problems in more recent areas where the requirement has arisen—in the manner of a current telephone capable of responding to a problem, through a multitude of functions from a coded data transmission/reception device.

We will argue here that the complex interface between the indoor *milieu* and the external one, together with the increasing demands of the user (for instance in terms of energy production or more generally comfort), requires rethinking the building as a whole in analogy with the cell membrane that receives information, treats it, activates substances and mechanisms that regulate the relationship between the inside and the outside of the cell to maintain homeostasis.

Intelligent building would therefore be, in our opinion, a concrete set in the sense developed above, which would consist of all the devices gathered and self-correlated to produce the desired relations, in real time, or almost, between interior and exterior with reference analogue to the membrane.

8 This 2nd Phase of 3rd Generation, Will Be Named *Eco-Mechano-Logique*

According to G. Simondon [13]:

Communication between technical objects and *milieu* is of ecological nature. (p. 85)

If we go back to the beginning of our remarks, we can say that the most emblematic current issue, as it is advocated, is that of energy stability. Nevertheless, if we translate it into *mechanistic* terms, it becomes relevant to emphasize on energy metastability for such a 2nd phase of the 3rd generation to respond to variations and uncertainties, through a close relationship between adaptation and self-correction, creating a productive relationship with the milieu.

8.1 About Invention

A few words—this part would be to develop:

The invention is here too and is not an addition. The invention creates both the object and its associated *milieu* and it is precisely the consciousness of the separation of the two, their coupling produces the invention according to Simondon [10].

The invention makes a new being happen, comments J. Y. Chateau [2]. To think of the invention as a process and a complex *being-milieu* in tension is perhaps what could solve the problem of the moral antagonism between a building and its environment, between artifice and nature, between the norm and the realization of a concrete device, allowing the formation of an eco-mechanical milieu (thermal, domestic etc.)

Simondon explains [12]:

In every age, normative inventions make a finding of compatibility for modes of existence that did not have a meaning or point of insertion in the preceding normative structures. (p. 158)

For the philosopher [12] this process also involves an author (or a team of authors) and the tension between the latter and his problem (the object and his environment to be constituted) which is considered to be at the same time the origin and the result, the beginning and the end of the process.

The problem is solved when a communication is established between the system of action of the subject for whom the problem arises and the regime of reality of the result; the subject is part of the order of reality in which the problem is posed; it is not part of that of the imagined result; Invention is the discovery of mediation between these two orders, mediation by which the action system of the subject may have taken over the production of the result by an ordered action. (p. 141).

Solving the problem by formalization creates an artificial object with properties that go beyond the problem (p. 173).

All scientific explanations do not overcome the invention. A particularly special dimension characterizes it. If invention produces a new being, an artifact that is both the origin and the fulfillment of itself, holding both a unique existence and total dependence, both being and middle associated *milieu*, then, from my point of view, the invention is here necessary to produce intelligent building.

8.2   Adaptive = Intelligent and Vice Versa

Our aim to define intelligent building was constructed on several steps. At the end of this tour, we may admit that passive houses and even houses with positive energy (additionally including elements of energy production as we recalled on the first page) as required by RT2020 French norm are not satisfying answers responding to the word *intelligent*. At best, we consider the second generation of machines, may be also the first stage of 3rd generation, as set of tools for energy transformation, ideal of reversibility of the transformations, control by negative feedback and indifferent state of equilibrium. Standards and norms stay coercive, due to low level of responsiveness to the diversity and richness of situations and needs. Intelligence is precisely what is missing.

The ambition for an intelligent building, if we accept the definition built above borrowing a lot to Gilbert Simondon philosophy of technics, requires to solve the problem of a steady dialog between indoor and outdoor building with the milieu and mainly the users. Therefore, it needs to build smart technical devices as a network able to produce, share and record information, acting in and with the *milieu* and the inhabitants. Of course, the recent developments of AI to treat big Data could be able to solve a part of this complexity. However, we shouldn't forget the two actors (users and milieu) are the key to go over standards and pure technical answers, introducing complexity, systemic design in relationship with social, behavioral, individual and even intuitive demands.

Beyond technical approach, Gilbert Simondon [11] searched for human being. He redeemed technics as a part of *individuation*. Intelligence supposes human being as main aim. It's why an approach of intelligent building as a part of human intelligence is a source of inspiration.

To answer to these intricate aims, or inventions as we present the term are needed. The building would become adaptive, an intelligent complex apparatus, where human being and milieu are the main actors. In the today's phase of technical and architectural evolution, adaptive building could be the definition of intelligent building. A step into lineage.

As Mario Borillo [1] mentions: After all, no matter the ontology that we assign to it, isn't an "intelligent" system primarily a program? (p. 16)

The advent of information techno-sciences in general, as invasive technologies, hybridizing and reorganizing all others in a network of data processing, storage and dissemination, undoubtedly allow the initiation of this technology.

The complete machine (self-regulating in the sense of Lafitte), this adaptive system that Gilbert Simondon described as the stage of the technique he saw emerge, is yet to be produced. It requires a greater co-operation between the different actors and researchers in the built *milieu*, beyond the prostheses produced today.

If we consider the complexity of the city, in the light of the concept of milieu, and compare it to a simple building, we can realize the magnitude of the task we face.

As we see, to establish this program, much remains to be done.

References

1. Borillo, M. (1984). *Informatique pour les sciences de l'homme: Limites de la formalisation du raisonnement* (p. 16). Paris: Editions Mardaga.
2. Chateau, J. Y. (2008). *Le vocabulaire de Simondon* (p. 80). Paris: Ellipses.
3. Ito, T. (2011). *Architecture words 8, Tarzans in the media forest & other essays,* (pp. 123–124). London: AA.
4. Lafitte, J. (1932). *Réflexions sur la science des machines.* Paris: Bloud & Gay.
5. La RT. (2020). Retrieved March 01, 2016 from: http://www.rt-2020.com.
6. Corbusier, Le. (1923). *Vers une architecture.* Paris: Crès et Cie.
7. Lecourt. D. (2008). *Georges Canguilhem* (pp. 83,184). Paris: P.U.F Que sais-je.
8. Piaget. J. (1970). *L'épistémologie génétique* (p. 22). Paris: PUF.
9. Simondon. G. (1958). *Du mode d'existence des objets techniques* (pp. 45, 47, 48, 57, 254). Paris: Aubier.
10. Simondon. G. (2005a). *L'invention dans les techniques* (pp. 25, 86, 101, 160–161, 180, 182, 232, 254). Paris: Seuil.
11. Simondon. G. (2005b). *L'Individuation à la lumière des notions de forme et d'information* (p. 29). Paris: Millon.
12. Simondon. G. (2008). *Imagination et invention* (pp. 141, 158, 171, 173). Paris: La Transparence.
13. Simondon. G. (2010). *Communication et Information* (p. 85). Paris: La Transparence.
14. Uexküll J. v. (1956). French edition (2010) *Milieu animal et milieu humain.* Paris: Bibliothèque Rivages.
15. Wiener, N. (2014). *French edition La Cybernétique, Information et régulation dans le vivant et la machine* (pp. 189–217). Seuil, Paris: Press Cambridge.
16. Varela, F., Thompson, E., & Rosch, E. (1991). *The embodied mind: Cognitive science and human experience.* Cambridge, MA: MIT Press.
17. Viollet-le-Duc, E. (1872). *Entretiens sur l'Architecture.* Paris: Morel.

Encouraging Energy Efficiency Among Residents of Smart and Green Buildings

Véronique Flambard, Josias Kpoviessi, and Rustam Romaniuc

Abstract Energy is an important aspect of a building that is monitored in real-time in smart and green buildings. Smart metering information systems provide new monitoring tools to encourage a two-way interaction between the building manager and its residents. Dynamic energy pricing; incentives; feedbacks or nudges can be introduced to encourage energy demand reduction and energy efficiency. We study the impact of a bonus system to reward responsible consumption of energy in the controlled environment of a lab experiment. Our results show that the bonuses act as focal points for subjects in their energy consumption. The least virtuous residents all reached the second bonus anchor. However, the intrinsic motivation of the soberest residents is partially crowded out by the bonus, stressing out the importance of taking into consideration behavioural factors. We conclude with policy recommendations.

Keywords Energy conservation · Financial incentives · Experimental economics · Environmental awareness · Smart metering information systems

1 Introduction

Eco-conscious designs and materials, as well as technology, are facilitators for energy efficiency and energy savings. Smart buildings are developed for housing towers, public housing, office buildings, and university campuses. The interest grows as business, government, energy providers and residential users see the benefits of energy conservation. Some experiments are conducted with pricing (time-of-use or real-time pricing) and behavioural nudges (feedbacks on energy consumption, social

V. Flambard (✉)
Université Catholique de Lille- FGES and LEM (UMR CNRS 9221), Lille, France
e-mail: veronique.flambard@univ-catholille.fr

R. Romaniuc
Burgundy School of Business, Université Bourgogne Franche-Comté, Dijon, France

J. Kpoviessi
Lyon, France

© Springer Nature Switzerland AG 2021
E. Magnaghi et al. (eds.), *Organizing Smart Buildings and Cities*,
Lecture Notes in Information Systems and Organisation 36,
https://doi.org/10.1007/978-3-030-60607-7_9

comparisons) to monitor energy consumption and are facilitated by smart metering or the presence of energy manager in smart buildings or smart energy communities. Energy conservation refers to the reduction of the consumption permitted by better energy efficiency and behavioural change.

In this contribution, we focus on energy behaviour, such as turning the light off when leaving a room, lowering room temperature, and adjusting the use of the dishwasher or other types of equipment [11] but not to energy retrofit or investment in more energy-efficient appliances.

Energy demand management (also called demand-side management or load management) aims to encourage consumers to shift energy consumption during off-peak times (during the night or week-ends) to reduce the need for network or power plant investments. The demand for energy is, in fact, a demand for an input used to produce services (heating, lighting, transportation, power) but not a consumption good for itself. Shifting use in time (the dishwasher during the night, for example) does not change the service provided by the dishwasher. The concept of energy efficiency is a different concept outside the scope of this study. The efficiency depends on the services produced per kilowatt-hour and depends on the building and appliances.

Factors influencing the energy consumption have been scrutinized, and scholars recognize the role of behaviour in addition to factors such as building and households characteristics, energy price or climate ([3], [4], [5], [6], [7], [23]). Energy behaviour responds to different interventions such as energy consumption feedback, financial incentives, symbolic rewards, use of default options, group-based emulation, and regulation or information campaigns. Interventions can reduce energy consumption by 5–15% (see the review of [27]).

Yue, Long and Chen [33] in a quantitative analysis based on a survey of 638 households, show socio-demographic factors (age, gender, income, the structure of the household, education) influence behaviours in terms of energy saving in China. Situational and geographic differences also matter to a less extent. Belaïd and Garcia [12] based on a French PHEBUS survey also highlight the importance of both environmental and socio-demographic factors. Households with the most frugal energy behaviour live in the worst performing energy buildings, in a warmer climate and tend to be less well off financially with lower social status. With respect to age, they find an inverted U-shape distribution. Younger households, with young children, tend to give priority to comfort for their children over energy savings. In the 45–56 age category, the priority is reversed. When households become older, they prefer comfort over savings, this time for their own comfort.

Jessoe and Rapson [25] compared, in a field experiment in the USA, the effect of sharp energy price increase and information. Households who suffered from the price increase and got information feedback decreased their consumption by twice as much as those receiving only price increase. Pellerano et al. [29] in a field experiment in Ecuador, evaluated the impact of financial incentives and social comparisons. Households who received information about the consumption of others reduced their consumption by about 1%. However, financial incentives did not help to reduce electricity consumption, and in some cases may have had perverse effects. It is consistent with the recommendation of ([19], and the work of [13], [9]).

Goal settings and information feedbacks help to reduce energy consumption. In an early study, Becker [10] reports about an experiment where consumers were given either an easy goal to reach (2% reduction) or a more difficult one (20% reduction). Some consumers were receiving *feedbacks* and others not. He found that only the households with more difficult goals and feedbacks significantly reduced their energy consumption by 15%. Yates and Aronson [32] recommended giving *salient examples* to residents to help them achieve energy savings. Some experiments use *challenges*. Under the effect of *competition*, McClelland and Cook [28] showed that the contest group consumed 6.6% less electricity than the control group who did not enter the competition. Harding and Hsiaw [24] in a field experiment evaluate to 4.4% on average the energy savings for customers who enter in a saver energy program. The persistent savings for those who set realistic goals are much higher at 11%. Abeler et al. [1] show that effort provision depends on goal settings: efforts are more intense if performance expectations are high than if they are low.

Andreoni [8] suggests that it is better to frame a programme as a *contribution to a public good* rather than a restriction from *taking* from a common resource (refraining from doing something bad). Indeed people are driven by the *"warm-glow" of contributing (for example to energy conservation) rather than the "cold-prickle" of refraining from polluting or wasting resources.*

Frey [19] warns that if residents are intrinsically motivated by the "warm-glow" of contributing positively to the environment (say, by investing in energy saving processes), then giving monetary incentives could reduce their personal motivation. He explains that tradable permits of gas emissions increase the price of energy and discourage consumption. However, this price signal crowds out *environmental moral* (the intrinsic motivation). To illustrate this, he compares the monetary instrument to the indulgences purchases in redemption for sins in the Middle Age. Therefore, a monetary instrument (for example an environmental tax) is efficient only if it is high enough to dominate the crowding-out effect.

In a recent contribution, Dellavigna and Pope [17] investigated the determinants of real effort task with an Amazon Mechanical Turk experiment (called MTurk hereafter), a platform where researchers can pay participants for small tasks. The MTurk participants had to press alternatively "a" and "b" keys for ten minutes, wining a point for each a-b sequence. In different treatments, they received either a flat payment (the payment did not depend on the effort or number of times they pressed "a-b" keys) or a 1 cent or 10 cents every 100 points they scored. They found that monetary incentives were effective: raising significantly performance from 1,521 points with a flat payment to 2,029 with a 1 cent a piece to 2,175 for 10 cents a piece. A low remuneration of 1 cent every 100 points did not crowd out effort and motivation. MTurk workers were not driven by the "warm glow of doing good" in the standard treatment (pressing keys had no social value per se). The authors also tested altruism. In two other treatments, the Red Cross Charitable Fund was given 1 or 10 cents for every 100 points scored by MTurk participants (but with no private gain for participants). The 1 cent given to charity resulted in an effort of 1,907 (above the flat payment but below the direct payment to the subject) and the 10-cent resulted in the same result as when the money goes to the worker. Other treatments were conducted with respect to time preference (MTurk workers were more responsive to payment today than 2 or 4 weeks later) and gain/loss (the effort was higher for a 40 cents framed as a loss than for a 40 cents framed as a gain). Finally, some treatments involved social comparison. They outperformed flat payments but were less effective than monetary incentives.

In this chapter, we seek to contribute to the research on energy conservation by testing the impact of financial incentives, goal settings and altruism. Based on the existing literature, we expect that consumers will reduce their consumption when social norms are activated; when useful information feedbacks are provided and when benefit from financial incentives are large enough to compensate for potential crowding-out effect. Bonuses, which provide goal settings, with salient points of energy consumption should reinforce the effects if the goals are not too easy to reach. The critical aspects we investigate here, controlling for the other factors, are the effects of financial bonuses and anchoring effects. Anchoring is the tendency to anchor or focus on one piece of information, for example, here a task goal or energy cost [31].

Behavioural responses to incentives may be evaluated with modelling of consumption choices, with evaluation of natural or field experiments, surveys or with laboratory experiments. Field experiments consist in studying the effect of some policy change in the targeted population's natural environment, while lab or online experiments are generally carried out in neutral and controlled environments with participants' knowledge that their behavior is under the experimenter's scrutiny. Controlled experiments are widely used in psychology, economics, biology, clinical tests. One or more parameters are manipulated (here the payment of the task/cost of energy use) in a fully controlled and randomized way. Lab experiments provide affordable and quick methods to gain insight on policies' impacts. This can serve as a testbed to assess the effect of policies in a simple and controlled environment. If participants respond poorly to the incentives, the policy is to be improved or dropped, if not, lessons can be drawn to test the policy in a more complex setting. Are financial bonuses an effective way for landlords of smart buildings to achieve energy conservation? To provide some insights to this question, we mimic in the lab, the daily routine of small gestures towards energy sobriety with a repeated real-effort task experiment. The only paper which comes close to our research question and experiment design is Dellavigna and Pope [18]. Our experiment adds to the latter by testing the effectiveness of goal settings (anchoring) in financial incentives when altruism is activated (through donation to an environmental association). Our experiment is also conducted in a lab (and not online with MTurkers as in [18]). Unlike MTurk participants who are not monitored and can perform several tasks/things at the same time or can be distracted by their day-to-day activities, lab participants perform their tasks in a controlled environment. Our paper hints that policy makers and building managers could possibly encourage the least motivated energy savers to improve their efforts with a bonus system and target levels of energy consumption.

The remainder of the paper is devoted to the experimental design (Sect. 2), the statistical analysis of the behavioural responses to the financial bonuses (Sect. 3) and the discussion and recommendations about this policy (Sect. 4).

2 Experimental Design

To study effort provision and performance, we use a real effort design by opposition to stated effort design. Charness et al. [16] discuss these two paradigms. In the first one, participants have to choose from a menu a combination of effort level and associated cost. Costs and benefits are clearly stated in this paradigm (see for example [15]). In the second paradigm, the performance is measured with the number of tasks actually performed by subjects (see for instance [1]). Tasks can then be of different types (visual search, puzzles, memory, physical, repetitive, cognitive...). The main advantage is that the effort is closer to reality and to the psychology of working. The drawback is that the cost of effort is not known to the researcher, only the payment per task in the lab is. Another advantage of real-task-effort design is that the experimenter can observe the changes in effort over time. Participants may reduce or increase their effort while performing the tasks over time (depending on learning, reactions to information, boredom...) which would not be captured with stated efforts. Finally, subjects do not necessarily behave similarly when deciding how much money to give or how much effort to make. With stated-effort-task we remain in the domain of money. For all these reasons, we opted for a real-task-effort experiment.

The experiment took place at the Laboratory for Experimental Anthropology, Lille, France, between May 18th and 22th, 2017. Participants were mostly students from Lille who had never participated in a similar experiment. The experiment consisted in four sessions run by the same experimenter with a total of 70 subjects invited via the ORSEE software [22]. Terminals were separated by lateral partitions to ensure complete anonymity. Subjects were paid at the end of each session, in a private room. Subjects earned an average 18.84 euros including show up fee. Sessions lasted one hour and a quarter, on average, including initial instructions and payment of subjects.

The experiment was rather decontextualized. The subjects did not know that the objective was to evaluate the impact of financial incentives on energy reduction. Instead, they were told that they would participate in a social experiment on decision making with real payments based on the number of tasks performed. The experiment took the form of a computer game. First, they had to read instructions. They had one hour to move a series of 50 light bulbs on a screen page from left to right (see Fig. 1). The tedious task had no intrinsic value for them and offered little learning possibility. We were confident that way the task would entail a cost for subjects.

After each series, subjects had the choice to start another page of tasks or to give up and surf on the internet for the rest of the 60 minutes experiment. Saving energy (and therefore money), day after day, requires repeated efforts. The repetition of the tedious tasks of sliding light bulbs icons from left to right was meant to measure the perseverance of the efforts. The payment of the subjects increased with the number of series of 50 tasks performed, called period hereafter. The amount paid per series of 50 tasks decreased by 20% every five periods. In this way, we wanted to duplicate a decreasing marginal benefit of energy savings (the first energy savings are achieved

TasksPage

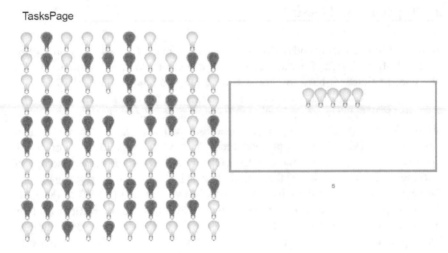

Fig. 1 Screenshot of computerized sliding tasks (one period)

at low comfort cost, while the following ones are increasingly costly in terms of comfort). The participants were divided into two groups.

A group of 30 persons, called the treated, were eligible to bonuses. The extra financial bonuses acted as target goals and incentives. Four levels of bonus could be achieved. If their effort (a proxy for energy consumption saving, such as turning off devices in standby mode, for example) reached a reference level they received the maximum bonus. They could also be eligible to lower bonuses: if their effort was 7.5% below the reference level (75% of the bonus), 15% below the reference level (50% of the bonus) and 30% below (25% of the bonus). We calibrated the thresholds so that the first one could be easily reached with small efforts and the last one could only be attained with a high but achievable level of effort.

Another group of 40 persons only received a payment based on the number of tasks performed, and did not receive target goals nor bonuses (Table 1).

Table 1 Description of experimental sessions	Session	Number of participants	Group
	1 (May 18th 2017, 12 h)	20	Control (without bonus)
	2 (May 18th 2017, 15 h)	20	Control (without bonus)
	3 (May 22nd 2017, 15 h)	14	Treatment (with bonus)
	4 (May 22nd 2017, 17 h)	16	Treatment (with bonus)

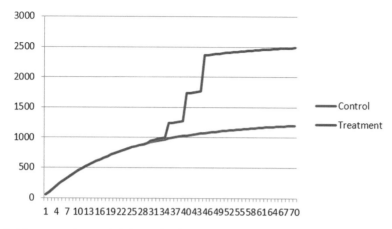

Fig. 2 Monetary gains per period completed per group

In order to raise awareness of the positive impact of their efforts on society (a positive externality), 5% of participants earnings (in the treatment and control group) were donated to a student association of environmental protection. This amount was not deducted from their own gain. The objective was also to give social value to the tasks.

The theoretical gain functions of the treatment and the control group are shown in Fig. 2.

Every 5 periods, the screen displayed the earnings in euros. Each subject had to confirm he had read the information before choosing between two possibilities. He could start another series of 50 tasks or give up the tasks, with no possibility of return and use his time as he wishes to surf on the internet or to relax while remaining seated.

The treated received, in addition to his remuneration based on the number of completed periods, the first level of a bonus payment at the 30th validated period. Then a second level at the 35th period, a third at the 40th period and the last level of payment at the 45 validated periods. These thresholds play the role of anchoring points or goal-setting points. The complete instructions are shown in appendix. After the experiment and before receiving their payments, subjects had to answer to a survey.

Approximately half of the subjects were women (36 out of 70), most of them were students (63 out of 70) and the average age was 22 years old. All subjects answered they understood well the instructions and had no difficulties performing the tasks. A majority of participants responded in the survey that their goal was to maximize the experiment's gains for themselves (40 fully agree and 21 rather agree) but they were divided when it came to maximizing gains for the environmental association (12 fully agree and 27 rather agree, so just slightly more than half of them rather or fully agree with this goal).

3 Main Findings

On average, the participants completed 46 periods in the control group with a decreasing but positive price paid per period with no premium. The treated group who could benefit from a premium in addition to the regular payment, achieved 48 periods on average (not statistically different from the 46 periods). A non-parametric test of Mann-Whitney confirms the average performance does not change with the bonus (Table 2). However, the distribution of the number of period changes from one treatment to the other (Fig. 3 and Table 2). In the group with a bonus, all participants exercised an effort level that allowed them to reach at least the second threshold of the bonus. A test of the variance of the two distributions confirms the variance is lower in the treated group relative to the control group (6 and 12 respectively). In the group with a bonus, all participants reached the second threshold of the bonus at 35 and do not exceed 58 periods while without the premium the number of periods varies from 11 to 66.

Reading note: (1) We test the null hypothesis that the subsidy does not change the number of tasks completed by the subjects. The statistical test concludes to no statistical significant difference with ($z = 0.048$, $p = 0.962$). (2) We also test the null hypothesis that the subsidy does not change the standard deviation of the number of tasks performed by the participants. The test concludes to a difference in standard deviations between the two groups.

We also take a look at the effect of the premium on the behaviour of certain "types" of individuals: those who are motivated to make efforts even in the absence of a premium, those who are moderately motivated, and those who drop out quickly.

Table 2 Descriptive statistics and hypotheses test about the number of completed periods

	Without financial incentives (control group)	With financial incentives (treated group)
Average period number	45.97	47.57
Standard deviation of period	12.48	6.25
[Minimum; Maximum]	[11; 66]	[35; 58]
Number of observations	40	30
Two-sample Wilcoxon rank sum Mann-Whitney test	Observed: 1424 Expected: 1420	Observed: 1061 Expected: 1065
	(1) $z = 0.048$, $p = 0.962$	
Standard deviation. Equality Test (2) $W0 = 9.00$ df(1, 68) Pr > F = 0.004 $W50 = 6.55$ df(1, 68) Pr > F = 0.013 $W10 = 7.52$ df(1, 68) Pr > F = 0.008		

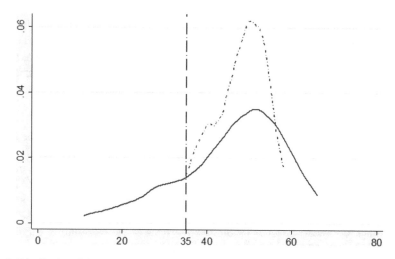

Fig. 3 Distribution of the number of completed period (The vertical dotted line corresponds to the minimum number of periods necessary to reach the first bonus for those eligible. The dotted line (respectively solid line) shows the distribution of the treated group who can benefit from a premium [the control group without premium])

The bonus acts as an effective mechanism that encourages the least motivated individuals to make more efforts (which generate both individual and environmental benefits). However, the bonus also reduces the level of effort that would have been achieved by the most motivated participants (if no bonus had been introduced). The medium performers do not seem to respond to the bonus, the average is unchanged and slightly exceeds the last anchor of 45 (respectively 46 without bonus and 47.6 with a bonus).

It confirms that people respond to goal settings. The bonus acts as a focal point for all participants: there is a convergence of behaviours in the range of bonus thresholds (in the treated group, 100% of participants reached the second bonus threshold and 66% went slightly beyond the fourth threshold and then stopped making efforts). This confirms the importance of the anchoring effect. All participants in the treated group reach at least the second threshold as mentioned previously but once the last threshold is reached, the effort decreases more rapidly in the group with the premium (dotted line, Fig. 3) than in the other group (solid red line, Fig. 3).

The additional financial incentives, given to the treated group increase the price or benefit of effort (this substitution effect encourages labour over leisure) and motivate them to reach the bonuses. However, with the financial bonus, income is earned quickly and people can stop efforts earlier to enjoy comfort. If this is the case, the income effect dominates the substitution one. Depending on which effect dominates, both behaviours are possible. The participants who increased their participation and in particular the least motivated persons who would not have reached the second threshold without the financial premium, have been more responsive to the price increase than to the income effect while it is the reverse for the others and notably for the most motivated ones. The phenomenon has been documented in the literature. For example, physicians paid with fee-for-services contracts have been shown to respond differently to the income and substitution effects. Income effects are not too high when prices are raised for specific services but become dominant with a broad and generalized price increase for services with a reduction in the labour supply of clinical services [30].

This experiment implies that financial incentives designed to promote energy conservation could have ambiguous effects. They could be efficient for the households for which the substitution effect dominates but inefficient for those for which the income effect is prominent. Policies toward energy efficiency, especially coupled with technological progress, should therefore be carefully designed. It is well known that behavioral responses to energy efficiency can reduce expected gains from technological progress. The size of this effect, known as the rebound effect (or in extreme cases, backfire effect) depends on the relative sizes of the substitution and income effect. With the improvement of energy efficiency, people substitute towards more energy-efficient goods and away from relatively more expensive non-energy goods (substitution effects) and with the increased purchasing power they may consume more of all normal goods (income effect) including energy goods. Therefore the energy savings from technological progress may be lower than expected due to a "rebound" effect [21].

We previously discussed the impact of the change in "price" of the effort focusing on purely financial aspects. The participants can also be eco-conscious and intrinsically motivated by energy conservation. If they were only driven by this environmental motive, and not responsive to financial incentives, their behaviour should not differ between the two treatments. But it does as we have seen. This could be solely the effect of extrinsic motivation (the financial bonus) or a mixed effect of the extrinsic and intrinsic motivation on efforts. The financial incentives can crowd-in or crowd-out intrinsic motivation. We only observe the total effect in this experiment since we did not add treatments to control for each of them separately. We observe that the less effortful participants increase their performance with financial incentives, therefore if there is a crowding-out effect it is dominated by the substitution effect. A crowding-in effect could also play a role. Frey [18] first showed in the literature that the substitution effect enhancing performance might be partially or completely offset by a negative effect called crowding-out effect in some conditions. This is particularly true if the person feels manipulated. This happens also for tasks or activities requiring personal initiative or intrinsic motivation, the perceived monitoring is then counterproductive. This has been observed if the reward is not high enough to outweigh the loss of intrinsic motivation. More recently the concept of crowding-in effect has been defined as conditions enhancing intrinsic motivation (for a literature review, see [20]). Lindenberg [26] explains that people are goal-oriented and that one goal will tend to supersede (the hedonic or normative frame fueled by intrinsic motivation or the financial frame involving comparisons of financial gains and effort costs). In sum, energy savings triggers a positive normative frame and "warm glow of doing good for the environment" and a financial frame (possible financial savings versus valuation of behavioral changes). The positive effect of the financial incentives will be reinforced if the normative and hedonic frame is not shattered by a perception of manipulation but on the contrary enhanced by a perception of achievement recognition. People are more performant if they perceive the financial bonus as a signal of the building manager's goodwill or as an appreciation of their energy-saving performance ([20] for a review in the context of wages).

At the end of the experiment, the participants answered a questionnaire, which shed light on their motivation. This survey revealed that the main motivations of the participants were monetary during the experiment (30% rather agree that they kept performing the tasks to increase their payments; 57% strongly agree). This is consistent with our previous observation that if participants had been only driven by environmental concern the results would have been the same in the two treatments. The environmental protection through the funding of the student association also pushed the participants to carry out tasks, but to a lesser extent than the revenue earned for themselves (50% rather agree that it was a main goal and 10% strongly agree). Therefore, we cannot exclude that the financial incentives did not reduce for some participants the overall effort performance, by driving attention to four-anchors of financial premium by opposition to endless effort for the environment.

4 Conclusions and Policy Recommendations

The results of the experiment suggest that the bonus acts as a focal point for individuals. This confirms previous work on goal settings ([1], [24]). The consumer is characterized by reference-dependent preferences and the bonuses in our experiment act as reference points. The findings are also consistent with results in social psychology that show that individuals are strongly influenced by "injunctive norm" which are moral benchmarks or guidelines about what the individual should do in a given context (see [14] for the role of social norms in energy reduction).

The results also suggest that policymakers and building managers can choose the focal points to push individuals to achieve a minimum effort relative to the situation without a financial bonus. However, our results show that the premium can have a perverse effect on those who without any premium were willing to make significant efforts (efforts far beyond what would have been necessary to obtain the highest premium). This is what psychologists and economists call an eviction effect whereas intrinsic motivations are shattered by extrinsic financial awards. This effect raises the question of the usefulness of a premium or the question of its targeting based on preferences. In practice, the idea is that if the individuals whose behaviour is to be changed have already internalized an environmental morality, the bonus can be counterproductive (the overall effect can, therefore, be negative). This also confirms that to obtain an average significant effect, the threshold or financial incentives have to be high enough. The goals have to be clearly set and not too easy to reach. In our experiment, the reference points for each bonus level were not high enough. In addition to the crowding-out effect already mentioned, the income effect may matter.

Some consumers may feel that when they have saved enough money, the marginal cost of additional effort is not worth it anymore.

The choice of an incentive mechanism (monetary or non-financial) depends on the households characteristics. The right incentive should be selected based on the households' lifestyles and degrees of concern for environment and energy-cost. People who are mainly concerned about monetary gains/costs represent a receptive audience for a bonus. On the contrary, for residents with a strong environmental moral, bonuses are likely to be counterproductive. For the latter, the salience of the social frame is replaced by that of the gain frame.

Smart buildings generate data which can serve as foundation for energy conservation. This experiment shows that it is necessary to go further and to gather information about consumer's preferences toward energy. Accenture [2] has shown that preferences vary widely among the population and across countries. This study segments consumers into six categories according to their preferences (based on savings sensitivity, ability and willingness to deal with bill complexities, sensitivity to social pressure, interest in reducing footprint on the environment, trade-off between comfort level and savings, acceptance of utility control and promptness to adopt new technologies). The six categories of consumers are skepticals, pragmatics, cost conscious, eco-rationals, proactives and indifferents. The consumers most sensitive to costs (cost conscious and to a lower extent pragmatics) would be more responsive to financial bonuses than the other categories. On the contrary, the bonuses would be less effective and could even be counterproductive for consumers identified as eco-rationales. Data can be used to identify consumer's profile and behavior and design consumer centric policies. Smart buildings and proactive management of energy use can provide a better consumer experience, reduce consumption and utility costs. This could be an additional argument to attract potential tenants in smart buildings.

Acknowledgements We would like to thank Flovic Gosselin who coded the experiment in oTree.

General Instructions for the Treatment of Control Without Bonus (Original Instructions Were in French)

This part in which you will participate is dedicated to the study of decision making. We request that you carefully read the instructions, they should allow you to fully comprehend this part. When all participants have read the instructions, an experimenter will proceed to read them one more time out loud.

All your decisions are treated anonymously. Indicate your choices with the help of the computer located in front of you. The total sums won in this part are expressed in points. Starting this moment, we would like to ask you to stop all communications. If you have any questions, raise your hand and an experimenter will come and answer them in private.

General overview

This part allows you to perform your tasks on the computer screen. A period is defined as a screen page containing 50 tasks. To validate a period and move to the next one, all 50 tasks must be completed successfully. Each task consists of turning-off a light bulb by moving it from left to right.

IMPORTANT: **you should turn off all the light bulbs to move on to the next step. You are free to complete as many periods as you wish.**

Your profit from this experience is proportional to the number of periods completed.

Example:

Suppose you validate 30 periods but while working on the 31st, you only complete 15 tasks out of 50. You do not validate the 31st period.

The first 5 periods validated will provide you with 50 points each. Periods 6 to 10, 11 to 15, 16 to 20, 21 to 25 and 26 to 30 provide respectively 40 points, 32 points, 26 points, 20 points and 16 points each.

Therefore, your earnings are equal to: (5*50 points) + (5*40 points) + (5*32 points) + (5*26 points) + (5*20 points) + (5*16 points) = 920 points.

Your earning decreases by 20% after each lot of 5 validated periods.

Important:

In addition, we are committed to allocate an amount equal to 5% of your earnings to a university student association promoting environmental practices (Eco-geste association). Of course, this contribution will not be deducted from your earnings, but collected from Anthropolab's budget. The association Eco-geste engages in promoting pro-environmental actions on campus through awareness and information campaigns.

Amount paid to the association Eco-geste:

For example, suppose you validate 27 periods during this part.

The first 5 periods validated will provide you with 50 points each. Periods 6 to 10, 11 to 15, 16 to 20, 21 to 25 and 26 to 30 provide respectively 40 points, 32 points, 26 points, 20 points and 16 points each.

Your earnings are: (5*50 points) + (5*40 points) + (5*32 points) + (5*26 point) + (5*20 points) +(2*16 points)= 872 points.

The amount paid to the association Eco-geste is therefore: 5%*872 points = 44 points.

Important: You have 60 minutes to complete as many periods as you wish.

Each period unfolds identically as the last one.

«Summary» screen:

At the end of each period, a «Summary» screen will appear on your screen. This screen will inform you of your earnings in points for this period, the number of periods validated, your cumulated earnings since the beginning of this part and the amount Eco-geste will benefit from thanks to your efforts. This screen will also provide you with a reminder of the conversion rate of the cumulated points in euros: 1 point = 0.015 euro.

Each 5 periods, the «summary» screen provides you with your earnings in euro.

Once you validated the «Summary» screen, a second screen will appear. You then have two possibilities: «Start the next period» or «Go to the Internet»

- If you click on the «Start the next period» button, another screen with 50 turned-on light bulbs appears and you can continue to turn-off the light bulbs.
- If you click on the «Go to the Internet» button, a web page will open automatically. You will therefore be able to go on the website of your choice (to consult your mails, go on Facebook or your usual websites). If you choose to click on the «Go to the Internet» button, you will not be able to complete the task, your decision becomes irreversible. Nobody knows which option you choose.

«History» screen

At the end of the time assigned for this part (60 minutes), you see a «History» screen appear.

This screen informs you of the total number of periods that you have completed, your total earnings in points and in euros cumulated for the duration of this part and the total amount in points and in euros that your efforts allowed the association Eco-geste to perceive.

****

General Instruction for the Treatment with Bonus (Original Instructions Were in French)

(The instructions are identical to the treatment of control without bonus, except for the description of earnings. We will therefore limit ourselves here to present example to illustrate the earnings with bonus)

Your earnings for this part are proportional to the number of periods effectively validated.

Example:

Suppose you validate 30 periods during this part.

The first 5 periods validated will provide you with 50 points each. Periods 6 to 10, 11 to 15, 16 to 20, 21 to 25 and 26 to 30 provide respectively 40 points, 32 points, 26 points, 20 points and 16 points each.

Therefore, your earnings are equal to: (5*50 points) + (5*40 points) + (5*32 points) + (5*26 points) + (5*20 points) + (5*16 points) = 920 points.

Your earning decreases by 20% after each lot of 5 validated periods.

Your earnings per period are diminishing but remain positive. In other words, each validated period accumulates to the amount that you will receive.

Important:

You receive a bonus starting from 30 validated periods. The maximum bonus, for 45 validated periods and above, is equal to 296 points.

Four thresholds are used to calculate the bonus. A first level bonus (equal to 28 points) is paid for 30 validated periods, a second level (equal to 111 points) for

35 periods, a third (equal to 222 points) for 40 periods and finally the last level (corresponding to the maximum level equal to 296 points) for 45 validated periods and above.

- If you validate a **maximum of 29 periods during this part, you are not eligible for the bonus.**
- If you validate between **30 periods and 34 periods, you receive an additional gain of 28 points corresponding to the 1st level of the graph.**
- If you validate between **35 periods and 39 periods, you'll receive an additional gain of 111 points corresponding to the 2nd level.**
- If you validate between **40 periods and 44 periods, you'll receive an additional gain of 222 points corresponding to the 3rd level.**
- If you validate at **least 45 periods, you'll receive an additional gain of 296 points corresponding to the 4th level.**

See Fig. 4

Amount paid to the association Eco-geste:

In addition, we are committed to allocate an amount equal to 5% of your earnings to a university student association promoting environmental practices (Eco-geste association). Of course, this contribution will not be deducted from your earnings, but collected from Anthropolab's budget. The association Eco-geste engages in promoting pro-environmental actions on campus through awareness and information campaigns.

For example, suppose you validate 37 periods during this part.

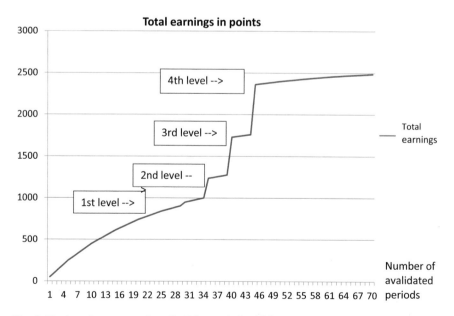

Fig. 4 Total earnings per number of validate periods with bonus payment

The first 5 periods validated will provide you with 50 points each. Periods 6 to 10, 11 to 15, 16 to 20, 21 to 25, 26 to 30, 31 to 35 and 36 to 37 provide respectively 40 points, 32 points, 26 points, 20 points, 16 points, 13 points and 10 points each.

You earnings without bonus are: *(5*50 points) + (5*40 points) + (5*32 points) + (5*26 points) + (5*20 points) + (5*16 points) + (5*13 points) + (2*10 points) = 1005 points.*

The amount paid to the association Eco-geste is then: **5%*1005 points = 50 points.**

Your total earning is the amount calculated above that served as a reference to subsidize Eco-geste plus the bonus of 111 points resulting to 1116 points.

****

References

1. Abeler, J., Falk, A., Goette, L., & Huffman, D. (2011). Reference points and effort provision. *American Economic Review, 101*(2), 470–492.
2. Accenture. (2010). *Understanding consumer preferences in energy efficiency, accenture end–consumer observatory on electricity management*, 2010 ACC10-0229, retrieved at https://www.accenture.com/t20160811t002327__w__/us-en/_acnmedia/accenture/next-gen/insight-unlocking-value-of-digital-consumer/pdf/accenture-understanding-consumer-preferences-energy-efficiency-10-0229-mar-11.pdf, on May 7, 2020.
3. Allcott, H. (2011). Social norms and Energy conservation. *Journal of Public Economics, 95*(9–10), 1082–1095.
4. Allcott, H. (2016). Paternalism and energy efficiency: An overview. *Annual Review of Economics, 8,* 145–176.
5. Allcott, H., & Kessler, J. (2019). The welfare effects of nudges: A case study of energy USE social comparisons. *American Economic Journal: Applied Economics, 11*(1), 236–276.
6. Allcott, H., & Mullainathan, S. (2010). Behavior and energy policy. *Science, 327*(5970), 1204–1205.
7. Allcott, H., & Rogers, T. (2014). The short-run and long-run effects of behavioral interventions: Experimental evidence from energy conservation. *American Economic Review, 104*(10), 3003–3037.
8. Andreoni, J. (1995). Warm-glow versus cold-prickle: The effects of positive and negative framing on cooperation in experiments. *The Quarterly Journal of Economics, 110*(1), 1–21.
9. Ariely, D., Bracha, A., & Meier, S. (2009). Doing good or doing well? Image motivation and monetary incentives in behaving prosocially. *American Economic Review, 99*(1), 544–555.
10. Becker, L. J. (1978). Joint effect of feedback and goal setting on performance: A field study of residential energy conservation. *Journal of Applied Psychology, 63*(4), 428–433.
11. Becker, L. J., Seligman, C., Fazio, R. H., & Darley, J. M. (1981). Relating attitudes to residential energy use. *Environment and Behavior, 13,* 590–609.
12. Belaïd, F., & Garcia, T. (2016). Understanding the spectrum of residential energy-saving behaviours: French evidence using disaggregated data. *Energy Economics, 57,* 204–214.
13. Benabou, R., & Tirole, J. (2006). Incentives and prosocial behaviour. *American Economic Review, 96*(5), 1652–1678.
14. Bradley, P., Fudge, S., & Leach, M. (2018). The role of social norms in incentivising energy reduction in organisations. In *Research handbook on employee pro-environmental behaviour*. Chektenham, UK: Edward Elgar Publishings.
15. Charness, G., & Kuhn, P. (2011). Lab labor: what can labor economists learn from the lab? *Handbook of Labor Economics, 4,* 229–330.

16. Charness, G., Gneezy, U., & Henderson, A. (2018). Experimental methods: Measuring effort in economics experiments. *Journal of Economic Behavior and Organization, 149*(C), 74–87.
17. Darby, S. (2006). *The effectiveness of feedback on energy consumption—A review for DEFRA of the literature on metering, billing and direct displays.* Environmental Change Institute, Oxford University. http://www.eci.ox. ac.uk/research/energy/downloads/sma rt-metering-report. pdf. Accessed 25 March 2010.
18. DellaVigna, S., & Pope, D. (2018). What motivates effort? evidence and expert forecasts. *Review of Economic Studies, 85,* 1029–1069.
19. Frey, B. S. (1999). *Economics as a science of human behaviour* (2nd ed., p. 247). Boston and Dordrecht: Kluwer.
20. Gagné, M., Weibel, A., Wiemann, M., & Osterloh, M. (2014). A behavioral economics perspective on the overjustification effect: Crowding-in and crowding-out of intrinsic motivation. In *The oxford handbook of work engagement, motivation, and self-determination theory.* Oxford University Press.
21. Gillingham, K., Rapson, D., & Gernot, W. (2015). The rebound effect and energy efficiency policy. *Review of Environmental Economics and Policy, 10*(1), 68–88.
22. Greiner, B. (2015). Subject pool recruitment procedures: Organizing experiments with ORSEE. *Journal of the Economic Science Association, 1*(1), 114–125.
23. Hahn, R., & Metcalfe, R. (2016). The impact of behavioral science experiments on energy policy. Economics of Energy & Environmental Policy, *International Association for Energy Economics, 0*(2).
24. Harding, M., & Hsiaw, A. (2014). Goal setting and energy conservation. *Journal of Economic Behavior & Organization, 107*(A), 209–227.
25. Jessoe, K., & Rapson, D. (2014). Knowledge is (less) power: Experimental evidence from residential energy use. *American Economic Review, 104*(4), 1–42.
26. Lindenberg, S. (2006). In D. Fetchenhauer, A. Flache, B. Buunk, & S. Lindenberg (Eds.), *Solidarity and prosocial behavior: An integration of sociological and psychological perspectives.* Amsterdam: Kluwer.
27. Martiskainen, M. (2007). *Affecting consumer behaviour on energy demand.* Final report to EdF Energy. Brighton, UK: Sussex Energy Group, 64 pages.
28. McClelland, L., & Cook, S. W. (1980). Energy conservation in university buildings: Encouraging and evaluating reductions in occupants' electricity use. *Evaluation Review, 4*(1), 119–133. https://doi.org/10.1177/0193841X8000400107.
29. Pellerano, J., Price, M. K., Puller, S. L., & Sanchez, G. E. (2017). Do Extrinsic Incentives Undermine Social Norms? Evidence from a Field Experiment in Energy Conservation. *Environmental Resource Economics, 67*(3), 413–428.
30. Shearer, B., Some, H. N., & Fortin, B. (2018). Measuring physicians' response to incentives: Evidence on hours worked and multitasking. *SSRN Electronic Journal.* https://doi.org/10.2139/ssrn.3211451.
31. Tversky, A., & Kahneman, D. (1974). Judgment under uncertainty: Heuristics and biaises. *Sciences New Series, 185,* 1124–1131.
32. Yates, S. M., & Aronson, E. (1983). A social psychological perspective on energy conservation in residential buildings. *American Psychologist, 38*(4), 435–444. https://doi.org/10.1037/0003-066X.38.4.435.
33. Yue, T., Long, R., & Chen, H. (2013). Factors influencing energy-saving behavior of urban households in Jiangsu province. *Energy Policy, 62,* 665–675.

The Obstacles of Circular Economy in the Real Estate Sector

Joanne Peirani and Nicolas Cochard

Abstract Kardham group offers services regrouping 3 main activities: real estate consultancy, architecture and development. Our group has decided to integrate the principles of circular economy in projects, more particularly in development projects. We therefore approached actors that were already present in this market and our operation teams to perform a first diagnostic. Apart from the evident opportunities that this approach provides, there are obstacles that we seek to identify in order to better overcome them. Despite the potential that circular economy represents and the presence of several actors in this domain, what are the obstacles that exist in the implementation of this type of operation? First of all, there are behavioral obstacles. Mentalities are evolving concerning environmental performance but there lies a need to convince the decision makers that circular economy represents a long-term value creation for the enterprise if integrated into the value chain. In addition, there are regulatory and legal obstacles. In the absence of adaptation to certain materials, we observe that they will be excluded from the reintegration market (absence of procedure reports attesting the performance). The lack of insurance and guaranty of certain equipment technique can also slow down the reuse and reintegration. If we want a holistic approach to circular economy, we think it is imperative that the market doesn't get compartmentalized... Finally, there are obstacles that exist in the implementation: we are only at the early stages of this step having very fluctuant volume of accessible materials. On the other hand, technical information on these materials often does not exist. We have feedback from building professionals based on their experience explaining that the diligent removal and refurbishing of materials involves overtime to integrate them into projects.

Keywords Circular economy · Materials · Equipment · Reuse · Sustainable development · Usage · Obstacles · Real estate · Value

J. Peirani (✉)
ACA Sustainable Development Project Manager, Groupe Kardham, Paris, France
e-mail: jpeirani@kardham.com

N. Cochard
Head of Research and Development, Groupe Kardham, Paris, France
e-mail: ncochard@kardham.com

© Springer Nature Switzerland AG 2021   159
E. Magnaghi et al. (eds.), *Organizing Smart Buildings and Cities*,
Lecture Notes in Information Systems and Organisation 36,
https://doi.org/10.1007/978-3-030-60607-7_10

1 Introduction

"Circular economy refers to an economic model whose objective is to produce goods and services in a sustainable manner, by limiting the consumption, the squander of resources and waste generation. This is about breaking-up the linear economic model for a circular economic model"[1] according the Ministry of Ecological and Solidary Transition.

Linear economy is based on 3 main stages "take, make, dispose of" [15]. This economic model has been the basis of many industries for centuries leading to a huge depletion of natural resources. According to the European Environment Agency [14], construction and demolition alone represent over a third of Europe's waste generation. The sector has a crucial impact on Europe's economy accounting for 9% of the EU's GDP [16], but is nevertheless one of the most wasteful. Therefore, through a wave of growing concern about linear economy and its lasting effects, circular economy increased its popularity amongst scholars doubling the number of publications yearly in the past 3 years [6].

The adoption of circular economy in the construction business is becoming inevitable in a world with scarce finite resources. Along that process, many countries have demonstrated their willingness through governmental support and incentives, research and development, and spreading awareness. According to the European Federation of Sustainable Business' report on circular economy (2019), leaders in this area such as the Netherlands and Germany have set an example through legislation and regulation favoring the implementation of circular economy throughout the different pillars of the economy. France is also considered as one of the top performers in Europe ranking 3rd in material reuse, 3rd in private investments and 2nd in patent creation based on Politico's 2018 Circular Economy Index. France has already elaborated a set of Extended Producer Responsibility (EPR) schemes in order to assign accountability over producers and manufacturers [20]. Nevertheless, the country is struggling to implement new schemes and regulations to the construction and demolition industry producing 80% of total waste [18].

Seven pillars of circular economy grouped in three areas were identified by the minister of Ecological and Solidary Transition. The first concerns the supply of economic actors and includes sustainable procurement, eco-design, industrial and territorial ecology and the economy of functionality. Sustainable procurement consists of taking into account the environmental and social impacts of the used resources. The eco-design is the consideration of the environmental impacts on a product's entire life-cycle while seeking to reduce them. Industrial and territorial ecology is the synergy and mutualization between several economic actors from their energy flux, material, water, infrastructure, goods or services in order to optimize the use of territorial resources. The economy of functionality concerns the fact of privileging usage instead of possession. The second area covers the demand and behavior of consumers and regroups responsible consumerism with the extension of usage duration. Responsible consumerism takes into account the environmental and

---

[1](*L'économie circulaire* n.d.) https://www.ecologique-solidaire.gouv.fr/leconomie-circulaire.

social impact in all the stages of a products' life cycle while making the choice of purchase. The extension of usage duration is done through referring to maintenance, sale or purchase of second-hand, donation, or for reintegration or reusage. The third and final area concerns waste management by improving the prevention, control and recycling of waste through reinjecting and reusing the materials generated from waste in the economic cycle.

First of all, the building is little compatible with durability because of its great consumption of resources and waste generation. In addition, the context is from the emergence of questions related to durability and environmental concerns in the real estate universe. Still embryonic, this reflection nurtures building-related careers most notably engineering and consultancy with a perspective, in accordance to the government's circular economy roadmap published on April 23, 2018, "of taking action by presenting concrete measures in order to achieve these goals."[2]

It is this context that urged our reflection. The following matter is a result of a professional and not a theoretic-conceptual approach. In addition, we do not pretend to communicate the general situation of the sector but more precisely our field experience in development projects that we manage. By "development", we mean the organization and design of an interior space in a tertiary building. Most commonly, clients demand a particular care to be provided for the comfort of the workers and the sorting of office waste. The questions relative to the materials or the recourse to second-hand or recycled products are still limited. Circular economy remains for the moment an element aiming to differentiate us from the competition during contentions and tender offers. Our enterprise wishes to be proactive in order to help the democratization of this practice in the development of interior spaces.

We decided to integrate the principles of circular economy in these projects but we were confronted by several obstacles in the implementation process. An obstacle blocks actions movement or hinders their progress.[3]

What are the obstacles that exist in the implementation of circular economy practices in development projects? What are the schools of thought that we can reflect upon to overcome them? Are professional feedbacks encouraging?

In order to examine this problematic, our methodology will consist of a dialogue between the theoretical approach, serving to provide a conceptual precision, confronted by our field approach as building professionals. We believe that this dialogue is particularly fruitful.

In first place, we will evoke our current practice of circular economy and the different actors with whom we are evolving, we will then unravel the internal and external obstacles that we have identified on the field.

In second place, we will transmit our preliminary feedbacks based on our professional experience.

---

[2] Roadmap for the circular economy [34].

[3] Retrieved from Cambridge Dictionary (*OBSTACLE|Meaning in the Cambridge English Dictionary* n.d.).

2 Literature Review

Nowadays, only few information is provided in literature on obstacles related to circular economy in the real estate sector in France. In fact, this concept is relatively recent and most published articles are institutional or fixated on the possible development axes of circular economy. We can note however that the French government, by publishing its "Roadmap for the circular economy" on April 23, 2018 gave its strategy for the development of this practice on a large scale.

Circular economy in the construction industry relies on several pillars in order to succeed, most notably on economic, behavioral, political, environmental, technological and social factors [29]. These externalities play a critical role in achieving the optimal building life cycle throughout all its stages: designing, planning, building, maintaining, refurbishing or reusing [29] According to Leising et al. [26], the life cycle of a building is an optimization of its useful lifespan through an integration of the building's end-of-life into the design phase whereby all materials act as inventory in the building, now considered a «material bank» [26]

Moreover, Geissdoerfer et al. [17] identified circular economy in construction as a creation of a closed-loop system adhering to an appropriate design, maintenance and refurbishing plan to regenerate resources and reuse materials. These elaborations of building life-cycle and estimations of efficiency revolve around the concept of LCA[4] presented by the European standard EN 15978:2011. The model allows the calculation of the 4 life-cycle stages represented by manufacture, construction, operation and end-of-life.

Europe has been demonstrating interest in the application of circular economy especially in the construction business. One of its most prominent projects, BAMB (Building As Material Bank), funded by the EU funded horizon program 2020, was initiated in 2015 to sponsor and support the use of circular economy through new standards and practices like RBD (Reversable Building Design) and "Building Material Passports" [3]. The project activated a wave of research towards developing new methods and tools to facilitate the implementation of circular economy in the complex world of construction ([10], [12], [13], [21], [27]).

Despite growing interest and an increase in publications around circular economy, the greatest challenge remains the lack of standards to implement circular economy in the construction sector [4]. In addition to the need of spreading awareness, Adams et al. [4] identified that government incentives for manufacturers and engineers to design products and buildings conformant with the requirements of circular economy are missing.

Hobbs and Adams [21] highlighted several barriers affecting the salvation and reuse of materials at the end of the building's useful life. These challenges represent in many ways a result of poor planning and design at the early stages of construction whether through the use of low quality materials or primitive technology [21]. Barriers also include a mismatch in supply and demand due to changes in quality and

---

[4]LCA: Life Cycle Assessment.

quantity, health and safety concerns in using manual deconstruction, time restrictions and availability of storage facilities [21].

Nevertheless, circular economy demonstrates multidimensional advantages mainly environmental and economic. In a circular economy, waste becomes a resource and the existing natural capital is preserved [19]. The salvation and the reuse of resources has allowed companies to introduce circular economy to their business models creating what Lacy and Rutqvist [35] referred to as «circular advantage». They demonstrated that the inclusion of circular economy in new business models favors resource productivity, decreases risks and costs, and most importantly creates a new income stream [24].

The ADEME[5] is a public establishment under the supervision of two ministers: the minister of Ecological and Solidary Transition and the minister of Higher Education, Research and Innovation. The agency participates in the implementation of public policies in the areas of environment, energy and sustainable development (*About ADEME* n.d.). On this occasion, it pilots scientific researches concerning circular economy on behalf of the French state. In fact, the objectives agreement which links the ADEME and the Minister of Ecological and Solidary Transition of 2009–2012 has already indicated without citing, the fabric of circular economy relative to the subjects of waste reduction, sustainable production and consumption, and eco-conception. The objectives agreement over the period of 2016–2019 devotes circular economy as a specific objective.

The ADEME published in December 2015 its report on a research called BAZED. The project aims at providing help for the preventative design of building waste. It addresses all active participants of a construction project by proposing actions for each step of the project. "Project BAZED is born from the conception of treating the issue of waste from its source and on the long term". This study involves a first phase audit of existing practices and most notably identifying the obstacles concerning the re-use due the precautionary principle [5].

In April 2016, a study dealing with the identification of constraints and levers of reusage was delivered by the ADEME. The study is named "Identification of constraints and levers of reclamation and reusage of construction products and materials". In addition to identifying the constraints and levers, it established an action plan to remove the former and activate the latter. In September 2016, the research project DEMOCLES aiming to advance the recycling of second-hand material was issued in a report by ADEME [11]. The research determines the constraints facing this type of recycling. In addition, the research program REPAR#2 [31], a sequel of REPAR#1 (2012–2014) which aimed at setting up reuse channels, published in 2018 its conclusions on the outlets that reusable products can find in architecture [32].

These different studies and research programs include for their majority either a roadmap, or an action plan, or a memo for the attention of the members of the building industry, allowing the theory to be concretely translated in practice.

---

[5]ADEME: ADEME is an active agency in the implementation of public policy in the areas of the environment, energy and sustainable development (Agence de l'Environnement et de la Maitrise de l'Energie en France).

3   The Evolution of Our Practices Towards Circular Economy and the Obstacles Encountered

Our enterprise indulged in circular economy at first as part of our business as developers. This business consists of organizing interior spaces in a tertiary building. Concretely, the first step of a project consists of creating a frame for the project by collecting input data and forming a multidisciplinary team to tackle the challenges of the project. In the second step, the team analyses the client's needs and performs a first non-detailed development plan called "macrozoning". It consists of formalizing the different spaces (meeting room, workspace, reprography area...) and their capacity in term of number of places. Once the draft plan is validated by the client, the third stage requires detailing the plan regarding the installation of partitions, furniture, etc.... The final step is relative to work implementation and performance monitoring.

We treat finishing-works assignments in two manners: either as general contractors, that is to say that we present a key provision to the client, either as project managers whereby we assist the client with the choice of companies that will execute the work. Our circular economy practice is recent since our enterprise started to take interest in circular economy based on a specific demand from a client at the end of 2018. In fact, the latter had requested a resource diagnostic of materials potentially reusable from the worksite. A resource diagnostic consists of performing a visit to the site and redeeming all materials in good shape and eligible for reintegration. A complementary analysis of the site's documentation should be performed in parallel to verify the technical results of the selected materials. A report is written to identify and list the material, its quantity, condition and location. Based on this demand from the client, we sought to develop our relative knowledge of circular economy. We reflected upon ourselves on the models' relevance in terms of our activity. Our reflection on the opportunity to set in place circular economy in our projects drove us to widely document the concept and to identify the ecosystem of actors present in France today and apply circular economy to buildings. Based on the client's request, we focused at first hand to identify what is in our capacity to answer. We identified a reusage platform that we contacted and has provided us with the know-how and the benefits of having recourse to these resource diagnostics. We made contact with the platform in order to answer the request of our client. After that meeting, we searched to identify the different actors present in the reusage market.

The historic actors of the construction industry are present. Namely, real estate agencies, promoters, assistants to the contracting authorities (ACA) and research bureaus. Other actors have emerged in the past years like the ACA specialized in circular economy or the material exchange platforms designated for reusage. To date, material exchange platforms act as circular economy ACAs in order to ensure the platforms' needs of material. Assisting a client consists of defining, piloting and exploiting the project. These ACAs handle resource diagnostics, which is equivalent to a material inventory. This step should take place at the beginning of the project during the research phase in order to integrate reusable materials from the conception phase. Therefore, the platforms can provide the site with materials. For this to happen, they contact demolition companies who are equally positioned in the safe removal market. This refers to a conscientious cleanse and storage of a building so that materials can be reintegrated or reused.

Associations have emerged like Circolab, "an association that aims at creating a community of actors in the real estate sector engaged in favor of circular economy and most notably reintegration".[6] The institute of circular economy has also been founded in 2014 and "has a mission to promote circular economy and accelerate its development through a collaborative dynamic".[7]

The various meetings that we were able to organize with other actors of circular economy, namely material exchange platforms, the ACAs of circular economy, the suppliers involved in the process and the fruitful exchanges that we were able to have with them, allowed us to better comprehend the challenges and objectives of each one of them. They all had an objective to reduce the amount of waste by prioritizing the extension of the materials' life-cycles. The challenge of reusage platforms is to be able to provide online a sufficient quantity of materials to intrigue the professionals in the construction industry. For the ACAs of circular economy, the challenge is to reconcile the environmental and social benefits of the process with the economic concerns of the project owners. For the suppliers and industrials engaged in this approach of circular economy, the free reclamation of raw material to reintegrate in their production line and the promotion of unsold or imperfect products are the main challenges. In this context where circular economy is requested by certain project owners, we had to build a network of partners with whom to evolve and on whom we could rely in the future. We had the opportunity to work with each of them on projects where we needed their expertise.

Simultaneously with these meetings, we confronted our job as developers to the seven pillars of circular economy in order to evaluate our scope of possible actions. The outcome of this study is that we can act on five of these pillars. First of all, concerning sustainable procurement, we are able to set in place a procurement policy which will integrate sustainable products into our basket of possible choices for our teams. Several headways are possible; prioritizing the recourse to certified products and materials, labelled or standardized by a third party like the product standard Cradle To Cradle[8] or the German eco-label Blue Angel[9] or to inquire with

our suppliers, principles of circular economy that they could integrate to their products. We can also recommend eco-designed products and furniture, i.e. that

---

[6](*Circolab—Laboratoire de l'Economie Circulaire—Les maîtres d'ouvrage dans le domaine de l'immobilier s'engagent en faveur de l'Economie Circulaire* n.d.).

[7]The institute is a collaboration between the public and private sector. (*Institut national de l'économie circulaire* n.d.).

[8]"Cradle to Cradle Certified™ is a globally recognized measure of safer, more sustainable products made for the circular economy" (*What Is Cradle to Cradle Certified^{TM} ?—Get Certified—Cradle to Cradle Products Innovation Institute* n.d.).

[9]"The Blue Angel is the ecolabel of the federal government of Germany since 1978. The Blue Angel sets high standards for environmentally friendly product design and has proven itself over the past 40 years as a reliable guide for a more sustainable consumption." (*Blue Angel* n.d.).

were subject to life-cycle analysis during their conception and whose objective is to reduce environmental and social impact. The eco-conception can also be applied on our scale by prioritizing materials or constructive systems that can be dismantled by mechanical assemblies for example and by excluding the recourse to adhesives and wet seals. Concerning the pillar relative to responsible consumption, it consists of organizing awareness campaigns to advise all the members of our company so they could determine, in their assigned projects, the possibilities of introducing circular economy. We are confronted by two possibilities concerning the pillar relative to the extension of usage duration. Either the project owner requests us to prioritize reusage and in this case we can for example resort to partners who build furniture from recycled wood, or reintegrate materials that are already kept in stock by the project owner. Or we advise the project owner on the possibilities that are made available to him of applying circular economy in his project. We study the most adapted way of having recourse to circular economy while responding to the projects' needs. Finally, concerning the pillar of waste management, we have to advise the project owner on his responsibility to treat the waste for his site. In fact, it is the project owner's legal responsibility to ensure that the waste generated for his project site are properly treated. Our company has to guide him through the options of the appropriate recycling channels and recommend a prior resource diagnostic when relevant in order to reduce the amount of waste to be treated.

Concerning our consulting activities, the environmental questions and more precisely those related to circular economy can be part of the mission at several levels of consideration. Undeniably, project owners have a certain degree of maturity or interest that is very heterogeneous with regard to these environmental issues. It is up to the ACAs to target the client's expectations by identifying this level of maturity and interest. A project that does not mention any consideration to the environment can reveal either a lack of interest or a lack of knowledge that does not always mean a lack of interest. This nuance should be decrypted so that the ACA can fully play his role and be proactive. The project owner is accompanied by the ACA in drafting the specifications document which is essential to the elaboration and implementation of a project because it does not just list the project's functionalities, or the client's expectations but it explains and demarcates the project and its conditions for accomplishment. It is this document that ensures the comprehension between the project stakeholders.

We intervene in two manners in the projects, either as project managers to conceive the development projects and help with the choice of companies to carry out the work on site, or as general contractors offering a complete mission of conception and implementation of the project. Our recommendations in favor of circular economy differ based on our company's role in the project.

Concerning the project management of a development, the mission consists of the conceiving the plans but does not include direct implementation of the work. A selection of companies may be provided but the responsibilities of deadlines and costs are within the client's hands. A project manager should therefore anticipate the exploitation, maintenance and upkeep or for example the recycling of waste. The client equally expects recommendations relative to products or materials deriving from circular economy that should be integrated in the specifications document for companies. Here, we mean recommendations relative to the manufacturing process such as the applied eco-design to furniture, or relative to sustainable procurement, for example through the recourse to materials from unsold for flexible floorings. Recycling is an integral part of the circular economy's loop defined by ADEME and must be considered jointly by the project owner and project manager.

Unlike the project manager, the general contractor is the only reference to the project because he assumes the totality of inherent obligations to the latter and to the project's management. In general contracting, the project owner expects an effort in identifying recoverable products and equipment as a particular care in their removal in order to recover them later on with the resale or reintegration in situ. The ideal is to stock up from the material platforms.

Nevertheless, we have to note that even though the previous remarks clarify the question of operational actors, they do not mention the necessary effort of "research and development" to supply a marketable offer. This element is quite important because it means that a company that wishes to invest in environmental issues is faced to invest beforehand in grey matter, therefore, if the investment occurs, companies hope to ultimately profit later-on, which explains the initial effort provided. In addition, this logic of research of development is naturally a process that cannot be limited in time but is rather continuous.

However, the remarks that we just made reveal a theoretical ideal that we'll have to confront in reality from our experience. This is what we now propose to detail.

4 The Obstacles Faced in the Integration of Circular Economy in Development Projects

We have identified four main types of obstacles from our expertise. To begin, we have observed obstacles related to behavior.

There is no study on the progress of environmental certifications in the French tertiary real estate sector. Nevertheless, our professional practice imparts that there is a slight increase in the number of project owners that request a certification for their project or consult us to implement sustainable development practices. However, this client profile remains marginal.

It is probable that certain project owners are not aware of such questions of circular economy and more broadly sustainable development. It is however possible that they do not know how these concepts can be translated into a development project. We have reflected upon this problematic and have adapted our initial scoping questionnaire that we perform at the beginning of each project. The questionnaire should allow the project team to fully comprehend the project's context, amass the client's needs, and analyze the site. It's on this occasion that the client will express his desire to include circular economy, a certification/labelling or sustainable development practices. By default, it will be up to the project team to offer awareness in order to inform the client, in the form of an exchange workshop, of the possibilities he possesses regarding his project. Following this awareness, the fully informed client will be able to make a clear decision. We are also confronted by a lack of knowledge in our operational teams on the concept of circular economy itself. It is only recently that circular economy was included in the curriculum of architecture and engineering schools. Based on this fact, an internal training program is necessary to increase the skills of the « knowledgeable » in order for them to adapt their work process and have a genuine role in consulting their customers.

Likewise, the research program REPAR #2, published in march 2018 and directed by Bellastock[10] in partnership with the CTSB[11] highlights obstacles relative to the lack of trust between the different partakers of a project which is translated by an absence of inter-site logistics and cultural and organizational constraints.

The project DEMOCLES, directed by Recylum[12] and the ADEME whose report took place in September 2016, aims at decrypting the difficulties encountered by the participants in construction concerning the recycling of end-of-work waste and to propose concrete and operational recommendations for the functions of project owners and project managers. The second work concerns all the non-constituent materials of the building structure. The plurality of types of materials generate low recovery rates even though they dispose of suitable recycling channels.

Constraints on access to deposit were detected by the project DEMOCLES by noting a lack of knowledge of recovery channels, the weight of the habits of participants prioritizing the mixture of elements to the detriment of alternative containers, and a rate of recovery from the sorting center which differs from the site's recovery rate.

We also note reluctance to change the way things are done, whether from our clients or our teams, on the questions of sorting the waste generated from the site or new practices to implement from an operational point of view. We have encountered in our field practice certain sites constrained by the lack of space or the impossibility of installing building tippers that could have led to questionable practices whereby the company implementing the work is encouraged to transport the waste generated from its site and treat them itself. This generates opacity in the chain of traceability of waste and can ultimately implicate the legal responsibility of the project owner.

It will be advisable to continue our approach of raising awareness to project owners and field teams in an attempt to remove these obstacles reflecting a lack of awareness of the possibilities offered by circular economy and their translation in our businesses, but also of the existing regulations, notably concerning waste management.

We are also confronted with a number of legal and insurance obstacles.

---

[10]Bellastock: association created in 2006 transformed into a Cooperative Society of Collective Interest in 2019 which practices the experimentation of the circular economy on the scale of the building and the city (*À Propos—Bellastock* n.d.).

[11]CSTB: Scientific and technical center of the building. It is a public establishment in France serving innovation in building and carries out 5 activities: research and expertise, evaluation, certification, testing and dissemination of knowledge (*Centre Scientifique et Technique Du Bâtiment* n.d.).

[12]Recylum: non-profit eco-organization responsible for collecting and recycling used lamps (*Recylum* n.d.).

In the absence of regulatory adaptation concerning certain materials, we observe that many of them will be excluded from the re-use market. If we want a holistic approach to circular economy, we believe it is imperative not to compartmentalize this market and allow all materials to be eligible for re-use. The case of fire doors is emblematic since a transcript is issued by the installer of these frames when they are installed because they require specific implementation. At the demolition phase of the building, these doors, requiring a greater amount of materials than a simple door, cannot be reemployed in their initial usage because no new transcript can be issued in the current state of the regulations.

In addition, the lack of insurance and warranty for certain technical equipment or materials can slow re-use. This is highlighted in the study of ADEME intitled "Identification of constraints and levers of reclamation and reusage of construction products and materials" published in April 2016, stating that "the platforms or resources dedicated to construction materials and products struggle to provide the products to the professionals. For the entities responsible of these structures, this defiance is linked to the problematic of the 10-year warranty, companies worry not being covered if they use reusable products". One of these reusage platforms has identified this obstacle and has partially remedied it by assuming a one-year insurance.

We observed obstacles related to the implementation of these materials in our projects.

We observe two possible scenarios for the implementation of projects. The first concerns the case where we are searching for materials on the reusable materials market through the exchange platforms or the industrials that apply destocking. The second scenario concerns the possibility made available to us by the resource diagnostic to reuse a certain number of materials on site directly. Our field experience has taught us that in the first scenario, the reuse of construction or development materials requires inquiring about product availability, quantity and their characteristics which are sometimes little known on the platforms or in limited stock. These problematics were raised by Bellastock and the CSTB in the research program REPAR#2: "unpredictability of the deposit in frequency, in renewal and in geometrical, mechanical and chemical requirements" [31]. The research project BAZED directed by NOBATECK, XB Architecture and ARMINES in partnership with the ADEME whose report, published in December 2015, also mentions this obstacle: "designing with reclaimable materials requires additional time: to locate the materials, recover them and recondition them. It is important to calculate if the additional time can be compensated by the profit on material prices" [5]. In fact, we observe in practice an extension of the project's conception time. The second scenario can pose difficulties for the weak current, for example. Technologies quickly evolve, this type of channel has to adapt. In our case of tertiary building developments, the replacement of this lot is often preferred. However, these materials may be suitable for another type of building that is less demanding.

In developments, materials are very heterogeneous since the project DEMOCLES has identified 24 categories of finished work waste making each site distinctive. Certain materials like the partition walls are generally built on measure based on their height because each project can have a different ceiling height. It is therefore easier to reuse them on the original site.

Each project is currently subject to the case-by-case rule. Field experience will certainly allow us to gain agility.

Finally, we notice market obstacles.

We hear by «market obstacles», the difficulties that we might encounter when a practice is relatively recent and supply and demand are only at their infancy. Reusage platforms were developed and organized but the volume of materials transited through them may not yet be enough to encourage project managers to systematically use them. The choice of materials is still limited. We hope that by democratizing the approach of circular economy and notably resource diagnostics, a sufficient number of materials will be able to circulate and make this approach even more attractive. Nowadays, the platforms have to ensure the role of circular economy ACAs to identify resource pools and therefore provide their sites with materials. The procurement of second-hand materials can equally be achieved by manufacturers, for example by organizing themselves to recover unsold stocks. Hence, these products are less costly but in limited quantities and forms. They can present a certain interest in projects with reduced surfaces and tight budgets.

As mentioned by Bellastock and the CSTB in REPAR #2, "the obstacles do not stop experiments today [...]. Learning through practice is a real way of doing things in the field of re-employment". We were also persuaded that it is field experience that will allow us to overcome the obstacles and make circular economy a regular practice, meaning that we will be able to systematically propose it to clients or integrate it in our work process.

5   First Feedbacks

In this second part, we will share our most significant feedbacks based on our professional experience and will try to take the measure of the difficulties encountered on the field during the implementation of circular economy in our development projects.

Our first feedback dates from the 4th trimester of 2018 and concerns a building of 15000 m^2 located at the 9th district of Paris owned by the landlord. The latter wanted to rent its premises once the work has been completed. This client profile has real estate financial profitability as a primary objective. The building was to undergo a rehabilitation of its facade as well as an interior renovation. We were solicited for a project management mission (architecture and engineering) as well as digital project management and BIM (Building Information Modeling). The client wanted to know the potential of reemployment of available materials on site. We therefore contacted a reusable materials exchange platform in order to numerically quantify a "resource diagnostic" mission. In fact, these platforms initially provide the role of circular economy assistants to the contracting authorities. Finally, we were not able to pursue the process because the cleaning procedure of the building's most interesting materials identified by the resource diagnostic had already been initiated. We were confronted by the problematic of project planning. Anticipation proves necessary when one wishes to include material reemployment. Resource diagnostics must be carried out in advance in order to estimate and identify the materials eligible for reemployment. A test of cautious removal has to be equally applied to ensure that materials react accordingly to this operation. In this case, we were not able to set up this removal test since the materials eligible for reuse had already been cleaned. In the future, clients should be aware beforehand of the planning in order not to skip a step and allow the procedure to take place sequentially. It is important to note that the demand to perform a resource diagnostic was done by an investor whose primary objective was economic profitability. This is a prominent example that suggests the economic relevance of this type of model.

Our second feedback concerns a leading company specialized in the production of professional electronic materials for whom we have conducted the development project of their new head office of 18000 m^2 in the Parisian region of Courbevoie in 2018. We assure a mission of general contracting, i.e. the equivalent of "key in hand", namely from the layout design to the completion of the project. This is a particular case because we applied circular economy practices without specific request from the client. A budgetary constraint pushed us to re-use a large part of the interior partitions. There were a multitude of consequences on the project. First of all, the planning was impacted since a cautious cleaning of these partitions had to be prearranged. Then the question of on-site storage arose by floor. And finally, the cleaning of partitions was not enough, the application of electrostatic paint on all surfaces was required. The paint generated specific protection issues for workers (masks), the implementation took place in staggered work hours in addition to the consequent time for drying. We can conclude from this experience that the environmental question was not in the center of concerns but that circular economy was imposed based on its economic interest. Even when taking into account the necessary adaptations in terms of planning, forecasting works and purchasing additional equipment and materials, the balance was tipped in favor of reusage. This demonstrates that from an economic point of view, circular economy can be pertinent. The scale of the project is certainly more suitable to this exercise than a smaller project.

Our third feedback concerns a French telecommunication company that had solicited us to carry out the interior development of one of its sites in the first semester of 2019. It was a general contracting mission on a 12000 m^2 building located in the Parisian area. The project owner had requested at the beginning of the project that we present him the principles of circular economy. This request is certainly based on his Corporate Social Responsibility (CSR) policy. In fact, our client is part of the companies that complied to the *Carbon Disclosure Project* (CDP) that aims at reducing the environmental impact of supply chains, from the procurement of raw materials to the delivery of products to the end-consumer, by taking into account all these flows. Moreover, as part of his certification ISO 14001,[13] the certifying entity

---

[13]ISO 14001 sets out the criteria for an environmental management system and can be certified to. It maps out a framework that a company or organization can follow to set up an effective environmental management system. (*ISO—ISO 14000 Family—Environmental Management* n.d., p. 14001).

had recommended to include circular economy more often in projects. The project team met with the client to present these elements and discuss how to integrate them into the project. However, it would seem that he had a hard time to contemplate ahead of the project since we were in the design phase. The client wished to see a budget and schedule comparative with a new implementation process. However, circular economy can be implemented by purchasing eco-designed products. This is what was proposed for furniture procurement in order to at least respect the essence of the initial project. Through eco-design, a new project can also benefit from circular economy with responsible purchasing. In addition, it will be interesting to reflect at enhancing the presentation of the principles of circular economy in the design phase to make the concept more understandable and help the project owner envision it more easily. An awareness of the project teams will allow a better understanding of the process so that we can then take ownership of it throughout the project and better transmit it to our customers.

The fourth feedback relates to the development of an office space at La Défense in the Paris region with a surface area of 356 m^2 for a French oil company in the first semester of 2019. It consists of a project management mission concerning architectural lots and office furniture. The project owner expressed, from the start of our collaboration, his desire to greatly include circular economy in the development project. We collected the testimony of the project's architecture manager; whose main lines are as follows. The project team successfully integrated a destocking carpet from two major specialist brands that have invested in the circular economy for several years. The choice of colors and textures is limited but pertinent from a financial point of view. Nevertheless, this requires additional time invested in research. This approach can prove to be very interesting in projects with tight budgets. We also had to make the "studio" aware of the matter of circular economy in order not to go outside the framework that was given by the client. The studio is a specialized pole within our company dealing with the artistic creation of layouts, that is to say that the interior designers give the identity of the project by selecting among others the floor coverings, the light fixtures or furniture. Their work process was inverted since a pre-selection of the materials, on which they had to build their visual identity of the offices, had already been made. Regarding carpentry arrangements, which are custom-made architectural elements, we called on recognized players in the reuse of materials. One of them is specialized in the creation of tailor-made furniture from reclaimed wood but in a collaborative manner with the teams intended to use these layouts. The furniture was also to be part of the elements issued by circular economy principles but due to budget constraints at the end phase of the work, the project owner decided to purchase part of the furniture himself through a framework contract with a furniture supplier for the whole group. Ergo, the furniture will not be exclusively issued from reused materials. Projects like this one allow us to make new professional encounters with partners that we had not identified beforehand. We have opened up to new practices, such as the destocking of materials, revealing interesting economic prospects. However, this project allowed us above all to capitalize, gain experience in circular economy, enhance our project teams' skills and by extension allow us to have our first feedbacks engaging our company definitively on the path of circular economy.

6 Conclusion

We can conclude by underlining that a circular economy approach can be undertook at first hand easily through the modification of the procurement policy by prioritizing eco-designed products. We have to pursue tackling each obstacle that we have mentioned in order to turn them into opportunities. Several among them (regulatory and legal obstacles) do not depend on us. We have to be patient for the legal system to take into account these new methods and facilitate them. However, we can react directly on other constraints like behavioral ones through properly training our teams. As designers and developers of facilities, we can also educate our partners and suppliers on our difficulties and operational needs so that they improve their products in the direction of eco-design.

The different constraints perceived in the market pose a challenge to both developers and governmental agencies to reduce the construction sector's environmental impact. Although several entities like the ADEME and the Ministry of Ecological and Solidary Transition are pushing towards circular economy, it remains an uncertain choice for developers and project managers alike due to its neoteric nature. That is why we feel that professional feedback and field experience are crucial at this stage of circular economy in order to help ease uncertainty for the different participants in the construction industry ranging from manufacturers to clients. In addition, an emphasis should be added to the importance of awareness of the benefits of circular economy from both an environmental and economic point of view. In this time, where circular economy is still emerging, the role of the government is as crucial as ever to promote this practice from a legal, regulatory and fiscal standpoint in order for the industry to benefit from "circular advantage". In turn, we as professionals, provide our experiences and observations to best serve the implementation of circular economy.

The first feedbacks are of good omen although for the moment limited or involuntarily circular.

References

1. *À Propos—Bellastock.* (n.d.). Bellastock. Retrieved May 18, 2020, from https://www.bellastock.com/a-propos/.
2. *About ADEME.* (n.d.). ADEME. Retrieved May 18, 2020, from https://www.ademe.fr/en/about-ademe.
3. *About bamb.* (2020). BAMB. https://www.bamb2020.eu/about-bamb/.
4. Adams, K., Osmani, M., Thorpe, A., & Thornback, J. (2017). Circular economy in construction: Current awareness, challenges and enablers. *Proceedings of the Institution of Civil Engineers—Waste and Resource Management*, 1–11. https://doi.org/10.1680/jwarm.16.00011.
5. *BAZED—Aide à la conception de bâtiments « zéro déchet ».* (2015, December). ADEME. https://www.ademe.fr/bazed-aide-a-conception-batiments-zero-dechet.
6. Benachio, G. L. F., Freitas, M. do C. D., & Tavares, S. F. (2020). Circular economy in the construction industry: A systematic literature review. *Journal of Cleaner Production, 260,* 121046. https://doi.org/10.1016/j.jclepro.2020.121046.

7. *Blue Angel.* (n.d.). Blue Angel. Retrieved May 18, 2020, from https://www.blauer-engel.de/en.
8. *Centre Scientifique et Technique du Bâtiment.* (n.d.). CSTB. Retrieved May 18, 2020, from http://www.cstb.fr/en/.
9. *Circolab—Laboratoire de l'Economie Circulaire – Les maîtres d'ouvrage dans le domaine de l'immobilier s'engagent en faveur de l'Economie Circulaire.* (n.d.). Retrieved May 18, 2020, from http://circolab.eu/.
10. Debacker, W., Manshoven, S., Peters, M., Ribeiro, A., & De Weerdt, Y. (2017). *Circular economy and design for change within the built environment: Preparing the transition.* https://repository.tudelft.nl/islandora/object/uuid%3A3f5ef013-fcef-499f-896e-2e4828526e4e.
11. *DEMOCLES: Les clés de la démolition durable.* (2016, Juillet). ADEME. https://www.ademe.fr/democles-cles-demolition-durable.
12. Durmisevic, E. (2016). *Dynamic and circular buildings by high transformation and reuse capacity.*
13. Durmisevic, E., Berg, M. van den, & Atteya, U. (2017). *Design Support for revisable buildings with focus on visualizing and simulating transformation capacity during initial design phase.*
14. EEA. (2020, January 16). *Construction and demolition waste: Challenges and opportunities in a circular economy* [Briefing]. European Environment Agency. https://www.eea.europa.eu/themes/waste/waste-management/construction-and-demolition-waste-challenges.
15. EMF. (2015, December 2). *Circular economy report—The circular economy—Towards a circular economy: Business rationale for an accelerated transition.* https://www.ellenmacarthurfoundation.org/publications/towards-a-circular-economy-business-rationale-for-an-accelerated-transition.
16. European Comission. (2016, April 1). *The European construction sector: A global partner* [Text]. Internal Market, Industry, Entrepreneurship and SMEs—European Commission. https://ec.europa.eu/growth/content/european-construction-sector-global-partner-0_en.
17. Geissdoerfer, M., Savaget, P., Bocken, N., & Hultink, E. (2017). The circular economy—A new sustainability paradigm? *Journal of Cleaner Production, 143,* 757–768. https://doi.org/10.1016/j.jclepro.2016.12.048.
18. Giorgi, S., Lavagna, M., & Campioli, A. (2018). Guidelines for effective and sustainable recycling of construction and demolition waste. In E. Benetto, K. Gericke, & M. Guiton (Eds.), *Designing sustainable technologies, products and policies: From science to innovation* (pp. 211–221). Springer International Publishing. https://doi.org/10.1007/978-3-319-66981-6_24.
19. Gutierrez, M. (2018, October 23). *Circular economy in construction is not just possible: It is necessary—Ferrovial's blog.* Blog. https://blog.ferrovial.com/en/2018/10/circular-economy-construction/.
20. Hird, A. (2019, July 11). *France drafts new chapter in the 'war on waste.'* RFI. http://www.rfi.fr/en/france/20190710-france-waste-recycling-circular-economy-environment.
21. Hobbs, G., & Adams, K. (2017). *Reuse of building products and materials—Barriers and opportunities.* https://repository.tudelft.nl/islandora/object/uuid%3Ad511af0d-2c03-4234-a6c2-ffb38ab0f232.
22. *Institut national de l'économie circulaire.* (n.d.). Retrieved May 18, 2020, from https://institut-economie-circulaire.fr/.
23. *ISO—ISO 14000 family—Environmental management.* (n.d.). ISO. Retrieved May 18, 2020, from https://www.iso.org/iso-14001-environmental-management.html.
24. Lacy, P., & Rutqvist, J. (2016). *Waste to wealth: The circular economy advantage* (p. 264). https://doi.org/10.1057/9781137530707.
25. *L'économie circulaire.* (n.d.). Ministère de la Transition écologique et solidaire. Retrieved May 18, 2020, from https://www.ecologique-solidaire.gouv.fr/leconomie-circulaire.
26. Leising, E., Quist, J., & Bocken, N. (2017). Circular Economy in the building sector: Three cases and a collaboration tool. *Journal of Cleaner Production, 176.* https://doi.org/10.1016/j.jclepro.2017.12.010.
27. Lowres, F., & Hobbs, G. (2017). *Challenging the current approach to end of life of buildings using a life cycle assessment (LCA) approach.* https://repository.tudelft.nl/islandora/object/uuid%3A4a76ed39-f40c-48f8-bdac-ab8086966f0b.

28. *OBSTACLE\meaning in the Cambridge English Dictionary.* (n.d.). Retrieved May 18, 2020, from https://dictionary.cambridge.org/dictionary/english/obstacle.
29. Pomponi, F., & Moncaster, A. (2016). *Circular economy for the built environment: A research framework.* https://doi.org/10.17863/CAM.7204.
30. *Recylum.* (n.d.). Retrieved May 18, 2020, from https://www.recylum.com/assets/sonepar/index.html.
31. *REPAR 2: Le réemploi passerelle entre architecture et industrie.* (2018, April). ADEME. https://www.ademe.fr/repar-2-reemploi-passerelle-entre-architecture-industrie.
32. *REPAR: Réemploi comme passerelle entre architecture et industrie.* (2014, March). ADEME. https://www.ademe.fr/repar-reemploi-comme-passerelle-entre-architecture-industrie.
33. *What is Cradle to Cradle Certified^{TM}?—Get Certified—Cradle to Cradle Products Innovation Institute.* (n.d.). Retrieved May 18, 2020, from https://www.c2ccertified.org/get-certified/product-certification.
34. https://www.ecologie.gouv.fr/sites/default/files/FREC%20anglais.pdf (in English). https://www.ecologie.gouv.fr/sites/default/files/Feuille-de-route-Economie-circulaire-50-mesures-pour-economie-100-circulaire.pdf (in French).
35. https://www.researchgate.net/publication/306234018_Waste_to_wealth_The_circular_economy_advantage.

Transforming the Catholic University of Lille Campus into a Smart Grid

Nicolas Gouvy, Jad Nassar, and Vincent Lefévère

Abstract Since the second World War, technological (r)evolutions have been further integrating our societies, causing a disruption not only in our life styles and know-how but also mentalities. Environmental awareness is a good example. Nowadays, everyone wants to be able to produce his/her own "green" and local energy. However, the French power grid, very centralized and hierarchical in its functioning, and requiring a lot of human intervention along its operations, was not thought of in this perspective of decentralization of energy. One of the solutions would be of course to create a new power grid. Another would be to use Information Technology to pilot the current power grid in a "smarter" way: this represents the Smart Grid. It is therefore a ubiquitous computer network parallel to the electrical network which must be built for communication. The Catholic University of Lille, a university in the heart of the city with a substantial and long-standing real estate heritage, has taken up this issue as part of its LiveTREE program.

Keywords Smart Grid · Smart Campus · Smart Building · LiveTREE · Wireless Sensor Networks

1 Introduction

Since 2008, Smart Grids (SG) have been at the center of the French research and development dynamic. The country has become a European leader in terms of investments, with over 108 demonstrators deployed on the French territory.

N. Gouvy (✉)
Université Catholique de Lille, Lille Cedex, France
e-mail: nicolas.gouvy@univ-catholille.fr

J. Nassar · V. Lefévère
Computer Science and Mathematics Departement, Yncréa Hauts-de-France, Lille, France
e-mail: jad.nassar@yncrea.fr

V. Lefévère
e-mail: vincent.lefevere@yncrea.fr

© Springer Nature Switzerland AG 2021
E. Magnaghi et al. (eds.), *Organizing Smart Buildings and Cities*,
Lecture Notes in Information Systems and Organisation 36,
https://doi.org/10.1007/978-3-030-60607-7_11

177

The SMILE (Smart Ideas to Link Energies) project aims to build a large intelligent power grid by 2020 in the departments of Morbihan, Ille-et-Vilaine, Loire-Atlantique and Vendée (*Objectifs et Enjeux|Smile* n.d.). It is supported by a consortium which brings together the regions of Brittany and Pays de la Loire, two cities, Rennes and Nantes, as well as 9 departmental unions for the distribution of electricity.

The FLEXGRID project, carried out by the PACA Region, combines 27 territorial projects and 5 cross-functional projects. The key themes of FLEXGRID are data management, the integration of renewable energies, electric vehicles, storage and intelligent buildings ("Le programme FLEXGRID" n.d.).

The YOU&GRID project of the Hauts de France region aims to deploy a range of services and technologies in smart grids in order to tackle energy transition challenges. This project should allow to test self-consumption on non-residential buildings on a large scale. The project also deals with the energy renovation of residential housing while managing the photovoltaic production and the integration of charging stations for electric vehicles in private parking lots (*You & Grid—Northern France|Enedis* n.d.).

2   Reinventing the City from Campus

Launched in 2013 by the Catholic University of Lille, LiveTREE represents the university's program for energy and social transition. It registers under Rev3—the Third Industrial Revolution in the Hauts-de-France region through a collaborative approach between the students, personnel, residents, companies and collectivities, the project aims to reduce the campus' carbon footprint and transform it to a living laboratory of social innovation (*Live Tree* n.d.).

LiveTREE intersects the disciplines and multidisciplinary functions of the University to experiment around energy, mobility, waste management, nature in the city or even social participation and new economic models.

The innovative solutions envisioned focus on the technical and human aspects of the transition and are tested in real conditions on the campus and its neighborhoods.

The energy aspects are particularly explored in LiveTREE, notably with the SoMEL SoConnected project which is part of YOU & GRID. The aim of this project is to enable the development of energy distribution networks to serve a territory through the connection of infrastructures. In light of that mission, the Faculties of the Catholic University of Lille and the Yncréa Hauts de France engineering school are developing self-consumption models of renewable energy in the non-residential sector.

3 Islet Replicable Strategy

Unlike the campus of many recent university sites mainly created on the outskirts of cities, the Catholic University of Lille has, since its creation in 1875, focused on the Vauban district of the city of Lille. This is in fact the Vauban campus of a university at the "heart of the city".

This Vauban campus represents around twenty buildings (a constantly increasing figure) for more than fifteen academic training entities, all belonging to the University federation. This represents a considerable and very heterogenous stock of real estate, ranging from individual townhouses converted into offices, to building complexes dating from the creation that have been little renovated or others that have been completely renovated.

The campus is centered around its historical "islet" formed by premises belonging to:

- The engineering school of HEI—Yncréa Hauts de France, whose last renovation dates back to 2013,
- The faculties of the Catholic University of Lille, namely the Academic Hotel, a historic building that was ultimately little renovated, and the newly renovated Rizomm in 2019.

It physically corresponds to the group of buildings surrounded by Rue du port, Rue de Toul, Rue Nobert Segard and the Vauban boulevard.

This historical islet also corresponds to an electric islet—the aggregate of buildings sharing a single point of power supply, this was the focus of the Smart Grid strategy carried by the University as part of the SoMEL SoConnected project. The underlying idea is to develop a reproducible approach on the other eight electrical islets identified on the perimeter of the Vauban campus.

The Rizomm building of the historical islet has therefore been heavily renovated and equipped with a photovoltaic power station with a surface area of 1500 m^2, whereas the Academic Hotel was equipped with electric vehicle charging stations.

On the HEI side, a more modest photovoltaic power station was installed.

In both cases, photovoltaic production is locally managed by the Technical Building Management (TBM) system to which the power station belongs. This will curb production (by degrading the conversion efficiency of inverters in photovoltaic power stations) so that it does not exceed the consumption of the associated building.

This functional approach has the merit of allowing a reduction in the energy consumption of the islet and contemplating the evolution of multiple buildings in the heart of the city from consumption points to mini self-consuming power stations without modifying the urban power grid.

Nevertheless, on the scale of a transformer station, that is to say of a district (or of a set of electrical islets), the overproduction of a building could potentially have been consumed by one of its neighbors.

For this reason, the power grid manager of the city of Lille, ENEDIS, has requested to intervene in the production management of the historic islet to provoke, at his request, and dynamically, the administration of the electric current produced in the metropolitan network based on the production forecast of buildings through their power stations, in addition to the consumption forecasts linked to the use of electric vehicle charging stations.

This is the demonstration project of Smart Grid SoMEL SoConnected.

The energy management considered within the framework of the SoMEL project requires numerous IT developments and full access to critical equipment such as building management systems which control and supervise electrical systems, heating and ventilation.

Initially, these approaches have been implemented by one of the leading Cloud companies to support the development and operation of IT systems using a "Software As A Service" approach. This means that the software solution developed to make the equipment controllable would be totally and exclusively executed on and for the company's Cloud platform.

4   A Dedicated Information System

It soon became apparent that the proposed approach lacked the necessary flexibility for a research project and stranded away from the partnership approach sought to move towards conventional service provision. The "loss of control" over the algorithms and data in a solution, the legal uncertainty linked to the provider's American origin and the functioning of the system, all in all, quite closed to developments, quickly posed a problem.

Ultimately, it was the unpredictability of recurring costs associated with a SAAS solution that convinced the need to develop a solution internally for the university.

It was then agreed that a dedicated LiveTREE Information System, common property of the participating entities, parallel to those operated in their own right, and managed accordingly with each department's information system, would be deployed and managed by IT researchers—for a budget lower than the cloud offer initially considered.

The system should be as reliable as possible (for a research project) while remaining open to future projects.

4.1   A Dedicated and Redundant Material Architecture

The reliability of an information system depends notably of its physical architecture. This refers to the number of servers used and the purpose of that use.

Hence, it was decided from the start to geographically distribute a set of identical and dedicated computer servers on two distinct sites: an already existing server room on the historic islet for one, and a nano server room created ex-nihilo for the other. A cross-backup system between the two sites is performed every night.

In each room, a dedicated server rack cabinet was installed in order to clearly distinguish between the entities' own equipment and the "common" equipment belonging to LiveTREE.

Each cabinet incorporates its ripple system in the event of a power outage, regardless of the site where it is installed. Each corrugated electrical outlet is monitored and operated remotely, making it possible to remotely stop/restart each server by controlling its power supply.

Each server is materially identical to the others, no matter its site.

The computing and storage power offered by the LiveTREE information system is therefore redundant on several levels: at the scale of each site and between the two sites. However, an asymmetry in the quantity of servers on each site was maintained to facilitate the operation of the software.

In order for these two sites to work together, it was necessary to connect them to each other and to the different buildings.

Similar to the means of calculation and storage, it was decided to deploy a LiveTREE channel between the various buildings of the different entities.

First of all, an optical fiber connection was devoted to link both information system sites. A redundant liaison through radio waves was established to secure this link.

To do this, inter-building optical fibers that were not used but were already installed have been put into service. An intra-building network is deployed in the buildings of the historic islet for the interconnection of equipment linked to SoMEL.

4.2 An Open Software Architecture

Technically, the LiveTREE information system will gain control over the different local control and command systems to propose a unique access point. It will thus settle at the interface between equipment and users to avoid conflicts in control and to include several software components to achieve this goal.

Basically, the system will have to include many, micro-service type, software components responsible for regularly interrogating consumption measurement equipment. This equipment uses multiple field protocols (REST API, ModBus TCP, KNX …) often specific to their manufacturer in their implementation and to the equipment in consideration.

These dedicated micro-services will generate time-stamped messages containing the measurement data. These messages will be entrusted to an open-source message broker like the Apache Kafka (*Apache Kafka* n.d.) or Mosquitto software [4].

A message broker is a system that will allow asynchronous communication between several software components. It will store messages to put them on hold in order to route them from producers to consumers.

The same mechanism is used inversely to send messages containing instructions to be applied on the equipment.

All the messages, whether control, command or simply containing a measurement, are archived in an Apache Cassandra type database (*Apache Cassandra* n.d.)

As the hardware architecture is physically distributed over two sites, we studied the technologies allowing us to similarly split the IT workload (micro-services, message broker, calculation, storage, process, etc.) of the hardware.

For this reason, we have made the choice of containerization with Docker (*Empowering App Development for Developers|Docker* n.d.) and Kubernetes (*Kubernetes* n.d.). These technologies, used collectively, make it possible to start (or restart), move, stop software components according to their level of stress or observed failures.

All the above is animated by the Linux operating system (*The Linux Kernel Archives* n.d.).

5   Research Perspectives

If the design and deployment of the LiveTREE Information System does not constitute a research topic in itself, a certain latitude has been left to the authors for the deployment of a research infrastructure within it.

In fact, if the SGs aim to transform the existing power grid to a "smart" grid with automated management and where energy production can be decentralized, this evolution of the power grid will only be possible through the massive, permanent and real-time exchange of data.

In the demonstrator framework, this aspect was resolved through the deployment of a dedicated wired grid representing several hundreds of meters of fiber optics for very elevated data rates with high reliability.

However, in the same way as it would have been utopian to create a new power grid to implement the SGs, there are no plans to deploy a fiber optic network (with all the necessary infrastructure) parallel to the power grid to allow its communication.

This is why the authors have deployed a set of 120 wireless sensors powered by batteries within the historic islet. These sensors will form a ubiquitous "ad hoc" communication network [10], that is to say decentralized and without infrastructure, dedicated to the transfer of data from the SG of the historic islet.

This network of sensors will make it possible to experiment in real conditions (radio interference, crossing thick walls, loss of signal, …) specific self-adaptive communication protocols necessary for managing a Smart Grid ([14], [15]): i.e. the differentiated routing of control orders and/or production or electricity consumption measures.

Indeed, SG applications are heterogeneous in terms of requirements, criticality and tolerance for delays [15], [3], [12]. As these applications generate different types of traffic (real time, critical, regular) (15), they require different levels of service quality and data prioritization [11] for their transmission by the sensor network. In fact, the latter is fundamentally slower in the transmission of data and less reliable while being limited by the capacity of the battery. New protocol approaches are therefore needed.

These approaches are evolving more and more to gradually shift decision-making from outside the grid (cloud computing) to its immediate proximity (edge computing) or even on the sensors themselves (fog computing). In fact, the energy consumption of a sensor is mainly due to radio communications, hereby requiring to limit them.

A first approach to experimentally validate consists of creating subsets called clusters in the grid, to aggregate the data or try to predict it, in order to limit the communications and therefore the saturation of the sensor network [11].

The Information System LiveTREE will therefore become a demonstrator of SGs at the scale of the historic islet. However, the system will itself be animated by a demonstrator of reprogrammable sensor networks which will allow the validation of theoretical research results on communication protocols by experiments in a real context [6].

6   Evolution and Challenges

The deployment of an Information System is a long-term project.

Nevertheless, the architecture developed in the SoMEL framework still seems today a pertinent approach that allows a real added value within the framework of new research projects by making it possible to aggregate the possibilities of control and command and by sharing the various data sets of the LiveTREE member entities.

Hence, the European research project H2020 eBalance + which begins and aims to work on the interoperability of different Smart Grid demonstrators, will exhibit the relevance of the initial architectural choices.

Finally, the open architecture of the system allows the consideration of making an open demonstrator for students by permitting the implementation of digital twins.

References

1. *Apache Cassandra.* (n.d.). Retrieved June 23, 2020, from https://cassandra.apache.org/.
2. *Apache Kafka.* (n.d.). Apache Kafka. Retrieved June 23, 2020, from https://kafka.apache.org/.
3. Davito, B., Tai, H., & Uhlaner, R. (2010). The smart grid and the promise of demand-side management. *McKinsey Smart Grid, 3,* 8–44.
4. *Eclipse Mosquitto.* (2018, January 8). Eclipse Mosquitto. https://mosquitto.org/.
5. *Empowering App Development for Developers\Docker.* (n.d.). Retrieved June 23, 2020, from https://www.docker.com/.
6. Gungor, V., Lu, B., & Hancke, G. (2010). Opportunities and Challenges of Wireless Sensor Networks in Smart Grid. *Industrial Electronics, IEEE Transactions On, 57,* 3557–3564. https://doi.org/10.1109/TIE.2009.2039455.
7. *Kubernetes.* (n.d.). Kubernetes. Retrieved June 23, 2020, from https://kubernetes.io/.
8. Le programme FLEXGRID. (n.d.). *Flexgrid.* Retrieved June 22, 2020, from https://www.flexgrid.fr/le-programme-flexgrid/.
9. *Live Tree.* (n.d.). Retrieved June 22, 2020, from https://livetree.fr/.
10. Nassar, J. (2018). *Ubiquitous networks for smart grids.*
11. Nassar, J., Berthomé, M., Gouvy, N., Mitton, N., & Quoitin, B. (2018). Multiple instances QoS routing in RPL: Application to smart Grids. *sensors (Basel, Switzerland), 18*(8). PubMed. https://doi.org/10.3390/s18082472.

12. Nassar, J., Miranda, K., Gouvy, N., & Mitton, N. (2018). *Heterogeneous data reduction in WSN: application to smart grids* (p. 6). https://doi.org/10.1145/3213299.3213302.
13. *Objectifs et enjeux\Smile.* (n.d.). Retrieved June 22, 2020, from https://smile-smartgrids.fr/fr/presentation/objectifs-et-enjeux.html.
14. Saputro, N., Akkaya, K., & Uludag, S. (2012). Survey a survey of routing protocols for smart grid communications. *Computer Networks: The International Journal of Computer and Telecommunications Networking, 56*(11), 2742–2771. https://doi.org/10.1016/j.comnet.2012.03.027.
15. Smart Grid Taxonomy. (2015). A system view from a grid operator's perspective. https://www.bkw.ch/fileadmin/user_upload/3_Gemeinden_EVU/gem_smart_grid_systematik_en.pdf.
16. Suljanovic, N., Borovina, D., Zajc, M., Smajic, J., & Mujcic, A. (2014). Requirements for communication infrastructure in smart grids. *IEEE Energycon 2014.* https://doi.org/10.1109/ENERGYCON.2014.6850620.
17. *The Linux Kernel Archives.* (n.d.). Retrieved June 23, 2020, from https://www.kernel.org/.
18. *You&Grid—Northern France\Enedis.* (n.d.). Retrieved June 22, 2020, from https://www.enedis.fr/yougrid-northern-france.

Correction to: Organizing Smart Buildings and Cities

Elisabetta Magnaghi, Véronique Flambard, Daniela Mancini, Julie Jacques, and Nicolas Gouvy

Correction to:
E. Magnaghi et al. (eds.),
Organizing Smart Buildings and Cities, Lecture Notes
in Information Systems and Organisation 36,
https://doi.org/10.1007/978-3-030-60607-7

In the original version of the book, the following belated corrections have been incorporated:

In Chapters 2 and 3 titled "Smart Cities: A Response to Wicked Problems" and "Big Data: An Introduction to Data-Driven Decision Making", respectively, the affiliation of the authors "Peter B. Duncan and David A. Edgar" has been changed from "Lancashire School of Business and Enterprise, University of Central Lancashire, Preston, UK" to "Department of Business and Management, Glasgow Caledonian University, UK". This has been corrected in the updated version.

The updated versions of these chapters can be found at
https://doi.org/10.1007/978-3-030-60607-7_2
https://doi.org/10.1007/978-3-030-60607-7_3

Printed in the United States
by Baker & Taylor Publisher Services